RACIAL MELANCHOLIA, RACIAL DISSOCIATION

RACIAL MELANCHOLIA, RACIAL DISSOCIATION

On the Social and Psychic Lives of Asian Americans

DAVID L. ENG & SHINHEE HAN

DUKE UNIVERSITY PRESS | *Durham and London* | 2019

Printed in the United States of America on acid-free paper ∞
Designed by Julienne Alexander
Typeset in Arno Pro by Copperline Books

Library of Congress Cataloging-in-Publication Data
Names: Eng, David L., [date] author. | Han, Shinhee, [date] author.
Title: Racial melancholia, racial dissociation : on the social and psychic
lives of Asian Americans / David L. Eng, Shinhee Han.
Description: Durham : Duke University Press, 2019. | Includes
bibliographical references and index.
Identifiers: LCCN 2018020450 (print) | LCCN 2018026363 (ebook)
ISBN 9781478002680 (ebook)
ISBN 9781478001256 (hardcover : alk. paper)
ISBN 9781478001607 (pbk. : alk. paper)
Subjects: LCSH: Asian American youth. | Asian Americans—Race identity. |
Model minority stereotype—United States. | Race—Psychological
aspects. | Asian American gays. | Asian diaspora. | Asians—United States.
Classification: LCC E184.A75 (ebook) | LCC E184.A75 E54 2019 (print) |
DDC 973/.0495—dc23
LC record available at https://lccn.loc.gov/2018020450

Cover art: Yayoi Kusama, *Late-night Chat is Filled with Dreams*, 2009.
Acrylic on canvas, 162 × 162 cm. © YAYOI KUSAMA. Courtesy of Ota
Fine Arts, Tokyo/Singapore/Shanghai; Victoria Miro, London/Venice;
David Zwirner, New York.

CONTENTS

PREFACE

We are bombarded today by celebratory discourses of multiculturalism and diversity in the face of intensifying racial discord and violence. In our putatively colorblind age we lack sufficient critical resources to analyze and explore the social and psychic conditions that give rise to such contradictions. In particular, we have few conceptual frameworks to understand their social and psychic effects on Asian Americans. *Racial Melancholia, Racial Dissociation* attempts to provide a theoretical account of these paradoxes of race.

The numerous case histories and commentaries on Asian American adolescents and young adults that comprise this book were written over twenty years. The present volume is the culmination of a comprehensive rethinking and rewriting of our various ideas about the social and psychic lives of Asian American students and patients we have encountered in the classroom and clinic across two generations—from Generation X to Generation Y. As a Chinese American humanities professor and Korean American psychotherapist, we have worked together to reconceptualize psychoanalytic theory in relation to specific historical moments and times—that is, to consider the shifting history of the Asian American subject in relation to the evolving subject of Asian American history. From the wake of the Cold War and civil rights movements to our current colorblind age under neoliberalism and globalization, we consider how psychic processes of racial melancholia and racial dissociation track and name the various ways by which Asian Americans in particular and other people of color in general are assimilated into, as well as excluded from, the social and political domains.

Having composed this book over the course of two decades, we have accumulated numerous debts of gratitude for the insights, friendships, and support we received along the way. First and foremost, we would like to thank Calvin Chin, María-Josefina Saldaña-Portillo, Karen Shimak-awa, and Michelle Stephens for their brilliance and generosity. These four wonderful friends and colleagues participated in a manuscript work-shop in 2016 that, along with the laser-beam insights of the magnificent Hirokazu Yoshikawa, transformed the theoretical structure and overall framing of this book at a crucial moment of its conceptualization.

Over many years, Hiro, Josie, and Calvin, as well as Ed Cohen, Neve Gordon, Janice Gump, Jack Halberstam, Amy Kaplan, Suvir Kaul, Da-vid Kazanjian, Homay King, Ania Loomba, Susette Min, the late José Esteban Muñoz, Mae Ngai, A. Naomi Paik, Ann Pellegrini, Camille Robcis, Catherine Rottenberg, Melissa Sanchez, Shuang Shen, Shu-mei Shih, Melanie Suchet, Joan Scott, Kaja Silverman, Serena Volpp, Priscilla Wald, Dorothy Wang, and Chi-ming Yang served as delightful and stead-fast interlocutors for this project. Dylan Verner-Christ provided exem-plary support with research, as did Derek Gottlieb with indexing. As al-ways, Teemu Ruskola was consistently present to think, support, cajole, and edit. The late Muriel Dimen's intellectual vision as embodied in the journal she helped to found, *Studies in Gender and Sexuality: Psychoanaly-sis, Cultural Studies, Treatment, Research*, has been an invaluable source of inspiration for us across theoretical and clinical domains. An earlier version of chapter 2 appeared in *Studies in Gender and Sexuality*, and an earlier version of chapter 1 appeared in *Psychoanalytic Dialogues*. We are grateful to these journals for providing an early home for our work.

At an important juncture in the writing of the last half of this proj-ect, Danielle Allen facilitated an excellent reading group at the Institute for Advanced Study in 2013 on what eventually became part 2 and the final couple chapters exploring the topic of racial dissociation. In con-junction, we would like to acknowledge the Institute for Psychoanalytic Training and Research in New York City and, in particular, Michael Moskowitz and Ben Kafka for their invitation in 2015 to reflect on the collaborations we have published over the years concerning psychoanal-ysis, race, and Asian Americans. Indeed, the warm welcome and encour-agement we received at IPTAR motivated us to complete this book. In this context, Patricia Gherovici has been an especially thoughtful and stimulating interlocutor.

Over the two decades in which these case histories and commentaries were written, we have given numerous presentations and workshops—

together and singly—at various universities, institutes, conferences, clinics, and community-based organizations. They are too numerous to name here separately, but we would like to express our deep gratitude to the multiple organizers and audiences whose serious engagement with the lives recounted and analyzed here has made our thinking all the better.

To our knowledge, *Racial Melancholia, Racial Dissociation* is the first monograph to bring together psychoanalytic theory and case histories with critical race studies and law. Moreover, it is the first coauthored book written across the domain of the clinic and the field of the humanities deploying as its primary source materials original case histories and commentaries on Asian Americans in a comparative racial context. That is, while the book is a timely and necessary expansion of psychoanalysis in relation to race, and vice versa, the project also insistently triangulates polarized black-white binaries of race and racism that often exclude Asian Americans and other people of color from critical analysis altogether.

Most of all, then, we would like to thank our students and patients for sharing with us their invaluable experiences and their courageous admissions of vulnerability, which are at the heart of this book and without which the project would simply not exist. We have been careful to disguise their identities: we have changed names, family backgrounds, hometowns, majors, and schools for the people described and discussed here. When at all possible, consent was received from those students and patients we were able to contact. Nonetheless, each case study incorporates aspects of not only one particular student or patient but also at times other students and patients who share similar experiences and dilemmas.

In chapter 1, case histories of Elaine and Nelson are composites of various students that we counseled (both in private practice and in the university clinic) and taught in our various Asian American lectures and seminars at the beginning of our careers. In chapter 2, the case history of Mina, a transnational adoptee from Korea, was written and published with her consent, as were the two case histories of Christopher and Neel, gay parachute children from China and India, in chapter 4. The case histories on Yuna and Yung, two other parachute children from Korea and China, composing chapter 3, are masked descriptions. Both Yuna and Yung were treated in university settings for brief periods, and it was impossible to locate either of them to obtain their consent, as their two case histories were composed long after their school files were sealed. All the students who agreed to be included in this book expressed a common hope that the pain underlying their distinctive social and psychic predicaments might somehow help other Asian Americans struggling in silence with similar troubles and crises. This, of course, is our hope as well.

Many thanks to Kusama Studio and the David Zwirner Gallery for permitting the use of our striking cover image. Yayoi Kasuma's art and her life as an Asian (im)migrant in New York City—she arrived in 1957 at age 27 and returned to Tokyo in 1973—anticipate in provocative ways many of the themes of this book. Last but proverbially not least, we would like to offer deep thanks to our longtime editor Ken Wissoker, and to Julienne Alexander, Elizabeth Ault, Mary Hoch, Sara Leone, and the other staff members at Duke University Press for their inveterate support of emerging, necessary, and difficult new scholarship in both psychoanalysis and critical race studies. We could not imagine publishing this book with anyone—or anywhere—else.

INTRODUCTION: *The History of the (Racial) Subject and the Subject of (Racial) History*

Racial Melancholia, Racial Dissociation represents an extensive and evolving collaboration that has lasted for two decades. This book is the result of a comprehensive reframing and rewriting of our various ideas about the social and psychic lives of Asian American adolescents and young adults we have encountered in the classroom and clinic across two generations, from Generation X to Generation Y. Over time, we have witnessed firsthand the shifting demographics, as well as the remarkable psychic transformations, of our students and patients in the face of an ever-growing politics of colorblindness in US society and a rising Asia under neoliberalism and globalization.

In this project, we present two distinct psychic mechanisms by which racialized immigrant subjects process problems of discrimination, exclusion, loss, and grief: racial melancholia and racial dissociation. We use the term "racial melancholia" to refer to histories of racial loss that are condensed into a forfeited object whose significance must be deciphered and unraveled for its social meanings. "Racial dissociation," in contrast, refers to histories of racial loss that are dispersed across a wide social terrain, histories whose social origins and implications remain insistently diffuse and obscure. We developed our theory of racial melancholia in the late-1990s in relation to Generation X (those born between 1960 and 1980). As we encountered a new cohort of students and patients—millennials from Generation Y (those born between 1980 and 2000)—we came to realize the historical and demographic specificity of our understanding of racial melancholia. Our novel theory of racial dissociation—to our knowledge, we are the first to explore the concept comprehensively—represents our attempt to understand, describe, and navigate the changing social and psychic landscape of race, racism, and race relations in the United States.

We—a second-generation Chinese American male professor in the humanities and a 1.5-generation Korean American female psychotherapist—originally met at Columbia University, where we worked in the mid-1990s in the Department of English and Comparative Literature and in Counseling and Psychological Services, respectively. A spate of suicides by Asian American students, and the gruesome murder of an Asian American law student by a former boyfriend, brought us together in collective sorrow. This grief was exacerbated by a feeling on the part of our students and patients that there was—and continues to be—little acknowledgment or understanding of the social violence and psychic pain afflicting Asian American communities. This fact is as true on the part of administrators, faculty, and students as it is, most poignantly, on the part of ourselves.

Indeed, the regnant "model minority myth," which we analyze and discuss throughout this book, persistently represents Asian Americans as nerdy automatons, technically gifted in math and sciences, continuously working, compliant, wealthy, and exempt from discrimination. Asian Americans in fact have the highest poverty rate of any racial group in New York City.[1] More often than not, racism against Asian Americans occurs without recognition and without provoking any serious outcry or protest.

Significantly, "Asian American" is an expansive term. It describes American-born citizens as well as foreign-born immigrants and citizens living in the United States from disparate national, geographic, cultural, education, class, and religious backgrounds who trace their ancestry to East Asia, South Asia, or Southeast Asia. Although students and patients tend to identify with their particular racial or ethnic group—as we do above—a long history of discrimination is what binds Asian Americans together as a collective, and the adoption of a coalitional Asian American identity is often a conscious, politicized choice. Paradoxically, while Asian Americans are always included in diversity statistics, they are largely excluded from affirmative action programs—a significant point of controversy in ongoing national debates concerning the politics of race and colorblindness. In short, we are seen as a homogenous and self-sufficient community in no particular need of assistance or support. This stereotype is the dominant way we are perceived—socially fixed and psychically formed as subjects. It is woefully inadequate to understanding the circumstances of our various social and psychic predicaments.

Some months after the last funeral at Columbia, we began to discuss the death of one of the students, Shirley Yoon, a popular and well-known senior whose suicide in 1998 affected both of us deeply though neither of us knew her personally. On reflection, her death was the emotional culmination in a series of unbearable losses the community suffered that year. Although dozens of students and family members participated in her burial service on Long Island, we, along with the University Chaplain, an African American woman, were among the few representatives of the university in attendance. We found this deeply unsettling.

In trying to come to terms with Shirley Yoon's passing, we became absorbed with one particular line in Freud's essay on "Mourning and Melancholia" (1917) in which he writes that the melancholic "knows *whom* he has lost but not *what* he has lost in him."[2] In contrast to what he initially describes as healthy mourning, Freud characterizes melancholia as a type of pathological mourning without end, in which the significance of the lost object remains unconscious and opaque: "In yet other cases, one feels justified in maintaining the belief that a loss of this [melancholic] kind occurred, but one cannot see clearly what it is that has been lost, and it is all the more reasonable to suppose that the patient cannot consciously perceive what he has lost either. This, indeed, might be so even if the patient is aware of the loss which has given rise to his melancholia, but only in the sense that he knows *whom* he has lost but not *what* he has lost in him."[3] In trying to understand what we had lost in Shirley Yoon, we eventually coauthored an article titled "A Dialogue on Racial Melancholia." That case history and commentary explored Freud's concept of melancholia in relation to depression and suicide among Asian American college students, and it sought to connect their interminable sadness with difficulties arising from immigration, assimilation, and the racialization they face on a daily basis.

"A Dialogue on Racial Melancholia" was originally published in 2000 in the clinical journal *Psychoanalytic Dialogues*. It comprises the first half of the title we have chosen for this book as it represents our initial joint endeavor to rethink both psychoanalytic theory and clinical practice so that they might be more useful for analyzing problems of race and racism for Asian Americans and other communities of color. In this book, we argue that what we describe as racial melancholia among Generation X and racial dissociation among Generation Y constitute two psychic mechanisms by which these different generations process social predicaments associated with discrimination and exclusion as well as psychic difficulties connected to loss and grief.

Importantly, by considering histories of immigration, assimilation, and racialization, as well as stereotypes such as the model minority myth and yellow peril, in terms of Asian American subject formation across two generations, we reconceptualize psychoanalytic theory in relation to specific historical moments and times. Throughout the book we investigate the history of the (racial) subject in relation to the subject matter of (racial) history. In this project, psychoanalytic theory is our primary theoretical tool for exploring the shifting history of the racial subject, while critical race theory is our primary theoretical tool for analyzing the evolving subject of racial history. That is, insofar as loss and grief are generated by juridicopolitical mechanisms configuring a long history of Asian American immigration and exclusion, the book pays particular attention to critical race theory's insights on law, structural racism, systematic bias, and social violence as a necessary supplement to our psychoanalytic investigation of the Asian American subject. From Cold War discourse and the legacy of the civil rights movement shaping Generation X's coming of age to our current colorblind moment under neoliberalism and globalization shaping Generation Y's coming of age, we consider how racial melancholia and racial dissociation identify and trace distinctive patterns by which Asian Americans and other people of color are assimilated into, as well as excluded from, the social and political domains.

In addition to depression, suicide, and racial melancholia among model minorities (chapter 1), we write about the politics of mothering and racial reparation in the practice of transnational adoption (chapter 2); racial dissociation, psychic nowhere, and the displacement of parachute children with the rise of Asia under neoliberalism and globalization (chapter 3); and panic attacks and the politics of coming out for gay

Asian parachute children in a colorblind age (chapter 4). We bring together different schools and paradigms of psychoanalytic thought, legal histories of race and racism, and the politics of Asian immigration and exclusion with the aim of creating a more sustained conversation about the lives of Asian Americans and Asians in the diaspora.

In retrospect, we have been investigating for two decades what might be described as the social and psychic structures of a comparatively privileged class of Asian American adolescents and young adults in private and public US institutions of higher education trying to recognize, narrate, and come to terms with what they have lost—as well as gained—in immigration, migration, displacement, and diaspora. It is worth emphasizing we do not presume to represent all Asian American subjects in this project. Nonetheless, we hope the specific case histories and commentaries of the particular students and patients presented here will shine critical light on some general social and psychic dilemmas that many Asian Americans endure. Thus, we hope to forge links among various groups to develop new critical approaches, clinical possibilities, and political coalitions.

The measured pace of our collaboration is due in part to the vicissitudes of our professional and personal lives, but it also stems from the comparative isolation of psychoanalysis and critical race studies as intellectual areas of inquiry largely independent from one another. On the one hand, race and racism are often conceptualized as sociological phenomena and problems of material inequality that have little to do with the formation of the psyche. As conventional psychoanalytic theory places sexuality at the heart of the development of individual subjectivity, it has relegated race to the periphery as sociology, in Kimberlyn Leary's words, "outside the purview of psychoanalysis altogether, or important only as categories of experience if translated into the metric of sexual desire or the vicissitudes of family life."[4] Farhad Dalal notes that, insofar as psychoanalytic theory typically approaches social conflict in the external world as a reflection of psychic distress in the internal world, racism is rarely conceptualized as an effect of larger social histories and cultural practices. Rather, it is seen as the result of individual neuroses, phobias, and prejudices.[5]

Psychoanalytic theory has consistently privileged the internal psychic world over the external social world. It has insistently focused on the "private" realm of family and kinship relations over the "public" realm of law and politics, and it has largely configured the internal psychic functionings of subjectivity as extraneous to the external world of the social. Broadly speaking, both psychoanalytic theorists and clinicians have been slow to examine how histories of race and colonial modernity implicitly frame their field's evolution—its dominant paradigms and theoretical assumptions. Even today the overwhelming majority of clinical case histories refer only to a patient's personal family history and interpersonal family dynamics rather than to the subject of (racial) history writ large. Social, political, legal, economic, and cultural factors are bracketed in the analysis of the history of the (racial) subject and the etiology of psychic pain. Put otherwise, psychoanalysis is focused on the mother but rarely considers the motherland; it is attuned to family dynamics but rarely thinks about the family of nations.

On the other hand, agendas in critical race studies have been largely governed by sociological, legal, and empirical accounts of race and racial subordination as *material* inequality—as a problem of political rights and representation as well as economic redistribution and justice. As a result, the field has not adequately considered how psychoanalysis as a critical heuristic for understanding how racial subjectivity is formed and created and race relations are reproduced and sustained as intertwined material and psychic phenomena. For instance, we argue in part II of this book that as race continues to slip into the collective unconscious in a colorblind age, the importance of a psychoanalytic approach that can frame and analyze the political stakes of this significant historical shift—the unconscious and hidden symptoms of what Stokely Carmichael and Charles V. Hamilton call "institutional racism"—only intensifies.[6] Similarly, in its largely domestic focus on the history of US constitutional law and black-white race relations, the field of critical race studies has not adequately explored new demographic trends among Asian Americans and other immigrants of color, such as transnational adoptees and parachute children. They are generally absent from analyses of race and racism.

At the same time, scholarly focus in critical race and ethnic studies on problems of *group* discrimination often overlooks critical insights provided by studying the predicaments of *individual* subjectivity.[7] Such an exploration is not only the hallmark of psychoanalytic practice and the case history but also at times the harbinger of (or impediment to) an emergent political consciousness—indeed, what Raymond Williams might describe as an emergent social formation and a will for historical change.[8] In slightly different terms, when identifying with others the individual is also invariably attaching him- or herself to larger group histories as well as social categories and collectives.[9] It is crucial, then, for both psychoanalytic and critical race theory to consider at once the psychic and social mechanisms of this interchange between the individual and the collective. From this perspective, the book is centrally concerned with psychoanalytic debates over the (biological) nature of the drives in terms of the actual social relations forming our psychic identifications with, attachments to, and investments in (racial) others.

Racial Melancholia, Racial Dissociation thus begins with the idea that race and racism are complex phenomena operating in and through social and cultural norms—that histories of race and racism must be approached as both a cause and an effect of individual subjectivity, agency, and will. Throughout the project, we employ insights from critical race theory. A branch of scholarship that grew out of the 1980s legal academy, critical race theory explores how law purports to represent abstract and equal liberal subjects while in fact *producing* racial subjects and hierarchies according to institutionalized structures of white power and privilege. Historically the law has codified racial identity as an instrument of both political exclusion and economic exploitation but, at the same time, it has refused to recognize group claims, embedding legal rights, recognition, and responsibility exclusively in the figure of the abstract individual and in relation to individual agency and intent. Today, under the mandates of neoliberalism and an ever-shrinking public sphere, the idea of entrepreneurial spirit justifies discrimination and racism, social inclusion and exclusion, as functions of economic rationality and private choice. In the process, neoliberalism conscripts law and politics to its instrumental logic of individual self-sufficiency—a topic that we explore at length in regard to Generation Y in part II of this book.

Throughout this project, we also employ insights from the humanities and interpretive social sciences in order to situate our legal histories and critical paradigms in relation to a troubled global history of colonialism, liberalism, and race binding together Europe and the Americas with Asia and Africa. Finally, we also turn to a number of authors, artists, and directors whose creative works offer alternative ways of narrating and thus understanding racial history in relation to psychic pain. Indeed, a humanities-based approach to psychoanalysis highlights the political and therapeutic dimensions of narration. Literary, historical, and psychoanalytic practices all converge in their potential to tell the story *differently*, with narration functioning as a kind of individual and collective talking cure in the face of the vicissitudes of law and politics.

In the past two decades, a small but growing number of influential books and articles exploring psychoanalysis and race have appeared in both the humanities and the clinical arena.[10] At the same time, there are a handful of publications in the field of critical race studies considering the place of psychoanalysis in jurisprudence.[11] Rarely, however, are humanities scholars and clinicians engaged in a sustained conversation about questions of race in psychoanalytic texts, case histories, clinical practices, classroom dynamics, cultural productions, and the larger social world. Even more rarely does this conversation focus specifically on the social and psychic lives of Asian Americans. To our knowledge, this is the first collaborative book written across the domain of the clinic and the field of the humanities deploying as its primary source materials original case histories and commentaries on Asian Americans. At the same time that this project is an expansion of psychoanalysis in relation to race, and vice versa, it also triangulates polarized black-white binaries of race and racism that often exclude Asian Americans and other people of color from critical analysis altogether, analyzing them instead in a comparative racial context.

In sum, *Racial Melancholia, Racial Dissociation* is committed to exploring how a more speculative humanities-based approach to psychoanalytic theory might supplement its clinical applications, and vice versa. In the context of race, racism, immigration, and diaspora—all of which remain undertheorized across various disciplinary deployments of psychoanalysis—such a critical endeavor continues to be especially urgent. As various race and postcolonial scholars have noted, psychoanalytic theory and practice remain largely unaware of their historical conditions of emergence and untroubled by the particular European colonial tradition by which they are framed and in which they inevitably participate.[12] At the same time, the lack of understanding in both Asian American and mainstream society of problems of social violence and psychic pain afflicting our communities demands a psychoanalytic vocabulary as one powerful conceptual tool—though not the only one—for critical analysis and change. The history of the (racial) subject has an ongoing and intimate connection to the subject of (racial) history, and it is this complex and shifting relationship that the book explores across two decades.

The remainder of this introduction is organized into three sections. The first section examines the subject of (racial) history through the idea of "race as relation" and what Cheryl Harris describes as a long history of "whiteness as property" in US law and jurisprudence tracing its origins to the establishment of the US nation-state through indigenous dispossession and the transatlantic slave trade. We start with the premise that race is not a "thing" as it is commonly understood—an unchanging biological trait, a bodily attribute, a difference of blood quantum or color, a static identity, a reflection of a natural order. Rather, we argue that race is a relation: a continuous, modulating historical relationship among subjects mediated by socio-legal processes of social inclusion and exclusion. Race is as much about skin color and physiological markings as it is about a wide range of disparate social and psychic experiences of segregation and assimilation, absence and belonging, integration and dissociation, inclusion and exclusion. While the first section does not directly engage with psychoanalytic theory, it provides a theoretical base from which to consider how US histories of race and racial conflict illuminate and reflect some fundamental concepts in psychoanalysis regarding problems of subject-object relations.

The second section of this introduction extends psychoanalytic theories of subject-object relations by exploring how race as relation and whiteness as property shape and configure the history of the (racial) subject. For instance, by describing race as processes of social inclusion and exclusion, we can reconfigure psychoanalytic theories concerning the nature of the drives and the constitution of subjectivity in similar terms. We are able to analyze our privileged objects of identification and desire as articulated in and through social norms and relations, in and through historically contingent ideals and prohibitions, rather than as unmediated representations of biological instincts divorced from larger social histories and lived realities.[13] We examine how race as relation and whiteness as property reconfigure universal paradigms in psychoanalytic theory such as the Oedipus complex and its privileged subject-object dynamics, while also investigating the intricate social and psychic transactions that work to support what the Swedish Nobel laureate Gunnar Myrdal labeled in 1944 as an "American dilemma." Myrdal describes this dilemma as the nation's paradoxical belief in the abstract equality of all American citizen-subjects in the face of a long history of racial disparity and despair.[14] In short, we consider how a repurposed psychoanalytic theory might provide powerful analytic tools for investigating the production of racial subjectivity and subordination, as well as race relations and segregation, in the United States, from which neither the spaces of the clinic nor the classroom are exempt. As Dorothy E. Holmes observes, the space of the clinic—and the university, we would emphasize—are no less prone than any other to keeping issues of race "repressed and unanalyzed."[15]

The third part of the introduction employs our critical discussions of the history of the (racial) subject and the subject of (racial) history to frame the four internal chapters—the case histories and critical commentaries—of this book in terms of the psychic mechanisms of racial melancholia and racial dissociation.

CRITICAL RACE THEORY AND THE SUBJECT OF (RACIAL) HISTORY

Race is a social relation with a long history in the United States. Modern genealogies of race trace themselves to the era of European colonization and, in particular, to the transatlantic slave trade—its biologization and commodification of human life. The "peculiar institution" of slavery associated with the United States and with ideas of US exceptionalism has configured the problem of race as a particularly American phenomenon, an American dilemma. This displacement of race from Europe to the Americas, along with the coterminous affirmation of a universal (European) liberal subject through the forgetting of indigenous dispossession in the Americas as well as the exploitation and exportation of human life from Africa (and later Asia), necessitates a more serious engagement with global histories of race attached to modern empire, European and otherwise, its tactics of colonial settlement, and its circulation of bodies, goods, and ideas of difference.[16]

In the context of the United States, the phenomenon of chattel slavery has often constituted the history of race as a problem of (white-black) *objectification*. After all, slaves were literally commodities—part of a slave ship's cargo manifest and insurable as such like any other goods.[17] In the process, chattel slavery also helped to shape the idea of race itself as object, as a "thing"—an unchanging identity; a fixed biological trait; a scientific difference of blood quantum and gradients of color immediately visible on the body and apprehensible to the naked eye; an ontology with attendant ideas of mind and matter, civilization and savagery, freedom and unfreedom that helped to justify the colonial enterprise and highly profitable business of enslaving other human beings. We might characterize this modern historical shift in biopolitics as a transition from the problem of anatomy to differences in physiognomy—from the problem of the body to the difference of appearance and skin (color). As race increasingly came to reflect a natural order of the species in the early modern period, race was considered less a verb than a noun. Similarly, color was transformed from an adjective into a noun.[18]

Today, we are more accustomed to thinking about race in terms of *cultural* differences, even in the face of increasing scientific advancements in genetics and related sciences in pursuit of a biological basis for and definition of race. Yet even cultural approaches to race tend to configure culture as a static object—culture as something particular racial groups possess and that certain racial groups must learn to relinquish with great difficulty and consequence. One only need glance at the Moynihan Report from 1965, *The Negro Family: The Case for National Action,* or, more recently, Samuel P. Huntington's *The Clash of Civilizations and the Remaking of World Order* to comprehend straightaway how culture becomes a fixed and intransigent "thing."[19] Such ossification helps to create and reinforce narratives of racial hierarchy and difference, whether it be in the form of a pathologized black family structure or a pathologized religion helping to fuel Islamophobia and the war on terror.

This history of race as objectification was, of course, always in tension with the fact that the slave was not just an object but also indeed a subject—an object possessing a subjectivity. In volume 1 of *Capital,* Karl Marx explores the nature of commodities, speculating as to what commodities might say if they could speak.[20] The problem of simultaneous objecthood and subjecthood embodied in the personhood of the slave—a commodity that *could* speak—was a lost opportunity for Marx to contemplate this provocative question in specific terms of race and the transatlantic slave trade. The deleterious effects of this confusion continue to persist in problems of race and racism in our time. The peculiar nature of the slave as a speaking commodity allowed Afro-diaspora scholars such as Cedric Robinson to take up Marx's call and to theorize the academic field of what is now known as "racial capitalism," the study of the intertwined relationships between race and capitalism in the evolution of US modernity.[21] The field returns us to the problem of universalism and abstraction in modern capitalism and democratic governance, to the American dilemma, in the enduring face of racial particularity, exploitation, and domination.

Debates in the field of race studies have often ended in an unproductive intellectual impasse, especially in early American studies, concerning the problem of historical causality. For instance, numerous scholars of early US history have deliberated at length as to whether racism is an effect of slavery (as a function of capitalism) or slavery is an effect of racism.[22] David Kazanjian observes that the terms of this discussion have been rather poorly posed, entangled as they are in a mechanical understanding of historical causality. Slavery and race, he notes, "are more usefully understood as coextensive formations feeding off of one another and requiring genealogical investigations of effects, rather than discrete entities functioning either as cause or effect and requiring presumptively positivist searches for a singular origin."[23] Kazanjian sets a different critical agenda by encouraging us to reframe such chicken-and-egg debates. He asks us instead to consider how slavery and capitalism were at once animated by and articulated with race and racial nationalism, and to what specific effects.

In a similar vein, we ought to consider how race is neither pure objectification nor pure subjectification but precisely both at once: a continuous modulating *relation* between object and subject, a coexisting and coextensive formation, a dynamic movement of sociality and casuality. In describing race as a relation, as a process rather than a thing, we treat it more as a verb than a noun. For us, race is a performance rather than an essence. Indeed, we might say that race is a historical effect of the social relations between objectification and subjectification. From a slightly different angle, to borrow from Lisa Lowe, race may be considered the historical trace of what remains between the affirmation of a universal (European) liberal human subject and the forgetting of a long history of African slavery, Asian indentureship, and indigenous dispossession on which that universalism was constructed.[24] These ever-shifting social relations are historically contingent: race as a verb, race as historical processes of *racialization*. Race as relation is thus one key approach to analyzing the subject of (racial) history.

It is useful to consider in greater detail some of the profound and enduring historical effects of slavery and race as coextensive social formations in US politics and law. In jurisprudence, problems of subject-object distinctions appear prominently in property law. We conventionally understand property as an object that a subject possesses, for example, a house or a car—or a slave. An owner—a subject—can purchase or relinquish, buy or sell, property at will. Indeed, liberal notions of property emphasize exclusive rights of possession, use, and disposition—property as, in William Blackstone's words, "that sole and despotic dominion which one man claims and exercises over the external things of the world, in total exclusion of the right of any other individual in the universe."[25] As an object, property is not connected to the subject in any intrinsic way—it is, in legal terms, *transferable* and *alienable*. To this day, ideas of alienability are at the conceptual heart of our commonsense notions of property.

Two fundamental shifts in theories of property law are critical to register here. First, in the early twentieth century, the jurist Wesley Newcomb Hohfeld (1879–1918) challenged the conventional idea of property as a subject-object distinction, insisting that property is, in fact, a *subject-subject* relation—at heart, a relational concept.[26] (From this perspective, we might suggest that Hohfeld's definitional shift of understandings of property law implicitly engages with the critical logics of psychoanalysis.) Put otherwise, the owner of a piece of land has not only the legal right to be on it but also the legal right to exclude others from being on it. In short, property is a subject-subject relation mediated by legal modes of social inclusion and exclusion.

Indeed, Hohfeld argues that the totality of property relations can be specified through a set of four juristic terms and their opposites: a group of entitlements (rights, privileges, powers, and immunities) and their correlatives (no-rights, duties, disabilities, and liabilities).[27] Given the long and continuing history of black-white racial segregation that overshadows US history and culture, we can apprehend immediately how race might be considered a key term, if not *the* key term, through which subject-subject relations of trespass—of inclusion and exclusion, of rights and no-rights, of privileges and duties, of powers and disabilities, and of immunities and liabilities—are mediated and negotiated.

Second, in the late twentieth century, legal scholars began to challenge the very concept of property as a tangible, physical object, a process that the legal historian Thomas C. Grey has described as "the disintegration of property."[28] For example, in the age of no-fault divorce, educational degrees and professional certificates such as medical and law licenses, which are intrinsically connected to the person who earned them and thus are not alienable in any typical manner as property, began to be considered as a form of property in dissolution of marriage agreements and divorce settlements. Due in part to feminist lawyers and legal scholars who successfully argued that a wife who financially supported her husband during medical or law school is entitled to a part of that degree or license as "property," we have more abstract notions of what might be considered property today. In a similar manner, the ever-expanding universe of information technology underscores how intangible things such as computer code, big data, and biometric records are increasingly monetized, valued, and legally protected as property—as abstract and intellectual rather than tangible and physical property.

Like educational degrees and professional certificates awarded to particular persons, race is conventionally thought of as *inalienable*, intrinsically connected to a person's body, although a long history of racial passing would seem to suggest otherwise. The disintegration of property in jurisprudence opens up a theoretical space to consider how race, too, might usefully be considered not as a tangible "thing" but as a type of intangible property, as a relation, as alienable, as a complex range of social and psychic interchanges and experiences. In 1992, critical race scholar Cheryl I. Harris published a field-defining article, "Whiteness as Property," in which she argued for the idea of race as a special kind of property right.[29]

Harris's article explores how "whiteness as property" facilitates a long history of subject-subject relations of social inclusion and exclusion, privileges and disabilities, produced and ratified by US law. Harris begins with the idea that the origins of property rights in liberal society are rooted in racial domination, noting that whiteness was the characteristic, the attribute, the property of free human beings. She writes,

> The origins of whiteness as property lie in the parallel systems of domination of Black and Native American peoples out of which were created racially contingent forms of property and property rights. I further argue that whiteness shares the critical characteristics of property even as the meaning of property has changed over time. In particular, whiteness and property share a common premise—a conceptual nucleus—of a right to exclude. This conceptual nucleus has proven to be a powerful center around which whiteness as property has taken shape. Following the period of slavery and conquest, white identity became the basis of racialized privilege that was ratified and legitimated in law as a type of status property. After legalized segregation was overturned, whiteness as property evolved into a more modern form through the law's ratification of the settled expectations of relative white privilege as a legitimate and natural baseline.[30]

Contrary to the idea of race as an unchanging thing, as intrinsic to the body, as biology, and as a reflection of a natural order, whiteness as property has functioned as a bundle of legal rights, powers, and immunities that has shored up (white) racial identity and privilege from the time of slavery and dispossession to the era of emancipation, and from Jim Crow segregation to the age of legal desegregation to our putatively colorblind moment.

What is especially powerful about Harris's argument is the ways in which it tracks different and historically contingent modes of social inclusion and exclusion among racialized subjects throughout a long history of US jurisprudence—indeed, modes of social inclusion and exclusion *creating* racialized subjects and legacies of racial privilege and domination in the United States. Her legal account of whiteness as property thus provides another key approach to investigating the subject of (racial) history in regard to the history of the (racial) subject.

Notably, Harris gestures to "parallel systems" of domination in histories of indigenous dispossession. However, she focuses almost exclusively in her examination of whiteness as property on a white-black polarity that dominates notions of race in US history, politics, law, and culture to this day. As we argue throughout this book, such polarities are unsustainable both socially and psychically. Racial dichotomies such as black and white fly in the face of social reality and ignore a multicultural US society defined by numerous and overlapping histories of race, racial epistemologies, and racial encounters. Similarly, psychic binaries such as love and hate are affectively untenable in their emotional extremity and repudiation of relationality. As Neil Altman observes, race and racism emerge from "dichotomized thinking."[31]

Psychoanalysis teaches us that the dyadic deadlock of the imaginary domain—you versus me, black versus white—is resolved and subsumed in the symbolic realm only through an analytic third, through symbolization, triangulation, and the emergence of proper social relations. Bringing together these insights with whiteness as property and other scholarship from critical race, ethnic, and postcolonial studies provides a critical foundation to explore how race as relation can be extended for a comparative analysis of the history of the Asian American subject in regard to the subject of history. The model minority myth and the middleman thesis—of the Asian indentured servant as social buffer between the black slave and the white colonial master—exemplify some of the long-standing patterns by which the figures of the Asian immigrant and colonial laborer have historically triangulated black-white power dynamics globally.[32]

In the main chapters of this book, we expand beyond Harris's discussion of slavery and emancipation to analyze an extensive history of Asian immigration exclusion and bars to naturalization and citizenship that subtend the historical emergence of black-white race relations and mark the specific racial formation of Asian (and Latino) immigrants in the United States as illegitimate and illegal.[33] We also examine how stereotypes of Asian Americans and Asian immigrants as "illegal immigrants," "yellow peril," "perpetual foreigners," "middle men," and "model minorities" are mobilized in relation not only to whiteness but also to blackness and other racial groups comprising US multicultural society in an ever-shifting network of historically contingent social relations. In our project, citizenship is examined as a key legal component of a sweeping history of whiteness as property that functions to exclude Asian Americans and Asian immigrants as alien(able), to bar them from full participation and belonging in US culture and society across different political movements, economic periods, and social encounters.

PSYCHOANALYSIS AND THE HISTORY OF THE (RACIAL) SUBJECT

Psychoanalysis has developed an extensive and sophisticated vocabulary for investigating subject-object relations and their associated dilemmas. Whether one engages with the classical drive theories of Freud, with the language-based analyses of Jacques Lacan, or with the relational approaches of Melanie Klein, these overlapping fields of psychoanalytic inquiry all offer methods for interrogating subject-object impasses that mark not only psychic life but also, we suggest, the long and troubled history of US race relations. Psychoanalysis begins with the premise that we enter the world through objects—whether they are the part objects of Freud, such as the father's penis; the mirror images of the self-same in Lacan; or the partial objects of Klein, most notably the mother's breast.

Psychic suffering stems in no small part from the refusal to recognize our objects as subjects. In the language of object relations, psychic violence and pain are a result of the infant's refusal to see the mother as a proper subject with her own agency and will rather than as a partial object to satiate its hunger and greed—that is, as a good and available or bad and unavailable breast. In sum, psychoanalysis delineates important methods to explore how we acknowledge our objects as subjects, recognize the other as other, and stage ethical encounters with others.

To align this analysis more closely with the legal histories of racial inclusion and exclusion examined above, psychoanalysis might be described as offering a thick vocabulary for evaluating the history of the (racial) subject as a continuous negotiation of subject-object relations, of material and psychic processes of objectification and subjectification, and the resolution of these dyadic structures through a social third. Whether one subscribes to Jacques Lacan's position on the impossibility of relationality or to D. W. Winnicott, John Bowlby, and W. R. D. Fairbairn's insistence on the human need for relationality and the importance of early external relationships in infancy to the development of a healthy internal psychic life, psychoanalysis offers a number of powerful theoretical paradigms for understanding how triangulation through symbolic processes is essential to mitigating subject-object, master-slave, you-me polarities leading to psychic deadlock and grievance. Yet it is only in recent years that psychoanalytic theorists and clinicians have begun to investigate these processes of triangulation and socialization in specific terms of race.[34]

We commonly understand triangulation through the universalizing model of the Oedipus complex and its privileged *sexual* triangle of mother, father, and son. To consider the history of the *racial* subject in relation to the subject of *racial* history therefore necessitates historicizing and rethinking the Oedipus complex and its privileged sexual objects (mother, father, son) in a longer racial history of European colonialism as well as US structures of race as relation and whiteness as property.[35] From a different angle, it demands an exploration of how law and psychoanalysis work to produce the uneven terrain of idealized racial subjects and objects.

To cite one important recent intervention in psychoanalysis, Gwen Bergner argues that the Oedipus complex not only encodes an incest prohibition but also a miscegenation taboo, one demanding that the little boy identify with not just the father but with the *white* father and displace his desire for the mother not just to any other woman but precisely to a *white* woman. In both theory and practice, psychoanalysis has not considered adequately how the universal subject of psychoanalysis is not just a gendered (male) but a raced (white) subject—a fact emphasized as early as the 1950s by the Martinique-born psychiatrist Frantz Fanon and Tunisian-born Albert Memmi in their critique of the psychopathologies of colonialism.[36] In other words, the Oedipus complex encodes both a sexual and a racial demand—both a sexual and racial taboo. From the perspective of US history and law, the incest taboo channels and configures the little boy's (hetero)sexual identifications and desires implicitly through an assemblage of racial prohibitions reinforcing and reinforced by a long history of whiteness as property: antimiscegenation prohibitions, fugitive slave acts, segregation laws, mob lynchings, and racial violence meant to facilitate the smooth transmission of property and privilege from one (white) generation to the next.[37]

If the Oedipal complex frames its (hetero)sexual dictates in the service of maintaining a white racial purity and hegemony, we can rethink W. E. B. Du Bois's writings on "double consciousness" in light of both race and sexuality.[38] Here, we can connect "double consciousness" to Freud's concept of "double inscription," the notion that the same idea can appear in the unconscious and (pre)conscious in different and seemingly unrelated forms.[39] That is, the traditional ways in which psychoanalysis has been interpreted as a theory of sex and gender relations may be considered the *conscious* manifestation of various *unconscious* ideas, prohibitions, and taboos associated with race. In the context of conventional psychoanalysis, we might describe race as the political unconscious of sexuality as, in the context of US history and legacies of whiteness as property, we might describe sexuality as the political unconscious of race. (We return to an analysis of this doubling in our discussions of colorblindness and racial dissociation in chapter 4.) If, as Lacan asserts, the unconscious is structured like a language, we ought to contemplate how the unconscious is specifically structured by a *racial* language throughout US history, law, and culture.

In other words, the racial subject does not just speak against objectification or rail against stereotypes. In a profound sense, he or she is already constituted and spoken through, indeed subjected to, the compromised racial language and history of an inherited culture—of race as relation and whiteness as property. Psychoanalysis insists that we are born into a world of others, that language precedes us, and that symbolic representations indexing a history of cultural norms and prohibitions frame our entrance to and existence in the world. Psychoanalysis thus alerts us to the fact that our agency is compromised and our will is limited from the beginning, that we are pregiven to and dependent on others, and that any assertion of an autonomous (racial) subjectivity, authenticity, or agency is an illusion already marked by and channeled through an otherness that will never translate into full psychic independence or social resistance. The racial subject, like any other subject, can speak only in and through a long history of prior race relations.

From this perspective, Kimberlyn Leary writes, "racialized experience must therefore be understood to be something that operates through people as cultural forms rather than simply as matters of individual intention and agency alone."[40] The political and ethical quandaries posed by assimilation and acts of passing, Anne Cheng observes in a similar vein, "may not be about whether it is right or wrong to act like someone else but rather about whether *acting like yourself* (here the idiom is itself revealing) may be fundamentally the same as *acting like someone else*."[41] These psychoanalytic insights are crucial to any investigation of the possibilities and limits of our political actions and psychic efficacy, and they are also indispensable for an analysis of entrenched and unconscious racial histories and stereotypes that continue to form the history of the (racial) subject and to dominate public debates concerning race and identity politics in a colorblind age. The purpose of this book is to draw conscious attention to the polarizing racial histories and scripts that both overdetermine and complicate our social and psychic relations in and with the world.

Stef Craps's recent intervention in the field of trauma studies applies to psychoanalysis in general. Craps argues that the single, catastrophic event-based model of trauma studies in which the Holocaust dominates—"an atrocity committed in Europe, by Europeans, against Europeans"—obscures different forms of incremental, long-term, and cumulative traumas connected to the structural violence of institutional racism occurring on a daily basis for various people of color.[42] On the one hand, the critical interventions of trauma studies implicitly underscore the ways in which catastrophic history shapes group identities as well as individual subjectivities. On the other hand, the problem of particular "chosen traumas," as well as the predicament of how violence comes to be recognized as violence, forecloses recognition of the ties between the social and the psychic, while obscuring the differential ways in which trauma is mobilized to address or to conceal histories of everyday, mundane, and quotidian violence against various subordinated groups.[43] For us, the specificities of the case history provide a unique portal to the hidden histories of everyday, mundane, and quotidian violence against Asian Americans.

Insofar as psychoanalytic theorists and clinicians remain blind to this everyday violence and, indeed, insofar as they remain ignorant of psychoanalysis itself as an integral part of history of liberal Enlightenment discourses of universalism refusing to take racial exploitation and difference into account, they naturalize the status quo and sacrifice therapeutic improvement. In such conditions, psychoanalysis becomes part of the problem rather than part of the solution, making it evident that psychoanalysis is not necessarily or inherently better equipped to address racism or to heal racial conflict than any other field or discipline.

Here, Michel Foucault's as well as Gilles Deleuze and Felix Guattari's critiques of psychoanalysis as a normalizing discourse in the history of sexuality and capitalism—and, we would add, in the history of racial domination and exploitation—are especially germane.[44]

In this project, we do not wish to idealize either the space of the clinic or the speculative dimensions of psychoanalysis as a panacea for racial conflict. Indeed, to the extent that a patient or clinician almost never initiates therapy to examine his or her racism, racism is not seen as a psychopathology but is rather normalized as an everyday practice. It thereby poses particular difficulties for therapeutic address and may be approached as a topic of enormous repression and resistance. In this book, we engage with specific case histories, "playing," to borrow a key term from Winnicott, with their specific intricacies in the hopes of creating a more responsive psychoanalytic theory and practice attuned to racial pain and the psychic predicaments of our Asian American students and patients. Indeed, our desire to address in a sustained manner race in psychoanalysis is powerfully motivated by a need for the field to remain theoretically relevant and clinically responsible to the changing demographics of an increasingly multicultural United States.

In sum, psychoanalysis provides extensive theories of how we misrecognize or disavow subject-subject relations as subject-object relations—a history of misrecognition and disavowal in which slavery, racial domination, and economic exploitation are some of the most prominent examples. That psychic suffering results from subject-object misrecognitions is an axiom in psychoanalytic theory and practice. That racial conflict is the consequence of such formative misrecognitions is also well recognized in critical race studies and identity politics. Yet psychoanalysis and critical race studies have not been in sufficient conversation with one another concerning this formative intersection. For instance, as Asian Americans have moved from voting largely Republican in the 1980s and early 1990s to voting firmly Democrat by the 2012 elections, we must consider how this political shift might mark an altered understanding of whiteness as property and exclusion in a colorblind age.[45]

In our analysis of the history of the Asian American subject, psychic processes of racial melancholia and racial dissociation name and mark histories of social inclusion and exclusion facilitating as well as foreclosing the possibility of reciprocal encounters among different racialized subjects. In part I, we explore racial melancholia as a privileged psychic mechanism for evaluating histories of interminable loss, grief, and exclusion associated with everyday processes of immigration, assimilation, and racialization for Generation X in the wake of the Cold War and movements for civil rights. In part II, we explore racial dissociation as a privileged psychic mechanism for understanding the possibilities and limits of creating a healthy illusion of "me-ness" and racial self in a colorblind and diasporic age for Generation Y.

Racial Melancholia, Racial Dissociation thus seeks to tell the story differently, all the while recognizing that race is one important master narrative in the modern age that frames social relations among different groups and constituencies. Just as the unconscious symptom recedes, evading capture and demanding continuous reinterpretation of its enigmatic kernel, we recognize that race cannot and will not explain all social relations and dynamics. This is an important theoretical caveat: to endow race with an all-encompassing explanatory value would effectively evacuate the racial subject of any agency or responsibility, universalizing the category of race in unproductive and ahistorical ways. It would render the racial subject a pure victim and thus reenact the totalizing effects of objectification and commodification that we have been careful to criticize and work through in these introductory remarks.

The goal of this collection is therefore to bring about a heightened critical awareness of the various modes of race and racism inscribing our social and psychic worlds. Nonetheless, at the end of the day there can only be, to borrow from the language of Winnicott, "good-enough" analyses of race. This insight generates an important but understudied question: how do we account for race in psychoanalysis in a manner that does not re-create a dialectic of objecthood that would render agency and responsibility of the racial subject moot while also asserting an all-encompassing, authentic, and autonomous racial subjecthood as the only and obvious solution? We hope to interrogate and to understand in much deeper ways the social and psychic production of the Asian American subject, the possibilities of its (racial) agency, and the limits of its (racial) will.

In addition to this introduction, *Racial Melancholia, Racial Dissociation* consists of four chapters and an epilogue. We have arranged them chronologically in two parts—crossing historically from Generation X (part I) to Generation Y (part II)—and we have organized the two parts under the rubrics of "racial melancholia" and "racial dissociation."

Throughout, we focus on both *intrasubjective* problems of subject-object distinctions and confusions (melancholia, fetishism, hysteria, paranoia, and the unconscious) and *intersubjective* problems of subject-subject conflicts (reparation, transitional objects, false self, dissociation, and attachment) overshadowed by shifting histories of loss that the concept of racial melancholia initially delineates. The book first engages with Freud's early work on melancholia, composed in the wake of World War I, and then turns to the later object relations theories of Klein and infantile theories of Winnicott, before connecting these critical analyses with more contemporary movements concerning affect theory, trauma studies, and relational psychoanalysis more broadly.

In short, the book moves from psychoanalytic theories of desire, repression, and internal models of neuroses-psychoses governing intrapsychic life to more relational models of attachment, conflict, and trauma organizing interpsychic lives. In revising our understandings of race from both the biological and cultural models to a model of race as relation, we are faced with an opportunity not only for more successful outcomes in the clinic but also for a productive coalitional politics of comparative race studies in our putatively postrace and postidentity moment. As such, we pay particular attention to psychoanalytic practice and the unstated racial dynamics of the clinic, crucial moments between analyst and patient when race becomes affectively charged, when analyst and patient are confounded by their racial positionings.[46]

While racial melancholia describes the politics of loss that overshadow the constitution of Asian American subjectivity for Generation X, the nature of this loss is not fixed but evolves historically over time and space as well as in terms of changing patterns of immigration and diaspora that create new social formations and psychic predicaments for their subjects. Each chapter explores the social and psychic politics of loss and exclusion in relation to a particular figure (the model minority, the transnational adoptee, the parachute child, and the gay millennial) and a particular psychic dilemma (depression, reparation, dissociation, and panic attacks) at a specific historical moment in time. The first two chapters comprising part I largely engage with second-generation immigrants in the wake of the Cold War and movements for civil rights (Generation X), during which problems of race and structural racism were keenly debated in politics, law, and society. The last two chapters comprising part II largely engage with first-generation immigrants, millennials coming of age under political assumptions of colorblindness and economic mandates of neoliberalism and globalization (Generation Y).

It is important to note that, while difficulties of race and racism appear at the heart of the psychic predicaments of the first two case histories on model minorities and transnational adoption, problems of race and racism recede in the psychic conundrums of the latter two case histories on parachute children and gay millennials. Like many millennials in Generation Y, parachute children rarely bring up issues of race or racism, a striking departure from those in Generation X for whom these topics were central points of discussion during treatment. We consider their social and psychic convergences and divergences in greater detail within the individual chapters themselves.

Indeed, we live in strange times: on the one hand, we inhabit a putatively colorblind and postracial society suffused with proliferating discourses of multiculturalism and diversity; on the other hand, we witness on a daily basis ongoing and escalating racial discord and violence, prominently underscored by the recent 2016 presidential election as well as the "Black Lives Matter" campaign that emerged in response to police racism and violence.[47] Predicaments of race as well as its putative disappearance in our colorblind age evidently require new psychic approaches and political strategies to narrate the politics of migration and loss. In the face of intensifying racial violence, with the imminent demise of affirmative action, and as the economic gap between the ultra-rich and the uberpoor continues to widen globally, the need to rethink the vocabulary of critical race studies through psychoanalytic inquiry remains urgent.

Chapter 1, "Racial Melancholia: Model Minorities, Depression, and Suicide," explores depression and suicide among Asian American college students and patients. We use melancholia, Freud's privileged theory of unresolved grief, as a conceptual key to analyze the sustained losses attendant to processes of immigration, assimilation, and racialization for Asian immigrants and their second-generation children as well as depression and self-annihilation that emerge from this psychic state. Freud writes that mourning comes to a conclusion with libido withdrawn from the lost object, place, or ideal to be invested elsewhere. In contrast, melancholia is temporally extended into an indefinite future—it is a mourning without end. Interminable grief and the internalization of loss as self-hatred results from the melancholic's inability to resolve the various unconscious psychic conflicts that forfeitures from immigration—encompassing family and language, home and property, and customs and culture—effect. Moreover, it stems from the melancholic's incapacity to (re)direct psychic investment into new objects, ideals, and places circumscribed by a long history of immigration exclusion and bars to naturalization and citizenship against Asian Americans.

Freud initially formulated melancholia as a pathological, individual, and intrasubjective psychic condition. In chapter 1, we describe racial melancholia instead as a depathologized "structure of feeling," to borrow another term from Williams, one exemplifying the everyday, collective psychic struggles of Asian Americans.[48] If experiences of immigration, assimilation, and racialization in the United States are fundamentally circumscribed by the relinquishing of lost but unspeakable Asian ideals as well as foreclosed investments in whiteness attached to histories of immigration exclusion and bars to national belonging, then we must not slot racial melancholia under the sign of pathology, permanence, or damage. Instead, we reconceptualize it as a normative psychic state involving everyday conflicts and negotiations between mourning *and* melancholia, rather than, in Freud's estimation, mourning or melancholia.

Chapter 2, "Desegregating Love: Transnational Adoption, Racial Reparation, and Racial Transitional Objects," explores mothering and transnational adoption from Asia. About a dozen years ago, more and more students and patients would "come out" to us in the classroom and the clinic—not as gay or lesbian but as transnational adoptees. In recounting their experiences, these students and patients would often employ the language of the closet and the vocabulary of shame. They emphasized how they felt invisible as transnational adoptees and how they felt compelled to come out of the closet time and again.[49] In this chapter, we discuss Mina, a transnational adoptee from Korea and a talented artist studying at a prestigious New York dance school. In her presentation, Mina expressed extreme antipathy toward all minorities, especially the Korean nationals with whom she attended classes. Along with the idealization of her white adoptive mother, Mina also vocalized an unrelenting hatred for her Korean birth mother.

We explore in our analysis of Mina how transnational adoption might be a particularly severe form of racial melancholia and self-hate, one not only excluding the transnational adoptee from larger society but also alienating her from intimate structures of family and kinship. Here we turn to object relations and to Klein, the theorist par excellence of infantile emotions, to analyze Mina's primitive and unrelenting splitting of love and hate. What is clear in this case history is the fact that for Mina splitting was not just a gendered but also a profoundly racialized dynamic: the segregating of love and hate between the good *white* adoptive mother and the bad *Korean* birth mother. As such, we use Mina's case history to argue that racial difference is central rather than peripheral to Klein's fundamental notions of splitting and idealization, depression and guilt, and reinstatement and reparation. For Mina, the reparative position ultimately entails the *racial* reparation of her lost and devalued Korean birth mother.

In chapter 2, we also consider more directly the racialized dynamics of the clinic as well as the race relations between the transnational Korean adoptee patient and her Korean American psychotherapist. We argue that the clinician (Dr. Han), who became pregnant during Mina's treatment, functions, to reformulate an idea from Winnicott, as a "racial transitional object" for Mina, as the Korean mother who keeps her baby and, in the process, helps Mina to renegotiate her volatile racial affects and boundaries. Winnicott argues that the clinic can be a privileged transitional space for negotiating the borders between internal and external worlds and thus helps to establish the existence of what he describes as a "true self."[50] Mina's case history underscores the need to investigate, as Carol Long suggests, how race and racial difference can also interrupt the therapeutic play of the clinic and by extension the larger world, how race poses particular challenges and obstacles to establishing any relation whatsoever between analyst and patient.[51] To the extent that racism often forces young children to confront social conflict prematurely, the formative psychic role of transitional objects and the formative psychic play of transitional spaces are short-circuited.

Chapter 3, "Racial Dissociation: Parachute Children and Psychic Nowhere," moves us into the study of Generation Y by investigating the phenomenon of parachute children—adolescents and children who migrate, often on their own, from different parts of Asia to Anglophone nations in the West in search of educational opportunities. Unlike prior populations of second-generation students we have taught and patients we have treated in Generation X, an increasing portion of our undergraduate students and patients today are first-generation parachute children, millennials who were neither born nor raised in the United States but have come directly from Asia for schooling often without the support of any intimate family structure. Parachuting creates divided families, separate households residing on different continents in social and psychic isolation. As Christy Ling Hom observes, parachute kids become *physically* autonomous from their parents once they move to the United States, yet it is less clear if they also become *emotionally* autonomous.[52]

Although originally an upper-class phenomenon associated with elites from Hong Kong, Taiwan, and Singapore, with the global rise of Asian capital parachuting is an increasingly middle-class phenomenon, with parents making considerable financial sacrifices to send their young children abroad. The dominant narrative associated with parachuting describes it as a transnational solution to an overly competitive Asian university system.[53] Parachuting is represented as providing underperforming Asian students with a "second chance" at success in the West. It thus reconfigures the model minority stereotype of academic and economic success by implicitly asking in regard to these young (im)migrant children: "How does it feel to be a problem? How does it feel *not* to be a model minority?"

Chapter 3 examines two case histories of parachute children, one from South Korea (Yuna) and another from China (Yung), in terms of Winnicott's notions of true and false self and Philip M. Bromberg's ideas of dissociation. False self and dissociation are often thought of as debilitating psychic conditions resulting in a lack of an authentic sense of true self and an absence of attachments to others. However, they also encompass healthy and positive aspects. Indeed, they can function as

psychic mechanisms of self-protection in the face of overwhelming social stress and pressure—for instance, through adopting the social cover
of the model minority stereotype as a form of self-protective camou-
flage. In Yuna's and Yung's cases, however, neither is able to find protection in racial stereotypes or to develop healthy illusions of me-ness—to
reconcile the ways in which they see themselves with the ways in which
others apprehend them. They are not only psychically nowhere but also
racially nowhere. Thus, we are faced with the challenge of understanding how shifting patterns of immigration under neoliberalism and globalization, as well as new immigrants, such as parachute children who
are racially nowhere, mark a different genealogy of colorblindness disconnected from the concept's largely domestic, Constitutional legal history. In short, chapter 3 and part II, more generally, explore the psychic
structures of colorblindness for millennials today.

Chapter 4, "(Gay) Panic Attack: Coming Out in a Colorblind Age,"
continues our discussion of race and racism in the age of neoliberalism
and global capitalism. We examine a series of case histories of academically accomplished parachute children from China and India in the diaspora, all of whom identify as gay men. Although living freely as gay
people in the West often constituted a key factor in these young men's
desires to immigrate, paradoxically they cited neither homophobia nor
racism as significant sites of conflict leading them to seek therapy. Most
suffer from debilitating panic attacks, high levels of anxiety that rendered them incapacitated and depressed with inexplicable bodily and
psychic pain. If sexuality and race remain largely tangential to their psychic predicaments what, then, is all the panic about?

Our analysis of (gay) panic attacks considers the contemporary
politics of coming out in the age of colorblindness. We turn to Freud's
theories of the unconscious as something we can know only through
its transformations and translations into consciousness in order to investigate the shifting relations between racism and homophobia across
two different generations—Generation X and Generation Y—that is,
historically from the age of AIDS to the era of queer liberalism and gay
marriage. In so doing, we consider the ways in which race continues
to function as the political unconscious of our colorblind age—a self-
enforcing social and psychic mechanism in which race constantly appears as disappearing. In our estimation, colorblindness signals not the

absence of racism or homophobia but is precisely the contemporary form in which structures of institutional racism and homophobia appear today. The ideology of colorblindness, we argue, has now been transformed into a collective psychic state of racial dissociation, posing significant challenges to how law and politics might address racial exclusion, exploitation and domination today. Ultimately, it forces us to rethink the ways in which queer liberalism reformulates race as relation and whiteness as property in a colorblind age, to apprehend the dissociated relations among race, sexuality, and economic precarity that define our contemporary multicultural moment under neoliberalism and globalization.

PART I

RACIAL MELANCHOLIA

CHAPTER 1

RACIAL MELANCHOLIA
Model Minorities, Depression, and Suicide

I wondered if whiteness were contagious. If it were, then surely I had caught it. I imagined this "condition" affected the way I walked, talked, dressed, danced, and at its most advanced stage, the way I looked at the world and at other people.

—DANZY SENNA, *CAUCASIA*

THE "CONDITION" OF WHITENESS

Configuring whiteness as a contagion, Birdie Lee, the narrator of Danzy Senna's novel *Caucasia* (1998), connects assimilation to illness and disease. Separated from her African American activist father, Birdie and her blue-blooded mother flee from the law in a racialized and radicalized Boston of the 1970s. Eventually, the two take up residence in New Hampshire, where Birdie passes as "Jesse" and for white. This assimilation into the whiteness of New Hampshire plagues Birdie, who wonders if she "had actually become Jesse, and it was this girl, this Birdie Lee who haunted these streets, searching for ghosts, who was the lie."[1] This vexing condition of whiteness alters the narrator's physical existence— the manner in which Birdie walks, talks, dresses, and dances. Moreover, it configures the sphere of the affective—the ways in which Birdie ultimately apprehends the world and its occupants around her. Physically and psychically haunted, Birdie/Jesse feels "contaminated."[2] This is the condition of racial melancholia.

A DIALOGUE ON RACIAL MELANCHOLIA

As noted in our introduction, part I of this book focuses on Generation X, largely second-generation and comparatively privileged Asian Americans attending public and private universities from the mid-1990s to the mid-2000s. Our psychoanalytic perspective is that of racial melancholia. This chapter is the outcome of a series of sustained dialogues on racial melancholia in which we engaged during the fall and winter of 1998. It was first published in 2000 as an article in the clinical journal *Psychoanalytic Dialogues*, and we have edited and updated it for publication here.

We originally wrote "A Dialogue on Racial Melancholia" as a critical response to disturbing patterns of depression we witnessed in a growing number of our Asian American students and patients. Not all Asian Americans are depressed, but several studies have shown higher levels of social isolation and depressive symptoms among Asian American adolescents in comparison to their African American, Latino/a, and white peers.[3] The article provided an opportunity for us not only to reflect on race and depression but also to consider more generally various approaches to investigating problems of race, immigration, exclusion, and loss in psychoanalytic theory and practice, a topic as important in 1998 as it is today.

As Freud's privileged theory of unresolved grief, melancholia presents a compelling framework to conceptualize registers of loss and depression attendant to social and psychic processes of immigration, assimilation, and racialization.[4] Freud typically casts melancholia as pathological. However, we are more concerned with exploring this psychic condition as a depathologized "structure of feeling," to borrow a concept from Raymond Williams describing emergent patterns of emotion still struggling for social form and recognition.[5] From this particular vantage, melancholia might be theorized in relation to our everyday conflicts and struggles with experiences of racial exclusion and discrimination. Furthermore, even though Freud conceives of melancholia in terms of individual loss and suffering, we are equally interested in approaching melancholia as a collective psychic condition—more interested, that is, in addressing group identities and identifications. How might a focus on racial identifications and differences in psychoanalytic theory allow us particular insights on the history of the Asian American subject in relation to the subject of history—to historical processes of immigration, assimilation, and racialization underpinning the formation of Asian American subjectivity?

ASSIMILATION AS/AND MELANCHOLIA

Freud's theory of melancholia provides a provocative model to consider how processes of assimilation work in the United States, and how the depression that characterizes much of contemporary culture for Generation X might be theorized in relation to race. In the United States today, assimilation into mainstream culture for people of color still means adopting a set of dominant norms and ideals—whiteness, heteronormativity, middle-class family values, Judeo-Christian religious traditions. The exclusion from these norms—the reiterated loss of whiteness as an ideal, notably—establishes a melancholic framework for assimilation and racialization processes in the United States precisely as a series of failed and unresolved integrations.

Let us begin with Freud's essay "Mourning and Melancholia" (1917), in which he attempts to draw a clear distinction between these two psychic states through the question of "successful" and "failed" resolutions to loss. Freud reminds us at the start of his essay that "mourning is regularly the reaction to the loss of a loved person, or to the loss of some abstraction which has taken the place of one, such as one's country, liberty, an ideal, and so on. In some people the same influences produce melancholia instead of mourning and we consequently suspect them of a pathological disposition."[6] Mourning, unlike melancholia, is a psychic process in which the loss of an object or ideal occasions the withdrawal of libido from that object or ideal. This withdrawal cannot be enacted at once; instead, it is a gradual letting go. Libido is detached bit by bit so that, eventually, the mourner is able to declare the object dead and to invest in new objects. In Freud's initial definition of the concept, melancholia is pathological precisely because it is a mourning without end. Interminable grief is the result of the melancholic's inability to resolve the various conflicts and ambivalences that the loss of the loved object effects. In other words, the melancholic cannot "get over" this loss—cannot work out this loss in order to invest in new objects and ideals.

To the extent that ideals of whiteness for Asian Americans and other people of color remain unattainable, processes of assimilation are suspended, conflicted, and unresolved. The irresolution of this process places the concept of assimilation within a melancholic framework. Put otherwise, mourning describes a finite process that might be reasonably aligned with the popular myth of the American "melting pot" for dominant Western European ethnic groups whose various differences are legally, socially, and psychically forged into an ideal of whiteness.[7] In contrast, melancholia describes an unresolved process that might usefully describe the compromised immigration and assimilation of Asian Americans into the national fabric. The suspended assimilation, the inability to blend into the American melting pot, suggests that for Asian Americans ideals of whiteness are perpetually strained—continually estranged. They remain at an unattainable distance, at once a compelling fantasy and a lost ideal.

In configuring assimilation and melancholia in this particular manner, it is important to challenge Freud's contention that melancholia ensues from a "pathological disposition"—that it emerges from the disturbance of an *intrasubjective* psychopathology rather than the disruption of an *intersubjective* relationship. In our analysis, the inability to get over unattainable ideals of whiteness is less an individual than a collective social transaction. Neil Gotanda notes that Asian Americans are racialized precisely as foreign.[8] US mainstream society typically perceives Asian Americans as perpetual foreigners largely based on physiognomy—on skin color and physical markings. Despite the fact that they may be native-born, or however long they may have resided in the country, or whatever their official legal status, Asian Americans are continually viewed as eccentric to the nation. Whether depicted as menacing yellow peril or applauded as model minorities, Asian Americans are cast as an economic threat and hyperproductive automatons and hence pathological to the US nation-state. In either scenario, mainstream refusal to see Asian Americans as part and parcel of the American melting pot is less an individual failure to blend in with the collective than a legally and socially sanctioned interdiction. Even Freud suggests in his essay that melancholia may proceed from "environmental influences" rather than internal conditions that threaten the existence of the object or ideal.[9]

Freud goes on to delineate the debilitating consequences of melancholia. When faced with unresolved grief, the melancholic preserves the lost object or ideal by incorporating it into the ego and establishing an ambivalent identification with it—ambivalent precisely because of the unresolved and conflicted nature of this forfeiture. From a slightly different perspective, we might say that ambivalence is precisely the result of the transformation an intersubjective conflict into an intrasubjective loss, as the melancholic makes every conceivable effort to retain the absent object or ideal, to keep it alive in the shelter of the ego. However, the tremendous costs of maintaining this ongoing relationship to the lost object or ideal are psychically damaging. Freud notes that the "distinguishing mental features of melancholia are a profoundly painful dejection, cessation of interest in the outside world, loss of the capacity to love, inhibition of all activity, and a lowering of the self-regarding feelings to a degree that finds utterance in self-reproaches and self-revilings, and culminates in a delusional expectation of punishment."[10]

In identifying with the lost object, the melancholic is able to preserve it but only as a type of haunted, ghostly identification. That is, the melancholic assumes the emptiness of the lost object or ideal, identifies with this emptiness, and thus participates in his or her own self-denigration and ruination of self-esteem. Freud summarizes the distinction between mourning and melancholia in this oft-quoted remark: "In mourning it is the world which has become poor and empty; in melancholia it is the ego itself."[11] He contends that melancholia is one of the most difficult of psychic conditions to confront and to cure as it is largely an unconscious process, one in which the significance of the lost object remains unconscious and opaque. To reprise our citation from the opening pages of our introduction, Freud observes, "In yet other cases, one feels justified in maintaining the belief that a loss of this [melancholic] kind occurred, but one cannot see clearly what it is that has been lost, and it is all the more reasonable to suppose that the patient cannot consciously perceive what he has lost either. This, indeed, might be so even if the patient is aware of the loss which has given rise to his melancholia, but only in the sense that he knows *whom* he has lost but not *what* he has lost in him."[12] Freud tells us that the depression often accompanying melancholia is extremely dangerous, characterized by the tendency to suicide. Here, we might add, suicide may not merely be physical; as in *Caucasia,* it may also manifest in the psychical erasure of one's identity—a self-imposed exile and exclusion. The effacing of a particular racial, sexual, or gender identity marks the emergence of a precarious social and psychic life.

NATIONAL MELANCHOLIA

For Asian Americans and other people of color, suspended assimilation into mainstream culture may involve not only debilitating personal consequences; ultimately, it also constitutes the foundation for a type of national melancholia, a collective national haunting, with destructive effects. In *Caucasia,* the ambivalence characterizing the narrator's passing into whiteness leaves her with the constant and eerie feeling of "contamination."[13] Writing about the nature of collective identifications, Freud notes in "Group Psychology and the Analysis of the Ego" (1921), "In a group every sentiment and act is contagious, and contagious to such a degree that an individual readily sacrifices his personal interest to the collective interest. This is an aptitude very contrary to his nature, and of which a man is scarcely capable, except when he makes part of a group."[14] Our analysis insists on a consideration of what happens when the demand to sacrifice the personal to collective interest is accompanied not by inclusion in—but rather exclusion from—the larger group. It reorients psychic problems of racial melancholia toward social problems concerning legal histories of whiteness as property and, in particular, exclusion laws and bars to naturalization and citizenship for Asian Americans as a type of property right.

As we know, the formation of the US nation-state entailed—and continues to entail—a history of institutionalized exclusions, legal and otherwise. Part of our introduction focused on the transatlantic slave trade and indigenous dispossession. Here, it is vital to consider the long history of legalized exclusion of Asian American immigrants and citizens alike—from Japanese internment and indefinite detention during World War II to earlier exclusion acts legislated by Congress, brokered by the executive, and upheld by the judiciary against every Asian immigrant group.[15] For example, from 1882 to 1943, Chinese immigrants experienced the longest legalized history of exclusion and bars to naturalization and citizenship—the first raced-based exclusions in US history. To cite but one specific instance, in 1888 the US Congress retroactively terminated the legal right of some twenty thousand Chinese residents to reenter the United States after visiting China. Those excluded from reentry were also barred from recovering their personal property remaining in the country, underscoring the ways in which race, citizenship, and property were simultaneously managed by the state to control and restrict flows of both Asian labor and capital.

This law was followed by a series of further exclusion laws, as well as accompanied by legislative acts against miscegenation and the ownership of private property, culminating in the National Origins Act (1924) and the Tydings-McDuffie Act (1934), which effectively halted all immigration from Asia for an indefinite period. As Teemu Ruskola notes, at the very historical moment when "the United States was pleased to refer to its China policy as Open Door . . . it hardly escaped the Chinese that the door swung one way only."[16] Yet, in our multicultural and colorblind age, few people remember this history of racially motivated discrimination against Asian Americans that laid the legal foundation for the emergence of the figure of the "illegal immigrant" and of "alien citizenship" preoccupying so much of political debate concerning immigration today. This history of exclusion is barely taught in US universities or high schools—indeed, colorblindness and the model minority myth demand a forgetting of these events of group discrimination in the name of abstract equality and individual meritocracy. A return to this history thus expands our prior analyses of race as relation and whiteness as property to consider how the legal mechanisms of citizenship have broadly functioned as a kind of restricted property right. For Asian immigrants, these mechanisms have mediated a long history of social exclusion and inclusion in US law and society. Racial melancholia can be seen as one profound psychic effect marking these histories of legal exclusion from the nation-state and prohibitions from national belonging.

Today, discourses of American exceptionalism and democratic myths of abstract equality and individualism demand a forgetting of these formative losses and exclusions, an enforced psychic amnesia that can return only as a type of repetitive national haunting—a type of negative or absent presence.[17] The contemporary model minority stereotype that defines Asian Americans is both a product of—and productive of—this negative or absent presence.[18] Asian American model minority discourse emerged in the postwar period after the lifting of legalized exclusion—in the wake of Cold War conflict, the US civil rights movements, and the reformation of the Immigration and Nationality Act (Hart-Celler Act) of 1965.

The Hart-Celler Act abolished the earlier immigration quotas based on national origins at the heart of US immigration policy for nearly half a century, replacing it with a system of preferences focused on the technical skills of immigrants and on family reunification. It dramatically shifted immigration patterns to the United States and spurred a "brain drain" of settlers from Asia (and Latin America). At the same time, Hart-Celler also created a vast and largely unacknowledged force of low-income and undocumented migrants from South Asia, new areas of China, particularly Fujian province, and Southeast Asia. This "yellowing" of the US nation-state reversed a long history of anti-Asian exclusion precisely under the banner of model minority citizenship and the collective forgetting of this history of exclusion and its unauthorized subjects.

The model minority myth identifies the academic success of second-generation Asian American immigrant children as dispositive of the United States as a land of equal opportunity free of racial discrimination or distress. Thereby, it functions as a national tool that manages and erases a long history of institutionalized exclusion by characterizing Asian American success precisely as the result—rather than something that occurred despite the lack—of equal opportunity in the United States. In turn, the deployment of the model minority myth configures the unequal status of African Americans in US culture and society as a self-inflicted injury. Resisting the invidious political juxtaposition of Asian American "success" with African American "failure," comparative race scholars have sought to reformulate this regulatory dialectic.

Over a hundred years ago, W. E. B. Du Bois asked African Americans in *The Souls of Black Folk* (1903), "How does it feel to be a problem?"[19] Today, comparative race scholars have revised Du Bois's earlier inquiry, asking Asian Americans, "How does it feel to be a solution?"[20] (We return to this dynamic in detail is chapter 3 on parachute children and psychic nowhere.) Put in terms of comparative race relations, Ellen Wu observes that during the prewar era of exclusion and yellow peril, Asians were defined as definitely not white. However, following the postwar era of inclusion, citizenship, and the emergence of model minority stereo-type, Asians were defined as definitely not black.[21] Understanding this triangulation is key to apprehending the ways in which racial binaries of black and white mask complex social relations of race while preventing political coalitions and alliances. Effacing unequal histories of racial discrimination, this divide and conquer strategy emerges most forcefully today in contemporary debates about affirmative action that seek to pit the interests of African Americans and Asian Americans against one another.

The model minority stereotype is a myth because it homogenizes widely disparate Asian American and Asian immigrant groups by generalizing them all as academically and economically successful, with no social problems to speak of. In this manner, the stereotype works to deny, in Lisa Lowe's words, the "heterogeneity, hybridity, and multiplicity" of various Asian American individuals and groups who do not fit its ideals of model citizenry.[22] The pervasiveness of the model minority stereotype in our contemporary national imagination thus works as one important melancholic mechanism facilitating the erasure and loss of repressed Asian American identities as well as histories of discrimination and exclusion. These identities and histories can return only as a type of ghostly presence. In this sense, the Asian American model minority subject also endures in the US historical imaginary as a melancholic national object—as a haunting specter to democratic ideals of inclusion that cannot quite get over these legislated histories of loss.

The psychic consequences that this model of national melancholia has exacted on the Asian American psyche are extensively explored and interrogated in Asian American cultural productions. One compelling example comes from Maxine Hong Kingston's *China Men* (1980). In Kingston's historical novel, an imaginary chronicle of several successive generations of male ancestors in the United States, the narrator speculates about the disappearance of the "Grandfather of the Sierra Nevada Mountains." After he helps to complete the transcontinental railroad, the greatest technological feat of the nineteenth century, Ah Goong vanishes. Kingston writes, "Maybe he hadn't died in San Francisco, it was just his papers that burned; it was just that his existence was outlawed by Chinese Exclusion Acts. The family called him Fleaman. They did not understand his accomplishments as an American ancestor, a holding, homing ancestor of this place."[23]

Kingston understands that the law's refusal to recognize Chinese immigrants as citizens "outlaws" their existence, subjecting them to legal erasure as well as institutional violence: "It was dangerous to stay," she observes in the context of the "Golden Spike" ceremony commemorating the railroad's completion. "The Driving Out had begun. Ah Goong does not appear in railroad photographs."[24] At the same time, Kingston also underscores how this historical repudiation of the Asian laborer gains its psychic efficacy through a simultaneous internalization of its interdictions on the part of those excluded themselves. That is, the grandfather's own family members refuse to recognize him as "an American ancestor, a holding, homing ancestor of this place." They cannot perceive the "Fleaman's" accomplishments building the transcontinental railroad as legitimizing his membership in the American nation. How, in turn, can it be possible to see themselves as legitimate members of this society?

In this regard, racial melancholia can be described as splitting the Asian American psyche. This cleaving of the psyche can be productively thought about in terms of an altered, racialized model of classic Freudian fetishism.[25] That is, assimilation into the national fabric demands a psychic splitting on the part of the Asian American subject who knows and does not know, at once, that she or he is part of the larger social body. In the same breath, fetishism also describes mainstream society's disavowal and projection of otherness onto a disparaged group that is then homogenized and reduced to a stereotype. In this manner, racial fetishism delineates a psychic process by which difference is assumed and projected and then negated and denied, returning us to social dynamics of Myrdal's "American dilemma."

In the early 1970s, psychologists Stanley Sue and Derald Sue (1971) reframed sociologist Robert Park's influential notion of the "marginal man" to describe an Asian American subject who desires to assimilate into mainstream American society at any cost. The marginal man faithfully subscribes to the ideals of assimilation only through an elaborate self-denial and repression of the daily acts of institutionalized racism directed against him. In "Chinese-American Personality and Mental Health," the Sues write about the complex psychological defenses and dissociations that the marginal man must necessarily employ in order to function within US society. The marginal man finds it "difficult to admit widespread racism since to do so would be to say that he aspires to join a racist society."[26] Caught in this untenable bind, the marginal man must necessarily become a split subject—one who exhibits a faithful allegiance to the universal norms of abstract equality and collective belonging at the same time that he displays an uncomfortable understanding of his disenfranchisement from these democratic ideals of national inclusion. This splitting of the racial subject leads to feelings of "contamination."

In *Caucasia,* Birdie's unresolved assimilation into the whiteness of New Hampshire provides another insight on the psychic effects of splitting on the level of the sign—at the site of nomination. Through the twinning of her name, the impossible mulatta child is marked by doubleness: Birdie (mulatta) → Jesse (white). Here, Birdie/Jesse is the object of melancholia for a nation organized by an ecology of whiteness. At the same time, she is the subject of melancholia—a girl haunted by ghosts. It is difficult not to notice that much of late-twentieth-century ethnic and immigrant literature in the United States is characterized by ghosts and by hauntings from both these perspectives—the objects and subjects of racial melancholia. For instance, the subtitle of Kingston's famous novel *The Woman Warrior* (1976) is *Memoirs of a Girlhood Among Ghosts*. Similarly, the Nobel laureate Toni Morrison observes that the African American presence is "the ghost in the machine."[27]

MIMICRY; OR, THE MELANCHOLIC MACHINE

Racial melancholia as psychic splitting and national dis-ease opens on the interconnected terrains of mimicry, ambivalence, and the stereotype. In his seminal essay "Of Mimicry and Man: The Ambivalence of Colonial Discourse," Homi Bhabha describes the ways in which a colonial regime compels the colonized subject to mimic Western ideals of whiteness. At the same time, this mimicry is also condemned to failure. Bhabha writes, "Colonial mimicry is the desire for a reformed, recognizable Other, *as a subject of a difference that is almost the same, but not quite.* Which is to say, that the discourse of mimicry is constructed around an *ambivalence*; in order to be effective, mimicry must continually reproduce its slippage, its excess, its difference. . . . *Almost the same but not white.*"[28] Bhabha locates and labels the social imperative to assimilate as the colonial structure of mimicry. He highlights not only the social performance but also its inevitable, built-in failure. This doubling of difference that is almost the same but not quite, almost the same but not white, results in ambivalence, which comes to define the failure of mimicry.

Here we elaborate on Bhabha's observations of mimicry with its intrasubjective internalization into the psychic domain through the logic of racial melancholia. It is important to remember that, as with Bhabha's analysis of mimicry in the colony, Freud marks ambivalence as one of melancholia's defining characteristics. In describing the genealogy of ambivalence in melancholia, Freud himself moves from the domain of the social to the realm of the psychic. He notes that the "conflict due to ambivalence, which sometimes arises from real experiences, sometimes more from constitutional factors, must not be overlooked among the preconditions of melancholia."[29] According to Freud, melancholia not only traces an internalized pathological identification with what was once an external but now lost ideal. In this moving from outside to inside, we also get a strong sense of how social injunctions of mimicry configure individual psychic structures as split and dis-eased. The ambivalence that comes to define Freud's concept of melancholia is one that finds its origins and routes in social history—in colonial and racial structures impelling performative displays of mimicry and man.

It is crucial to extend Bhabha's theories on colonial mimicry to the domestic landscape of race relations in the United States—a postcolonial nation itself—in order to consider how we might usefully explore this concept for Asian Americans. One potential site of investigation is the racial stereotype discussed above—the model minority myth. In an earlier essay titled "The Other Question: Stereotype, Discrimination, and the Discourse of Colonialism," Bhabha aligns ambivalence and splitting with the stereotype, suggesting that the performance of mimicry and the phenomenon of the stereotype be considered together. The stereotype, Bhabha writes, "is a form of knowledge and identification that vacillates between what is always 'in place,' already known, and something that must be anxiously repeated . . . for it is the force of ambivalence that gives the colonial stereotype its currency."[30]

If we conceptualize the model minority myth as a privileged stereotype through which Asian Americans appear as subjects in the contemporary social domain, then we gain a better understanding of how mimicry specifically functions as a material practice in racial melancholia. That is, Asian Americans are forced to mimic the model minority stereotype in order to be recognized by mainstream society—in order to be, in order to be seen at all. However, to the extent that this mimicry of the model minority stereotype functions only to estrange Asian Americans from mainstream norms and ideals (as well as from their own histories), mimicry can operate only as a melancholic process. As both a social and a psychic malady, mimicry and the model minority myth distance Asian Americans from the mimetic ideals of the nation. For Asian Americans, mimicry is always a partial success as well as a partial failure to assimilate into regimes of whiteness.

Let us analyze this dynamic from yet another angle. Although Asian Americans are now largely thought of as model minorities exemplifying the "American dream," this stereotype of material success is partial because it is configured primarily as economic achievement (in spite of extreme poverty in various Asian American communities) rather than social or cultural belonging. The putative success of the model minority subject comes to mask the limits of his political representation and agency. It covers over her inability to gain "full" and "well-rounded" subjectivities—to be politicians, athletes, artists, and activists, for example—to be recognized as a "typical American," to invoke the exact title of Gish Jen's novel from 1991.

To occupy the model minority position, Asian American subjects must therefore submit to a model of economic rather than political and cultural legitimation. To this day, widespread social and parental pressures often dictate that Asian American students must opt for "safe" professional and upwardly mobile careers—doctor, engineer, lawyer—often at the expense of individual desires and psychic well-being—"doing well versus feeling well."[31] They must not contest the dominant order of things; they must not "rock the boat" or draw attention to themselves. It is often difficult for our Asian American patients and students to articulate or to acknowledge their desires, as the model minority stereotype demands not only an enclosed but also a passive self-sufficiency and compliance. Drawing from Jacques Lacan's idea of the subject as a desiring subject, Antonio Viego has described a similar prioritizing of needs over desires in the context of Latino immigration. He describes this process as the psychic production of a "dead subject," the creation of a subject dead to his or her desires.[32] Insofar as both social and parental pressures emphasize needs over desires—necessity over extravagance in Sau-ling Wong's elegant formulation—melancholia and the death drive cannot be far behind.[33]

The model minority stereotype also delineates Asian Americans as academically successful but rarely well-rounded—well-rounded in tacit comparison to a normative white student body. Here is another example of Bhabha's concept of mimicry as nearly successful imitation. This not quite successful performance attempts to cover over that gap—the failure of well-roundedness—as well as that unavoidable ambivalence resulting from this tacit comparison in which the Asian American student is seen as lacking and not fully assimilated. This social failure incites a psychic ambivalence that characterizes the racialized subject's identifications with dominant ideals of whiteness as pathological. This is an ambivalence that opens upon the landscape of melancholia and depression for many Asian American students. Those Asian Americans who do not fit into the model minority stereotype are altogether erased from—are not recognized by—mainstream society. Like Kingston's grandfather in *China Men,* they are often rejected by their own families as well.

The difficulty of negotiating this unwieldy stereotype is that, unlike most negative stereotypes of African Americans, the model minority myth is considered to be a "positive" representation—a model of social achievement and exceptionalism. In this regard, not only mainstream society but also Asian Americans themselves become attached to, and divided by, its seemingly admirable qualities without sufficiently recognizing its liabilities—what the political theorist Wendy Brown describes as a "wounded attachment."[34] According to Bhabha, in its doubleness the stereotype, like mimicry, creates a gap embedded in an unrecognized structure of ambivalence. In Jen's *Typical American,* for instance, we encounter Ralph Chang, who chases the American dream through his attempts to build a fried-chicken empire, the "Chicken Palace." Eventually, the franchise fails, and the first "a" falls off the "Chicken Palace" sign which becomes "Chicken P_lace." This falling off is the linguistic corollary to the gap in the American dream that Ralph unsuccessfully mimes. Perhaps it is in this gap—in this emptiness—that melancholia emerges and comes to inhabit. It is also where the negotiation between mourning and melancholia is staged.

MOURNING/MELANCHOLIA/IMMIGRATION

The structure of mimicry gestures to the partial success and partial failure to mourn our identifications with whiteness. Moreover, it also gestures to our partial success and partial failure to mourn our identifications and affiliations with Asian cultures. Thus far, we have been focusing on the loss of whiteness as an ideal structuring the assimilation and racialization processes of second-generation Asian Americans. However, the lost object can be multifaceted. Since the reformation of the Immigration and Nationality Act of 1965, demographically there are more first-generation Asian American immigrants living in the United States today than any other generations of Asian Americans (these patterns are shifting noticeably under globalization today, a topic of further discussion in part II). Examining Asian American experiences of exclusion from the mid-1990s, this chapter focuses on the second-generation offspring of these first-generation immigrants who at that time filled our classrooms and clinics. Hence, it focuses on the psychic dynamics of mourning and melancholia in relation to problems of immigration and intergenerational losses between first- and second-generation Asian Americans. Generationally, racial melancholia delineates a psychic process by which an intersubjective subject-subject relationship between mainstream and minority groups as well as between the first- and the second-generation Asian American parents and children becomes configured as an intrasubjective psychic predicament of loss and exclusion.

The experience of immigration itself is based on a structure of mourning. When one leaves one's country of origin—voluntarily or involuntarily—one must mourn a host of losses both concrete and abstract. These include homeland, family, language, identity, property, status in community—the list goes on. In Freud's theory of mourning, one works through and finds closure to these losses by investing in new objects—in the American dream, for example. Our attention to the problematics of mimicry, performance, ambivalence, and the stereotype, as well as our earlier analysis of the legal history of exclusion and bars to naturalization and citizenship for Asian Americans, reveals a social structure that prevents the immigrant from fully assimilating into the American melting pot. From another perspective, it denies him or her the capacity to invest in new objects. The inability to invest in new objects, we must remember, is part of Freud's definition of melancholia. Given the ways in which Asian American immigrants are foreclosed from fully assimilating into mainstream culture, are they consigned to a perpetually melancholic status? If so, how do we begin to address Freud's notion of melancholia as pathological? Clearly not all Asian Americans are consigned to melancholy or depression. If this is the case, how do first-generation immigrants negotiate and mitigate their losses? How do their second-generation offspring inherit and inhabit these losses?

If the losses suffered by first-generation immigrants are not resolved and mourned in the process of assimilation—if libido is not replenished by the investment in new objects, new communities, and new ideals—then the melancholia that ensues can be traumatically passed down to the second generation. At the same time, can the hope of assimilation and pursuit of the American dream also be transferred? If so, we might say that mourning and melancholia are reenacted and lived out by second-generation children in their own attempts to assimilate and to negotiate the American dream. Here, immigration and assimilation characterize a process involving not just mourning or melancholia but the intergenerational negotiation between mourning and melancholia. Configured as such, this notion begins to depathologize melancholia by situating it as the intersubjective unfolding and outcome of the mourning process that underwrites the various psychic investments and losses connected to the immigration experience.

CASE HISTORY: ELAINE

Let us turn to a clinical example. Elaine, a US-born Korean American female college student, grew up in Texas. Her father is a professor, and her mother is a homemaker. An academic dean referred Elaine to me (Dr. Han) in 1997 because she was at risk of failing her first year in college. In a tearful presentation, Elaine reported, "My parents have sacrificed everything to raise me here. If my parents had stayed in Korea, my mom would be so much happier and not depressed. She would have friends to speak Korean with, my father would be a famous professor, and we would be better off socially and economically. I wouldn't be so pressured to succeed. They sacrificed everything for me, and now it's up to me to please them, and to do well in school." When asked the reasons for her academic probation, she responded, "I didn't do well because at a certain point, I didn't care anymore, about myself or anything else."

Elaine's case is an illustration of an intergenerational transference between immigrant parents and a child that might be usefully described through the logic of racial melancholia. The loss experienced by the parents' failure to achieve the American dream—to achieve a standard of living and a level of social acceptance greater than what they could have putatively achieved in Korea—is a loss transferred onto and incorporated by Elaine for her to work out and to repair. In particular, Elaine reenacts these losses through her relationship with her mother. Elaine's depression is a result of internalized guilt and residual anger that she not only feels toward but also identifies with in her mother. Through this incorporation, she also functions as the placeholder of her mother's depression. This mother-daughter predicament has been widely debated in feminist circles.[35] Here, the question is how race intersects and reconfigures what is considered a strongly gendered dynamic.

This intersection of sexual and racial difference in first- and second-generation intersubjective conflict is a common narrative in Asian American literature as well. Numerous stories portray the first generation (and often the second generation) as being a lost generation—bereft, traumatized, with few material or psychic resources.[36] Is it, however, only at the moment in which the first generation acknowledges its disappointments and failure to achieve the American dream that this theme of first-generation sacrifice then emerges to be retroactively projected onto the second generation? In other words, are Asian American parents as completely selfless as the theme of sacrifice and ideals of Confucian filial tradition suggest, or is this idea a compensatory gesture that attaches itself to the losses, disappointments, and failures associated with immigration? Could the ambitions of Elaine's father to become a professor in an American university have motivated the family's immigration, or was it perhaps his inability to succeed in Korea—especially because of constraints on opportunities connected to various military conflicts during World War II and the ensuing Cold War? Sacrifice, it is important to remember, is built on the assumption of nonequivalence and the melancholic notion that what is forfeited and lost can never be recuperated. In turn, do children of immigrants "repay" this sacrifice only by repeating and perpetuating its melancholic logic—by berating and sacrificing themselves?

But could sacrifice also be considered the displaced residue of hope— a hope for the repairing of melancholia, of achieving the American dream? Can hope, too, be transferred from parent to child, or from child to parent? Elaine's case evokes Rea Tajiri's moving documentary film *History and Memory* (1991).[37] *History and Memory* is about a young Japanese American girl whose parents endure internment during World War II. Whereas the girl's mother has repressed all memories of the internment experience, the daughter has nightmares that she cannot explain— recurring images of a young woman at a watering well. The daughter is depressed, and the parents argue over the etiology of her depression. Eventually, the daughter discovers that these nightmares are reenactments of the mother's histories in camp. Ironically, the mother has history but no memory, while the daughter has memory but no history. For both mother and daughter, history and memory do not come together until the daughter visits the former site of the internment camp, Poston. There she realizes that it is her mother's history that she remembers.

Tajiri's film is an eloquent disquisition on racial melancholia. It is a compelling example of the ways in which historical traumas of loss, grief, and forgetting are passed down from one generation to another unconsciously—how, as Freud remarks in his essay "The Unconscious" (1915), "the unconscious of one human being can react upon that of another, without passing through the conscious."[38] The daughter's psychic predicament illustrates Freud's observation that the most difficult losses suffered in melancholia are unconscious ones, psychic forfeitures that cannot be properly grieved and for which Freud could offer no simple solution or remedy. Yet, at the same time, it also diverges from Freud's conception of the disease insofar as it posits a theory of melancholia that is not individual but that is intergenerationally shared among members of a social group, Japanese American internees. It also departs from Freud's definition of melancholia as pathology and permanence. Here, the hope for psychic health is stitched into the fabric of melancholia but only as an optative gesture that must be redeemed by subsequent generations. In contrast to Freud's contention that melancholia is a classic intra-subjective psychic condition, Tajiri's version of melancholia approaches this condition from a different perspective. It refines our theory of racial melancholia as a psychic state focused on bonds of displaced love and hate among a collective—an intersubjective collective—that might be addressed and resolved across generations. Indeed, in *History and Memory* the daughter's return to Poston initiates an incipient healing process in her mother.

In melancholia, the subject's turning from outside (intersubjective) to inside (intrapsychic) threatens to render social history invisible. What is striking in both these examples, of Elaine and of *History and Memory,* is the manner in which the daughters' bodies and voices become substitutes for those of the mothers—not just the mothers' bodies and voices but also something that is unconsciously lost in them. To return to Freud, the melancholic "knows *whom* [s]he has lost but not *what* [s]he has lost in [her]."[39] Elaine's narrative and the Japanese American daughter's nightmares are not their own histories. These daughters have absorbed and been saturated by their mothers' losses. The mothers' voices haunt the daughters. These losses and voices are melancholically displaced from the external world of the social into the internal world of the psyche. The anger that these daughters feel toward the loved object is internalized as depression and anger toward the self. Freud's essay reminds us that the reproaches against the self are, in fact, displaced reproaches against the loved object that have been shifted onto the individual's own ego.[40]

In this respect, racial melancholia highlights a particular subject-object confusion, as it traces a trajectory from love to hate of the lost object, indeed orienting the production of racial hatred over love. In the course of moving from the outside world into the domain of the psyche, this hate is brought into the shelter of the ego, identified with the self, and subsequently transformed into self-hate. As such, the internal monologue that the daughters direct toward themselves should rightly be an external dialogue between daughter and mother—indeed, toward the larger social world around them. If racial melancholia traces the social exclusions of immigration, assimilation, and racialization as form of self-hate, how might we address the problem as a subject-subject relation, a subject-subject (com)plaint?

In the *Psychic Life of Power*, Judith Butler writes, "The melancholic would have *said something*, if he or she could, but did not, and now believes in the sustaining power of the voice. Vainly, the melancholic now says what he or she would have said, addressed only to himself, as one who is already split off from himself, but whose power of self-address depends upon this self-forfeiture. The melancholic thus burrows in a direction opposite to that in which he might find a fresher trace of the lost other, attempting to resolve the loss through psychic substitutions and compounding the loss as he goes."[41] This turning from outside to inside threatens to erase the political bases of melancholia, and to obscure the history of the melancholic (racial) subject in relation to the subject of (racial) history, precisely as it configures hate as a displaced residue of love. To approach this dynamic from another angle, when Asian American students seek therapy, their mental health issues are overwhelmingly perceived as intergenerational familial conflicts. That is, they are often diagnosed as being exclusively symptomatic of cultural rather than social or political conflicts. By configuring Asian values and

Confucian filial tradition as the exclusive source of all intergenerational dis-ease, a pathologized Asian culture comes to serve as an alibi for a panoply of mental health issues and symptoms.[42]

These predicaments may in fact trace their etiology not to questions of Asian cultural difference but rather to historical forms of institutionalized racism and economic exploitation—to the subject of (racial) history. The segregation of Asian American mental health issues into the domain of cultural difference covers over structural questions of institutional violence and inequality, as well as histories of whiteness as property, as they circulate both inside and outside the therapeutic space of the clinic. For instance, not to account for a history of Japanese internment and indefinite detention when analyzing Tajiri's mother-daughter family conflict serves not only to repress and to deny this history but also to redouble and to intensify the source of the daughter's melancholia and depression.

Lowe writes in *Immigrant Acts*, "Interpreting Asian American culture exclusively in terms of the master narratives of generational conflict and filial relation essentializes Asian American culture, obscuring the particularities and incommensurabilities of class, gender, and national diversities among Asians. The reduction of the cultural politics of racialized ethnic groups, like Asian Americans, to first-generation/second-generation struggles displaces social differences into a privatized familial opposition. Such reductions contribute to the aestheticizing commodification of Asian American *cultural* differences, while denying the immigrant histories of material exclusion and differentiation."[43] A therapeutic process that solely attributes Asian cultural differences to intergenerational conflict may result in the failure to cure; even more, it may also serve to endanger further the mental health of the patient.

CASE HISTORY: NELSON

This discussion on intergenerational dilemmas of immigration and assimilation brings us to the related issue of mourning, melancholia, and language. Nelson, a first-generation Japanese American student who emigrated from Osaka to New Jersey when he was five, sought therapy with me (Dr. Han) in 1996, presenting chronic struggles with depression associated with racial conflict. Nelson is the eldest child and has two siblings, a brother and a sister, both of whom were born in the United States. Before Nelson entered school, his mother spoke only Japanese to the children. When Nelson started kindergarten, his teacher admonished his mother to replace Japanese with English at home if she wanted her children to assimilate and to become successful students. Despite the mother's broken English, she followed the teacher's instructions assiduously, speaking only English to her children.

Nelson recounts a story that took place later in grade school. During a reading lesson, he mispronounced "crooked" as "crookd" (one syllable). His teacher shamed him publicly for his failed speech act—his failed act of mimicry—and demanded to know where he learned to mispronounce such a simple word. Nelson reluctantly replied that he learned this pronunciation from his mother. Nelson remembers, in particular, feelings of social embarrassment and shame from the ridicule of his teacher and classmates.

What we learn about Nelson's case history is that, although his original connection to the primary object (the mother) was through the Japanese language, this connection was interrupted by a foreign property, English. The mother's poor mimicry of English severed and revised the earliest mother-child attachment, one brokered in Japanese. As such, Nelson could no longer mirror himself from his mother, in Japanese or in English. This estrangement from language, both native and foreign, is a double loss. Although acquiring a new language (English) should be perceived as a positive cognitive development, what is often not acknowledged sufficiently is the concomitant psychic trauma triggered by the loss of what had once been a safe, nurturing, and familiar language to the young child (Japanese).

The loss of Japanese as a safe and nurturing object reveals another way to think about racial melancholia in relation to processes of immigration and assimilation. In Nelson's case history, melancholia results not only from a thwarted identification with a dominant ideal of unattainable whiteness but also a vexed relationship to a compromised Japaneseness. Nelson's situation reveals how on two fronts ideals of whiteness and ideals of Japaneseness are lost and unresolved. Here the problem of accent marks an impossible social compliance. In both instances, language is the privileged vehicle—the privileged property— by which standards of successful assimilation and failed integration are measured. In this sense, language itself might be thought of as a kind of property right and stereotype, demanding a flawless mimicry on the part of the young Nelson, whose failed performance leads him to shame and self-abasement at a crucial moment of social and psychic development.

Nelson's transition from Japanese to English is another example of the negotiation between mourning and melancholia in the immigration and assimilation process. That is, although he suffers a loss and revaluation of his mother tongue, his transition into the adopted ideal of the English language is anything but smooth. We need to emphasize that the shaming ritual to which the grade-school teacher subjected Nelson—one all too common in the Darwinian space of the classroom—is one that not merely makes his transition into English difficult but also demonizes and repudiates the mother (and the mother tongue and accent) at the same time. What was once a loved and safe object is retroactively transformed into an object of shame and insecurity. To the extent that the figure of the mother originally represents safe notions of "home," Nelson's estrangement from his mother, and from his mother tongue, renders her *unheimlich*—unhomely, unfamiliar, uncanny—a topic that critical race scholar Mari Matsuda has explored in her legal analyses of accent discrimination.[44]

The relationship between language, pedagogy, and assimilation into a mainstream national citizenry is examined also in a short story by Monique T. D. Truong. "Kelly" (1991) is about a young Vietnamese refugee, Thuy-Mai, who finds herself in the improbable space of a North Carolina classroom of 1975. Truong's narrator composes a distressing epistolary monologue to her one and only (and now absent) friend from that dark period of her life, Kelly. In doing so, she reenacts the melancholic logic discussed above. That is, an intersubjective external dialogue meant for two parties is melancholically internalized and transformed into an intrasubjective monologue of one remarkable for its anger and solipsism. What is an epistolary, after all, other than an impassioned (but not necessarily answered) plea to the other?

Truong's narrator recalls their grade-school teacher:

Kelly, remember how Mrs. Hammerick talked about Veteran's Day? How about the Day of Infamy when the Japanese bombed Pearl Harbor? Mrs. Hammerick, you know, the mayor's wife always had a sweet something surrounding her like she had spent too much time pulling taffy.... Kelly, you only knew that she liked the Beths and the Susans cause they wore pink and never bulged and buckled out of their shirt plackets. I was scared of her like no dark corners could ever scare me. You have to know that all the while she was teaching us history she was telling, with her language for the deaf, blind, and dumb; she was telling all the boys in our class that I was Pearl and my last name was Harbor. They understood her like she was speaking French and their names were all Claude and Pierre.[45]

Truong's story expands our discussion of language and its performative effects on the constitution of good and bad national subjects. Here, Mrs. Hammerick's common language for the "deaf, blind, and dumb"—a language from which Thuy-Mai is emphatically excluded—is used to create and then separate good students from bad students within the institutionalized space of the classroom. The Susans and the Beths, the Claudes and the Pierres, are all, as Louis Althusser would put it, "interpellated" by the mayor's wife as good citizen-subjects of the classroom and nation-state.[46] Truong emphasizes how education is a primary site through which narratives of national identity and belonging are established and reinforced through pedagogical compliance. At the same time, the Vietnamese refugee, Thuy-Mai, is pathologized as Asian enemy, dismissively labeled "Pearl Harbor," erroneously conflated with the Japanese, and implicitly rendered a menace to the coherence and integrity of the US nation-state.

Mrs. Hammerick is, of course, not literally speaking French (though Vietnam was of course colonized earlier by France), but Truong's attention to language underscores the ways in which an unconscious discourse of colonialism and race, of national inclusion and exclusion, is circulated in the classroom. Furthermore, as Lowe points out, Mrs. Hammerick's nationalizing tract is simultaneously a gendered discourse: "The narrator's observations that the teacher's history lesson addresses 'all the boys' further instantiates how the American nationalist narrative recognizes, recruits, and incorporates male subjects, while 'feminizing' and silencing the students who do not conform to that notion of patriotic subjectivity."[47] Racialized subjects, such as Nelson and Thuy-

Mai, become "good" citizens when they identify with the paternal state and accept, as Lowe summarizes, "the terms of this identification by subordinating [their] racial difference and denying [their] ties with the feminized and racialized 'motherland.'"[48] In the following section, we turn to Melanie Klein's theories of good and bad objects, of good and bad mothers and motherlands, to explore the politics of aggression and destructiveness, of guilt and reparation, as they configure the psychic limits of racial melancholia and expand on Freud's account of loss and interminable mourning.

ON GOOD AND BAD (RACIALIZED) OBJECTS

In Nelson's case history, the teacher's shaming of the mother and mother tongue brings her image into explicit crisis, such that she returns to Nelson in the transformed guise of a bad mother. Like Elaine, Nelson, as the child of immigrant parents, becomes the arbiter not only of his own ambitions and losses but also those of his mother. His attempts to reinstate and repair his first love-object and caretaker (the Japanese mother) as well as his first language (Japanese) are torturous and compromised.

Nelson's case history invokes the work of Melanie Klein and object relations, which can be usefully considered in terms of our discussions of racial melancholia for Asian Americans. In "Mourning and Its Relation to Manic-Depressive States," Klein extends Freud's theories on mourning the lost object in terms of early infant development: "While it is true that the characteristic feature of normal mourning is the individual's setting up the lost loved object inside himself, he is not doing so for the first time but, through the work of mourning, is reinstating that object as well as all his loved *internal* objects which he feels he has lost. He is therefore *recovering* what he had already attained in childhood."[49]

For Klein, states of mourning in adult life are negotiated and resolved through the alignment of the lost object with all the "loved internal objects" of early infancy. This alignment and clustering of the lost and loved object with the good objects of the past represents an attempt to recover and hence to reinstate the securities of infancy before the mother was split into a good and a bad object—an impossible but necessary and life-sustaining enterprise. This clustering thus marks an unconscious process by which the lost and loved object is "preserved in safety inside oneself" so that the depressive position can be negotiated and melancholia can be repaired.[50]

Klein's formulation for mourning and her prescription for psychic health depend on the introjection of the lost object, on preserving and retaining it through a melancholic logic of internalization, but one that attempts to reinstate the lost object by aligning it with a cluster of good internal objects. Klein warns, however, of the difficulties often accompanying the reparative process—this rebuilding of the inner world, as the infant alternates among the paranoid, depressive, and reparative positions. Depression will surely prevail, Klein warns, if the lost and loved object cannot be clustered with the good objects of the past.

In particular, Klein writes about the advent of depression through the forfeiture of the "good" mother. In "A Contribution to the Psychogenesis of Manic-Depressive States," she observes that from the "very beginning of psychic development there is a constant correlation of real objects with those installed within the ego. It is for this reason that the anxiety which I have just described manifests itself in a child's exaggerated fixation to its mother or whoever looks after it. The absence of the mother arouses in the child anxiety lest it should be handed over to bad objects, external and internalized, either because of her *death* or because of her return in the guise of a *'bad'* mother."[51] Nelson's case illustrates what happens when the mother returns in the guise of a "bad" mother precisely through the loss—the death—of "Japaneseness." Nelson's "good" mother of infancy returns as a "bad" mother of childhood at the moment of the teacher's linguistic interdiction. After this childhood trauma, Nelson cannot easily repair and realign an image of a "bad" Japanese mother with his earlier perceptions of this nurturing figure.

Klein summarizes, "In some patients who had turned away from their mother in dislike or hate, or used other mechanisms to get away from her, I have found that there existed in their minds nevertheless a beautiful picture of the mother, but one which was felt to be a *picture* of her only, not her real self. The real object was felt to be unattractive—really an injured, incurable and therefore dreaded person. The beautiful picture had been dissociated from the real object but had never been given up, and played a great part in the specific ways of their sublimations."[52] Nelson's case history challenges us to consider what must be shorn away from the real object—the shamed Japanese mother—in order to reinstate her to a world of loved internal objects, in order to create from her a "beautiful picture." In this instance, it would seem that it is racial difference—Japaneseness itself—that must be dissociated and split off from the figure of the injured and dreaded mother in order for this reinstatement to occur. Through the shaming of his mother and mother tongue and, in turn, his attempts to repair them, Nelson's own Japanese identity becomes alienated and dissociated from him, transformed into a persecuting and bad object. In sum, Nelson's case history underscores the way in which attachments to a good primary object within the family romance can be threatened and transformed precisely through histories of race defining the family of nations.

What we are proposing here is the refinement of Klein's theories of gender and mothering into an account of "good" and "bad" *racialized* objects. Nelson and his mother are bound together as mourners. Nelson's mother becomes associated with guilt through her broken English. She transfers the burden of this trauma as well as hope onto Nelson's shoulders. Nelson attempts to redeem his mother and himself by reinstating her as good object, one necessitating the arduous reparation of a racial splitting. Nelson's fixation with perfecting his English—he later declares an English major—is indicative of an obsession that negotiates the depressive position for him, as he embraces the mimicry of whiteness. Nonetheless, this process of perfecting English might also be seen as Nelson's displaced attempt to preserve the image of the beautiful Japanese mother—to make good on her hopes and failures. Nelson's effort to reinstate an image of beauty is an ongoing process of repair. This process cannot be fully satisfied or resolved—for him or for anyone. However, these attempts are a necessary failure, for Klein warns that if this image of beauty is removed completely—if the death wish against the dreaded Japanese mother is fulfilled—then guilt is not reduced and the depressive position not repaired but melancholia is in fact heightened and redoubled through this splitting.

Indeed, the racial melancholia that underwrites Nelson's unresolved loss of the Japanese mother renders the attempt to reinstate her as a good object extraordinarily tenuous. This compromising of Nelson's efforts vexes the proper work of mourning, leaving him in a state of anxiety and depression. Klein states, "The ego endeavours to keep the good apart from the bad, and the real from the phantastic objects."[53] However, it may be that the racial melancholia and depression that ensue for Nelson can be avoided only through the most difficult psychic process of dissociation—the splitting off Japaneseness from the figure of the mother as well as segregating of racial and sexual difference. Klein comments, "The attempts to save the loved object, to repair and restore it, attempts which in the state of depression are coupled with despair, since the ego doubts its capacity to achieve this restoration, are determining factors for all sublimations and the whole of the ego development."[54] Nelson's sustained depression and ambivalence toward his mother indicate the torturous process of reinstatement that impedes proper ego development and psychic health. Even more, his case history emphasizes how certain losses are more difficult to negotiate due to the absence of social support and in the face of social institutions such as the school. It is the history of the (racial) subject in relation to the subject of (racial) history that must be addressed here.

DEPATHOLOGIZING MELANCHOLIA

The process of assimilation is a negotiation between mourning and melancholia. The Asian American subject exemplified by Elaine and Nelson does not inhabit one or the other—mourning or melancholia—but mourning and melancholia coexist at once in processes of assimilation and the negotiation of social and psychic borders. This continuum between mourning and melancholia allows us to approach racial melancholia as conflict rather than damage. Indeed, we must investigate further the condition of racial melancholia as the intrasubjective displacement of a necessarily intersubjective dynamic of conflict and trauma in all its various social manifestations. We have described racial melancholia among Asian Americans in Generation X as tracing a trajectory from love to hate of the lost object, a hate that is subsequently transformed into self-hate in the course of moving from the external social world into the internal domain of the psyche. If racial melancholia traces the history of social exclusions relating to immigration, assimilation, and racialization for the Asian American subject and configuring that exclusion as an intrasubjective psychic form of self-hate, then how might we reverse this trajectory and address this condition as an intersubjective subject-subject relation?

The attention to racial melancholia as conflict rather than damage not only renders it a productive category but also removes Asian Americans from the position of solipsistic "victims" singularly responsible for their own psychic maladies. We are dissatisfied with racial discourses and clinical assessments that pathologize people of color as permanently damaged—forever injured and incapable of being "whole." In contrast, our exploration of intersubjective conflict—between mainstream and minority cultures as well as on the intergenerational level—draws attention to race as relation by expanding Klein's notion of reparation and reinstatement to a communal level.

Our discussion of immigration, assimilation, and racialization pursued here develops them as issues involving the fluid negotiation between mourning and melancholia. In this manner, melancholia is neither pathological nor permanent but, to return to Williams, "a structure of feeling," a structure of everyday life. In *Disidentifications: Queers of Color and the Performance of Politics* (1999), José Esteban Muñoz observes that, for queers as well as for people of color, melancholia is not a pathology but an integral part of daily existence and survival. Muñoz provides, as we do, a corrective to Freud's vision of melancholia as a destructive force and states that it is instead part of the "process of dealing with all the catastrophes that occur in the lives of people of color, lesbians, and gay men. I have proposed a different understanding of melancholia that does not see it as a pathology or as a self-absorbed mood that inhibits activism. Rather, it is a mechanism that helps us (re)construct identity and take our dead with us to the various battles we must wage in their names—and in our names."[55]

Within the continuum of mourning and melancholia is a productive gap inhabited by the various issues under discussion here—immigration, assimilation, and racialization; mimicry, ambivalence, and the stereotype; sacrifice, loss, and reparation. The social and psychic negotiations of these various issues are the internal conflicts with which Asian Americans have struggled on an everyday basis. This struggle does not necessarily result in damage but is in the final analysis a necessary process of political engagement and action. It is the work of renarrating loss and rebuilding communities. "Suffering," Klein offers, contains productive capacities:

> It seems that every advance in the process of mourning results in a deepening in the individual's relation to his inner objects, in the happiness of regaining them after they were felt to be lost ("Paradise Lost and Regained"), in an increased trust in them and love for them because they proved to be good and helpful after all. This is similar to the way in which the young child step by step builds up his relation to external objects, for he gains trust not only from pleasant experiences but also from the ways in which he overcomes frustrations and unpleasant experiences, nevertheless retaining his good objects (externally and internally).[56]

We would like to think about the numerous difficulties of Asian American immigration, assimilation, and racialization processes in terms of "Paradise Lost and Regained." The reinstatement of lost and loved objects in a racist world that would not have them encompasses the productive capacities of racial melancholia. It also indexes the possibilities of hope and the will of the racial subject—its abiding fidelity to the beautiful picture.

In the work of racial melancholia lies an important ethical and political project. In "Mourning and Melancholia," Freud describes the melancholic's inability to get over loss in negative terms. We instead focus on the melancholic's absolute refusal to relinquish the racial other—to forfeit alterity—at any costs. As Hannah Arendt suggests, and as the case history of Nelson eloquently underscores, an accent is the refusal to give up the mother or mother tongue.[57] Put otherwise, the development of pride in one's culture, as Beverly Greene points out, can be an important if complex source of psychic resilience, alternately a site of psychic vibrancy or shame.[58] Freud lays out in his essay the provocative idea that in melancholia "the shadow of the object fell upon the ego."[59] This idea is notable for, throughout the Freudian oeuvre, it is the ego that holds sway; the narcissism of "His Majesty the Ego" reigns supreme.[60] Equally so, Lacan emphasizes this narcissism of the ego, reversing Freud's formulation in "Mourning and Melancholia" by insisting that it is always the shadow of the ego that falls on the object.[61] In our present discussion, however, we have the loved object rather than the ego holding sway. Racial melancholia thus delineates one psychic process in which the loved object is so overwhelmingly important to and beloved by the ego that the ego is willing to preserve it even at the cost of its own self. In the transferential aspects of melancholic identifications, Freud suggests, "is the expression of there being something in common which may signify love."[62]

This community of love—as W. R. D. Fairbairn, Jessica Benjamin, Christopher Bollas, and others have noted—is possible only through the aggressive and militant preservation of the loved and lost object.[63] Hence, the melancholic process is one way in which racially disparaged objects and others live on in the psychic realm. This behavior, Freud remarks, proceeds from an attitude of "revolt" on the part of the ego.[64] It displays the ego's melancholic yet militant refusal to allow certain objects to disappear into social oblivion. In this way, Freud tells us, "love escapes extinction."[65] This preservation of the threatened racial object might be seen, then, as a type of ethical hold on the part of the melancholic ego. The mourner, in contrast, has no such ethics. The mourner is perfectly content to kill off the lost object, to declare it to be dead yet again within the domain of the psyche. We might describe this dynamic as a historical politics of love and hate in racial melancholia—indeed, a psychic pedagogy of surviving hating and being hated in a long history of race and whiteness as property.[66]

While the ambivalence, anger, and rage that characterize this preservation of the lost object threaten the ego's well-being, we do not imagine that this threat is the result of some existential tendency on the part of the melancholic; it is as we have been arguing throughout this chapter a decidedly social threat. Ambivalence, rage, and anger are the internalized refractions of an institutionalized system of whiteness as property bent on the exclusion and obliteration of the racial object. If the loved object is not going to live out there, the melancholic emphatically avers, then it is going to live here inside of me. Along with Freud, "we only wonder why a man has to be ill before he can be accessible to a truth of this kind."[67] It is the melancholic who brings us face to face with this social truth. It is the melancholic who teaches us that "in the last resort we must begin to love in order not to fall ill."[68]

Both Butler and Douglas Crimp isolate the call of melancholia in the age of AIDS—the historical period of this chapter's case histories—as one in which the loss of a public language to mourn a seemingly endless series of young male deaths triggers the absolute need to think about melancholia and political activism. Muñoz highlights the communal nature of this activist project—the community-oriented aspect of collective rather than individual losses, of collective rather than individual identifications, and of collective rather than individual revolt: "Communal mourning, by its very nature, is an immensely complicated text to read, for we do not mourn just one lost object or other, but we also mourn as a 'whole'—or, put another way, as a contingent and temporary collection of fragments that is experiencing a loss of its parts."[69] A series of unresolved fragments, we come together as a contingent whole. We gain social recognition as a racial collective in the face of this communal loss.

There is a militant refusal on the part of the ego—better yet, a series of egos—to let go, and this militant refusal is at the heart of melancholia's productive political potentials. Paradoxically, in this instance, the ego's death drive may be the very precondition for survival, the beginning of a strategy for living and for living on. Butler asks of melancholia, "Is the psychic violence of conscience not a refracted indictment of the social forms that have made certain kinds of losses ungrievable?"[70] And Crimp ends his essay "Mourning and Militancy" with this simple and moving call: "Militancy, of course, then, but mourning too: mourning *and* militancy."[71] We pause here to insert yet another permutation of this political project in relation to the Asian American immigration, assimilation, and racialization processes we have been discussing throughout this essay: mourning *and* melancholia.

LIVING MELANCHOLIA

This chapter and book is an engagement with psychoanalysis and racial difference that belongs neither in the humanities nor in the clinical arena proper. Rather, like our theory of racial melancholia, this project exists in a gap—in the space of creative play—between two disciplinary deployments of psychoanalysis, and it seeks to establish a productive relationship between them for the analysis of race as relation. We explore racial melancholia with the hope of proffering a number of new critical interventions significant to both areas and with the desire to understand better our students and patients, our wider communities, ourselves and others.

Moreover, our dialogue—crossing into the disparate realms of the literary and the clinical—is an exercise in new models of collective interpretation and political creativity entailed in the everyday living out of racial melancholia by Asian Americans. Much of this chapter reexamines the ways in which the genealogy of racial melancholia as individual pathology functions in terms of larger communal group identities contingent of the vicissitudes of history. Poignantly, histories of legalized exclusion attached to Asian American immigration, assimilation, and racialization configure psychic belonging and the promise of citizenship as a type of loss and self-hate. It is the naming of these losses that transforms difference into a politicized identity. Indeed, it is our belief that the refusal to view identities under social erasure as individual pathology or permanent damage lies in the reappropriation of melancholia, its refunctioning as a structure of everyday life. This reappropriation annuls the multitude of losses an unforgiving social world historically enacts and enables.

CHAPTER 2

DESEGREGATING LOVE

Transnational Adoption,
Racial Reparation, and
Racial Transitional Objects

We didn't know that we could never be good enough,
so we kept trying to do the impossible.

—JANE JEONG TRENKA, *THE LANGUAGE OF BLOOD*

Around 2000 we began to notice an emergent pattern in both the class-room and the clinic: a growing number of our students and patients started to "come out" to us—not as gay or lesbian but as transnational adoptees. In recounting their experiences, they would often employ the language of the closet and the vocabulary of shame, emphasizing how they felt invisible and how they felt compelled to come out as transna-tional adoptees time and again. They also admitted how such personal disclosures exacerbated their anxieties of being stigmatized and of feel-ing neither adequately Asian American nor sufficiently white. Finally, they stressed how such ambivalence provoked fears that they were being disloyal or ungrateful toward their adoptive parents.[1]

The complexity of these issues sparked a series of extended discus-sions between us: Is the transnational adoptee an immigrant? Is she Asian American? In turn, are her white adoptive parents Asian Ameri-can? The original version of this chapter was published in *Studies in Gen-der and Sexuality: Psychoanalysis, Cultural Studies, Treatment, Research* in 2006.[2] Although the original case history remains largely unedited, we have expanded our critical commentary for this book. In the process of analyzing transnational adoption, we came to realize that our theories of racial melancholia were not adequate to explaining the various psychic predicaments of transnational adoptees. As such, we turned to Melanie Klein's influential ideas about infantile development and reparation as well as D. W. Winnicott's suggestive concepts regarding transitional ob-jects and spaces to supplement Freud's formative theories concerning loss and interminable mourning.

Transnational adoption involves the intersection of two very power-ful origin myths—the return to mother and to motherland. In this case history of a Korean transnational adoptee, Mina, issues relating to Asian immigration, assimilation, and racialization are central to the patient's psychic predicaments. As noted in chapter 1, problems of racial melan-cholia between first-generation Asian immigrant parents and their sec-ond-generation American-born children entail intergenerational pro-cesses, influenced and configured by the social forces of history. Hence, the conflicts they present are *intersubjective* and external rather than just *intrasubjective* and internal. However, transnational adoptees often struggle with such predicaments in isolation. In Mina's case history, she mourns the loss of her birth mother and motherland—a repressed past prior to her "official" arrival and history in the United States—as a profoundly unconscious and intrasubjective affair.

Moreover, in Mina these significant losses trigger a series of primitive psychical responses such that we are forced to rethink, as we began to in Nelson's case, Klein's theories of object relations—of good and bad objects, as well as good and bad mothers—in terms of good and bad *racialized* objects, as well as good and bad *racialized* mothers. That is, Mina's case history demands a consideration of race as constitutive of, rather than peripheral to, Klein's fundamental notions of infantile development—her theories of splitting and idealization, depression and guilt, and reinstatement and reparation. In short, we come to recognize that Klein's developmental positions are also *racialized* positions. For Mina, the reparative position ultimately entails the *racial* reparation of her lost and devalued Korean birth mother.

Finally, Mina's case history draws further attention to the clinic as a racialized space—in D. W. Winnicott's terms a potential space of play—and to the materiality of the therapist as a racialized and gendered subject. In particular, we consider how the transference-countertransference dynamic between the transnational adoptee patient and her Korean American therapist is framed not only by the visibility and public fact of their shared racial difference but also by the visibility and public nature of the analyst's pregnancy during the course of Mina's treatment. We examine how Dr. Han's pregnancy constitutes her, to reformulate Winnicott, as a "racial transitional object" for Mina. In the process, we reconsider Winnicott's theories concerning object usage in terms of Mina's use of her Korean American therapist to transition to a reparative position for race. Ultimately, racial reparation allows Mina to resignify her vexed identifications with both a disparaged Koreanness and an idealized whiteness. Psychic health for the transnational adoptee involves creating room in her mind for two "good-enough mothers"—the Korean birth mother and the white adoptive mother. Such a resignifying project, we argue, belongs to the creative processes Winnicott associates with transitional space and play, leading us to explore race as transitional space.

Mina is a twenty-three-year-old transnational adoptee from Korea. She is a dancer in a renowned New York City ballet company. One of Mina's mentors referred her to me (Dr. Han) in 2001 as she was beginning her first year with the ensemble. Mina carries herself with the natural grace of a ballerina. During our consultations, however, she often sat at the edge of her seat. She is a smart and articulate, though rigid, young woman who sought psychotherapy to better understand the problems in her romantic relationships as well as the "whole adoption thing." She believes that the two are somehow connected.

In her presentation, Mina recounted that, since age thirteen, she had had a series of white boyfriends. Every relationship was marked by some degree of abuse, mostly verbal. Furthermore, although she boasts of her sexual power over men, Mina believes that she was often coerced into sexual relationships with her partners much sooner than she desired. At the start of her sessions with me, she was not in a relationship because she felt that she needed to "figure out" herself first. Mina had a theory that her birth mother had been a college student when she found herself in a precarious and perhaps abusive relationship with a boyfriend. This boyfriend subsequently abandoned her mother when she became pregnant with Mina. Mina spoke angrily about her previous boyfriends and recounted her fantasies concerning the circumstances by which her birth mother had become pregnant. At the same time, Mina blamed herself for consistently choosing bad boyfriends. Collectively, these failed relationships have had a negative impact on Mina's self-regard. Despite her formidable artistic talents, she suffers from low self-esteem while often displaying excessive intolerance toward others.

During our initial consultation, Mina asked how much I knew about Korean transnational adoption as well as "what kind of Korean" I was. She immediately wanted to figure out my attitudes toward adoptees: she wondered if I were adopted, a recent immigrant, born in the United States, from an affluent background. She believes that the overwhelming majority of Koreans in Korea and Korean Americans in the United States are prejudiced against Korean adoptees. She stated that she does not like Koreans at all. In particular, the Korean nationals with whom she attended dance school "made her sick" with their "Gucci, Louis Vuitton, and Chanel accessories," as well as with their "garish and ugly" makeup. She felt especially disconnected from them because they spoke only Korean to one another. "They are in America," she remarked. "Why don't they speak English?" Finally, she accused them of being disingenuous. "These girls all have white boyfriends. And they sleep around all the time," she stated. "But they act virginal around other people, as though no one can tell how slutty they really are."

Before I could respond to Mina's statements, she told me that she thought I was a Korean American, but not the type she described. (I am, in fact, a "1.5 generation" Korean immigrant, having moved to the United States when I was thirteen.) I took this as a warning not to carry my designer purse to work. At the same time that I wondered, to borrow a key concept from Winnicott, if I were going to be a "good-enough" Korean for Mina, I also realized that in all likelihood she did not consider herself a "good-enough" Korean for me.[3] I decided to share with Mina my prior experience with Korean transnational adoption, in particular, my specialty as a postadoption social worker assisting both transnational adoptees and their parents. Skeptically, she replied, "Good." Because of her angry, aggressive, and defensive attitude, I felt unsure if our relationship would continue beyond our initial consultation. "She's a tough one," I concluded. I thought to myself that I should be careful, or Mina would group me with those Koreans she hates, or even worse create a new negative category of Korean just for me.

A white couple from Philadelphia adopted Mina when she was eleven months old. She has a younger brother, also adopted from Korea, who was at that time a first-year student in a small liberal arts college in the Northeast. Mina describes her brother as an easy-going kid who does not seem to have many issues concerning his adoption or Koreanness. She is not very close to him. Mina's mother is a freelance journalist who often writes for travel magazines. Although her mother was once a full-time reporter, she quit her office job to raise Mina and her brother at home. Mina describes her relationship with her mother as very close. They talk on the phone at least once or twice a day. She discloses "everything" to her mother, including her boyfriend problems as well as adoption issues. While Mina feels that her mother has good insight into her life, she also worries that her mother "knows too much" and therefore cannot be objective in her advice. Mina looks and sounds confident when she says that her mother would do "anything and everything" she wants her to do. Mina's father is a professor of applied mathematics. She describes him as somewhat distant and clueless about her life. Both, however, are actively involved in Mina's flourishing dance career and often travel from out of town to attend her performances.

Mina reported that her adoption file contained very little information. She was found in a tattered basket at the doorstep of a church in Inchon City, near Seoul, in South Korea. The minister and his wife took Mina to a local police station. From there she was taken to an orphanage. One week after Mina was found, a young woman visited the church to inquire about the infant left at the doorstep. Mina wondered if this woman were her birth mother. She hypothesized that her birth mother was perhaps not a college student, after all, but a "poor whore" who lived in a nearby city. And she stated angrily, "Why didn't the bitch leave just a little more information about me? Like, my name and her name! Did she even think to give me a name?"

Mina stated that she has two questions for her birth mother if and when she finds her: "What's my name?" and "Why did you give me up?" After these answers are furnished, she claims she wants nothing further to do with her birth mother or Korea. Mina's anger toward her Korean birth mother was palpable. Unlike other transnational adoptees I have previously treated, youths as well as adults who often created idealized pictures of their lost birth mothers, Mina's negative attitude toward hers was remarkably raw and unrelenting.

During the years at her dance academy, Mina's engagement with her adoption issues waxed and waned, often displaced by pressing school demands. She was the only one of her classmates chosen to join her ballet company upon graduation. Mina was surprised by this achievement. Her teachers had been telling her that, while her technique was superb, she needed to work more on her emotional expression. Shortly after joining the ballet company in the fall, she began treatment with me. Four months later, Mina started seeing a young choreographer, Henry, who was already in another relationship. It started off as a friendship, which quickly evolved into a romantic relationship. This relationship spun Mina's emotions wildly. Her volatile moods were largely contingent on Henry's continued but failed promises to break up with his girlfriend.

As their tumultuous affair progressed, a noticeable pattern emerged. Mina became increasingly dependent on Henry. She organized her daily schedule around his, while also taking care of Henry's housework, doing his laundry and cleaning his apartment. Gradually Mina grew exhausted and resentful, although she could not bring herself to end the affair. She wondered if her birth mother had found herself in similar circumstances, resulting in her pregnancy with Mina. A couple of months later, Henry abruptly ended the relationship by announcing that he had decided to become engaged to his girlfriend.

At the time Henry broke up with Mina, I was four months pregnant. As I was in my second trimester, my pregnancy had become noticeable to a few patients. I wondered if Mina had detected my physical change. I was due to give birth at the end of summer, around the time that Mina was scheduled to return from her summer tour. Before she departed, however, I decided to discuss my pregnancy with her. When I told her, Mina's reaction was very controlled and polite. And when I asked Mina directly how she felt about my pregnancy, she answered, "Oh, it's fine. You having a baby has nothing to do with my adoption. You're a professional. You'll come back to the office and we will work together as usual."

Despite her initial nonchalance, as my belly swelled, Mina often asked how I was feeling, how much weight I had gained, and if my pregnancy had been planned. "I know nothing about you," she said. "But I know that you are well educated and independent. So, I don't know if you're having this baby alone, with a man, or even a woman." On further exploration of her fantasies about me, Mina added, "I think you're married and this is a planned pregnancy. You wouldn't be so stupid and just get knocked up." It seemed important to Mina that my baby have two (heterosexual) parents who would love and care for him and, most important, keep him.

As her summer tour approached, Mina wanted to know if we could schedule phone sessions while she was away—"just in case." I reassured her that I would be available until I gave birth. At the moment, I wanted to explore with Mina any possible feelings of abandonment, and of unacknowledged feelings of envy toward my unborn child. I feared that my pregnancy might raise doubts about our relationship, and I wondered whether Mina harbored a secret wish to be my baby. But as much as I attempted to raise these topics, Mina showed little interest in discussing her fantasies or anxieties. She left for her summer tour soon after these conversations.

During Mina's tour, we more or less kept to our weekly sessions over the telephone, until a couple weeks before I gave birth. After giving birth, I took maternity leave and was not in contact with Mina for two months. Upon resuming our sessions in late fall, Mina immediately asked if my baby was a boy or a girl and offered warm congratulations. She then delved into her big news: she had just attended an adoption camp. Following the dance tour, Mina had decided to volunteer as a camp counselor for adopted children from Korea as well as China. There, for the first time, she spent an extended period with other Korean adoptee volunteers who had either found their birth mothers (and families) or were contemplating such a search. She experienced an intense drive to absorb their stories, and she began to reconsider her own search for her birth mother. Mina's shift in attitude made me wonder how much of her recent actions were related to my pregnancy and motherhood.

That fall, Mina joined a Korean adoptee support group as well as a mentoring group for young adopted Chinese girls in New York City. While she expressed envy toward the social and cultural support that these white parents collectively provided to their Chinese daughters, her feelings toward her adoptee support group were quite negative. She described them as a "bunch of screwed-up Korean adoptees who are obsessed with their adoptions." She fears that there is something deeply wrong with her because, like these screwed-up peers, she too was adopted.

Indeed, throughout her treatment, Mina expressed blatant prejudices against many different racial groups—African Americans, Latinos, Jews, and Asian Americans—as well as gays and lesbians. For instance, she characterized African Americans as "those lazy blacks who are all in gangs and only know how to steal and kill." She described Latinos as the "dumbest racial group" and Jews as "those who sniff money all day." Gays and lesbians were "abnormal" and "flamboyant" people obsessed with sexual display. As for Asian Americans, she embraced the ostensibly positive model minority stereotype, observing, "At least Asian Americans are academically successful and work hard and don't bother anyone."

It was very difficult for me to endure Mina's tirades and rants against these various groups. As Mina's prejudices intensified over the course of treatment, I continued to hold her anger without any direct verbal confrontation, although I grew increasingly concerned about the ways in which my negative countertransferences might affect her. However, as I learned more about Mina, I began to understand that her racism and bigotry were deeply connected to the fear of being seen by others, and of accepting herself, as a minority. Mina's emphasis from the very beginning of our work together had been, "I'm an American! I have an Asian face but I'm white! My parents are white, and I grew up in a white suburb, and I feel most comfortable around white people." Under this tough and brittle surface, though, Mina felt extremely vulnerable and conflicted about her own racial identity, as evidenced not only by her aversion to Koreans in general but also by her vexed identifications with her new friends as "a bunch of screwed-up Korean adoptees" in particular. Hence, as I began to feel more empathetic and protective toward Mina, I made a conscious effort to police my disapproval as it arose.

During that fall, Mina spent more and more time with her new Korean adoptee friends. She reported that most of their conversations revolved around what they all called "the search" for their birth mothers and the ways the search often provoked intense rivalry around the amounts and quality of information discovered. For the first time, I began to notice Mina's deep struggle with the idea of beginning her own actual search for her birth mother, one motivated in part by competitiveness with, as well as by a desire to belong to, this group. It became increasingly clear that Mina was starting to come to terms with the great psychological difficulties associated with initiating the search process.

During this period, Mina also volunteered to be a spokesperson at a local adoption agency. There she met with potential parents to talk about the dos and don'ts of transnational adoption. Mina told these potential parents to embrace the culture and language of their children as their own. In our sessions, she began to express new feelings toward her adoptive parents: "I'm so angry at them for not exposing me to Korean things. I told my mom maybe I'm screwed up because I didn't have anything Korean when I was growing up. I asked her why she didn't do this, and she just says she doesn't know why. It didn't occur to her. How can she say that?"

It seems that Mina's de-idealizing of her adoptive mother stems from a feeling that she had intentionally kept Mina away from all things Korean, including her birth mother. In fact, as Mina has become more involved in these various adoption activities, it has become increasingly noticeable to me that she has been regressing and is in greater conflict with her adoptive mother. Nonetheless, Mina calls her mother every morning and evening to complain about being lonely and unhappy. She blames her mother for her agitated state of mind. But, at the same time, she feels more dependent on her. As a result, her mother has made extra visits to New York.

A year and a half into our sessions, Mina's desire to take action on the search congealed. She decided to go to Korea for a big adoption conference during the upcoming summer, and she planned to stay afterward to look for her birth mother. Again, Mina expressed her frustration and anger about having such limited information about her adoption. She also had a long list of anxieties and complaints: "How long will it take? Where will I stay—in Seoul or Inchon City? How will I get around when my Korean is barely good enough for ordering food in restaurants? I'll be so lonely. I don't really know anyone there and I don't want to see anyone from the dance school. Who will really help me? How will I know if someone is really genuine or just wants to take advantage of rich Americans?" I replied, "It sounds as if you'd feel more secure if I went there to search with you." She smiled and quietly acknowledged, "I guess so." When I asked her how she felt that I could not go with her, she immediately responded, "Oh no! I wasn't asking or thinking that you could go with me. Besides, you have a baby to take care of."

Trying to refocus our discussion on the issue of her birth mother, I suggested that, if we followed Mina's fantasies about her, she might currently be around my age. Mina looked at me with great surprise and said, "Wow, that could be true. I just never thought of it that way." My comment seemed to introduce to Mina the idea that her birth mother is a real, living person rather than a fantasy. Mina added, "I just always imagined her as a twenty-something-year-old girl like me . . . but I guess she isn't anymore." On further exploration, Mina admitted, "I want her to be married but with no kids. I don't want any siblings, not even half-siblings. I don't want to be the one she didn't keep." Mina hoped that her birth mother was okay, "living a normal life, but not too happy." Despite her curiosity about her birth mother's current circumstances, Mina continued to feel angry that her mother had not tried to search for her. And she envied those adoptees whose birth mothers had sought them out first. She feared that she had been erased from her birth mother's memory from the moment after she was dropped off at the church doorsteps.

In the following session, Mina introduced yet another fantasy concerning her stuffed animals. Mina has been collecting ducks since she was a toddler. Mina takes one female duck, Suzette, with her wherever she goes. Indeed, Suzette has now traveled around the world with Mina on tour (a lucky duck). When Mina was nine, Suzette got "married" to Tommy and gave birth to three baby ducklings. However, Suzette did not like her babies because all they did was whine and cry, demanding attention. Suzette pecked and hurt them, and finally she abandoned them. As a consequence, Tommy was left to take care of these "ugly ducklings" along with another duck, Jane. Mina describes Jane as a sort of nanny. It was only recently that Tommy, Jane, and the ducklings have been reunited with Suzette and joined her in Mina's New York apartment. Still, Mina asserts, Suzette "hates" these babies.

Mina told me that she also hates babies because they are such helpless creatures. When I suggested that perhaps she feels that her helplessness as an infant contributed to her birth mother's abandoning her, Mina expressed great shock. After some silence, she asked, "How could I not have thought of this possibility? I have been blaming myself all this time without realizing it. My mother gave me up because I couldn't do anything. I didn't have any skills." Mina understands that this is the reason why she has become so independent—strong willed and intent on taking care of herself and no one else (Henry notwithstanding), not even a husband if she later marries.

I asked Mina what kind of skills she could have possibly possessed as an infant. She replied matter-of-factly, "I should have known how to feed myself and how not to rely on my mother. Be toilet trained, so she didn't have to change my dirty diapers." She speculated that perhaps she cried too much, and, as a result, her birth mother had to give her up. After this revelation, Suzette stopped abusing her ducklings. Instead, she "bathed and cleaned them up."

Currently, our primary focus is on Mina's preparations for her search. Mina plans to put advertisements this coming summer in Korean newspapers. In addition, she has brought in her adoption file to share with me and to look for possible clues. As Mina mentioned earlier, there is little information in the file that we could use to make her advertisement distinctive. Finally, Mina has decided to participate in a Korean television program that reunites lost relatives. She repeatedly states, "I'm all for results. That's all I care about, and I don't care what I have to do to find her." In this regard, Mina requested that I call and talk with the church couple who discovered her. She has also asked her adoptive mother to go with her to Korea to help with her search. Mina is determined to find her birth mother and to demand answers about their brief life together. She has become increasingly agitated about her abandonment. And she wants answers.

TRANSNATIONAL ADOPTION AND RACIAL MELANCHOLIA

Is the transnational adoptee an immigrant? Is she Korean? Is she Korean American? Are her adoptive parents, in turn, immigrants, Koreans, or Korean Americans?

Mina's case history provides some provocative and vexing answers to these questions. Mina does not consciously see herself as an immigrant, as a Korean, or as a Korean American. She insists that, like her adoptive parents, she is an "American." Although she has an "Asian face," she nevertheless feels "white." "My parents are white, and I grew up in a white suburb, and I feel most comfortable around white people," Mina reasons. Indeed, she repudiates Koreans categorically—the "ugly," "garish," and "slutty" Korean nationals at her dance school who speak only Korean to one another as well as Koreans and Korean Americans who are "prejudiced against Korean adoptees."

We know that such extreme feelings of disavowal and aversion often represent for the patient unconscious and ambivalent identifications with the excoriated object. In this regard, Mina's struggles with the "whole adoption thing" raise a number of issues regarding immigration, assimilation, and racialization that are in many ways consistent with the psychic dilemmas of Asian immigrants and their second-generation children examined in the prior chapter. To begin, not unlike Mina, many second-generation Asian Americans from Generation X exhibit a heightened ambivalence or conflicted relationship to race. For example, they might strongly identify with a dominant white mainstream society (that often would not have them) while disidentifying with their immigrant parents as dreaded or disadvantaged racial others. We might think of this scenario as a psychic variation of the "marginal man" thesis from the previous chapter.

How can we bring greater psychic specificity to Mina's case history and to the historical phenomenon of transnational adoption from Asia in particular? Let us return to the dynamic of racial melancholia to note that Mina negotiates her vexed identifications with both Koreanness and whiteness in social and psychic isolation. Let us recall that for second-generation Asian Americans the numerous political, economic, and cultural conflicts arising from the difficulties of immigration, assimilation, and racialization processes are typically configured as intergenerational and intersubjective struggles. Let us also recall that these conflicts are usually interpreted through a master narrative of intergenerational *cultural* struggle between immigrant parents and their American-born children, between the Asian-born first generation and the US-born second generation. Reducing all conflicts, including those resulting from institutionalized racism and the contingencies of history, to intergenerational cultural struggles threatens to displace them into the private space of family and kinship as personal issues and pathologies, the result of internal distress rather than external realities. In the process, such displacements deny what are necessarily collective social issues and collective public problems by absolving the state and the larger community from political response, economic redress, and shared responsibility for structural inequality.

While we flag this danger, what we must emphasize in Mina's case history is the suspension of this intergenerational and intersubjective process—the loss of the communal aspects of racial melancholia. To the extent that Mina's parents do not recognize her as an immigrant, a Korean, or a Korean American ("I'm so angry at them for not exposing me to Korean things. I told my mom maybe I'm screwed up because I didn't have anything Korean when I was growing up"), and to the extent that Mina herself does not affectively *feel* herself to be an immigrant, a Korean, or a Korean American, the numerous losses relating to her birth, birth mother, abandonment-relinquishment, adoption, and immigration to the United States remain unaffirmed and unacknowledged by her own family or self.[4] All the more, they remain unaffirmed in the face of the public nature of her adoption. That is, unlike the biological Asian immigrant family, which is seen if not always felt as an integrated racial unit, the transnational adoptee disrupts the aesthetic continuity of the white nuclear family. She cannot pass, as her bodily presence draws immediate attention not only to her racial difference but also to the fact of her adoption.

Nonetheless, unlike histories of racial passing (from black to white) or sexual passing (from gay to straight), in which marginal subjects attempt to conceal the differences for which they would be punishable through slavish attempts to imitate the norm, Mina's racial difference is instead effaced by those around her and, most notably, by Mina herself. For Asian Americans who are often depicted as either adjunct to whiteness or "whiter than white," the model minority stereotype only exacerbates this collective denial of difference. This is the genealogy of racial invisibility that frames the phenomenon of coming out—coming out into difference—for the Asian transnational adoptee.

Mina mourns her significant losses in solitude. As we have noted, she negotiates them not intersubjectively with her adopted family but, rather, intrasubjectively and, equally important, *unconsciously*. Furthermore, to the extent that adoptive white parents today may recognize their transnational adoptees as immigrants or racialized subjects (Mina envies the Chinese adoptees whose white parents provide social and cultural support for their young daughters) yet do not consider themselves immigrants or racialized subjects in turn, we witness an affective cleaving of tremendous significance within the private space of the family. While transnational adoptees identify with their parents' whiteness, their parents do not necessarily identify with their children's Asianness. Such a failure of recognition threatens to redouble racial melancholia's effects, severing the adoptee from the intimacy of the family unit, emotionally segregating her, and obliging her to negotiate her significant losses in isolation and silence.

As we observed earlier, melancholia is one of the most difficult psychic conditions to treat, as it is largely an unconscious process in which the patient "knows *whom* he has lost but not *what* he has lost in him."[5] Mina knows that she has lost her Korean birth mother, but she does not know exactly what she has lost in her. Through the unspecified and thus ungrievable nature of this loss, we come to witness in Mina a remarkably severe form of racial melancholia, one displaced and externalized in patterns of racial enmity and idealization segregated between Korean-ness and whiteness. In short, Mina's racism stems from her incapacity to integrate love and hate across extreme polarizations of a racial divide. Indeed, from a slightly different perspective, we might speculate that for Mina hate marks a closed system of racial segregation, loss, and survival.

Before returning to Melanie Klein's notions of loved and hated (racial) objects, let us emphasize that Mina's white adoptive mother is, in fact, warm and loving. She is an empathetic, conscientious, and responsive woman. Mina discloses "everything" to her, and she feels that her mother would do "anything and everything" for her. Indeed, as Mina's treatment evolved over time, and as Mina came into greater conflict with whiteness and her white adoptive mother, Mina's mother was able to hold effectively her daughter's rage and attacks. She did not retaliate against Mina's frequent regressions and tirades but, in fact, provided increased emotional support by making herself available for extra phone calls and by making numerous visits to New York City. She also agreed to go with Mina to Korea to search for her birth mother.

The adoptive mother's "failures," if they can be described as such, are more social than individual. Although psychoanalysis has developed strong theories about mechanisms of projection underlying hatred, the field has been slow to analyze racial difference in regard to hatred and projection, in part because conventional psychoanalytic theory approached race as sociology rather than psychology. As such, it lay outside the purview of psychoanalysis.[6] Like our case histories in chapter 1, Mina's case history underscores the necessity of analyzing her psychic struggles and hatred in the context of her particular individual family dynamics while also considering their relation to larger historical problems of immigration, assimilation, and racialization. How do these histories affect the developmental trajectories of the Asian transnational adoptee and configure her mourning of mother and motherland as a profoundly isolated psychic enterprise, as a melancholic affair?

Put otherwise, Mina's case history demands a sustained consideration of how social and psychic configurations of race influence core developmental issues concerning processes of identification, projection, and introjection central to the establishment of subjectivity and identity. As we have observed, there remains much work to be done on how his-

tories of race as well as the particularities of both analyst and patient—
including their individual histories and family dynamics, not to mention
their race, ethnicity, gender, religion, education, and class—constitute
subjectivity and are instrumental in framing the clinical dialogues and
particular themes that emerge during the course of treatment. In the
following two sections, we expand on both of these points.

RACIAL REPARATION

What we so strikingly witness in Mina's case history is that the "return" to
origins—the return to mother and to motherland—that invariably marks
the psychic evolution and development of the transnational adoptee occurs through the emphatic dissociation of mother from motherland,
through primitive mechanisms of splitting and idealization regarding
not only gender but also race. Mina's case history offers a striking opportunity to advance our prior discussion in chapter 1 of Klein's theories of
infantile development in relation to race—and to problems of racism and
racial hatred—as a hindrance to individual psychic growth.

Standard interpretations of Kleinian object relations provide a narrative of infantile psychic development governed by mechanisms of introjection and projection.[7] According to Klein, because the mother is the
original source of sustenance for the child, her absence is registered by
the frustrated infant through the introjection and splitting of the breast
into good object and bad object—good when the breast is available and
the infant can obtain it, and bad when the breast is unavailable and it
fails him. While the good object is loved and idealized, the bad object
is hated and aggressed. The primal violence of splitting—what Klein
calls the "paranoid position" of projection, persecution, and defense—
destroys the mother as a hated object, but it simultaneously gives rise
to an acute anxiety that the mother as a loved object has perished in the
process as well.

As the infant attempts to come to terms with the psychic havoc it
has wreaked, the depressive position emerges as a response to the guilt
arising from psychic destruction and anxiety. If the infant can successfully negotiate this guilt, the reparative position ensues and the mother
is reinstated as a separate object—indeed, a separate subject—with
agency and will. In this manner, the infant learns to integrate love and

hate, initiating an object relation not only with the mother but also with the rest of the world beyond her and the many other subjects in it. In slightly different terms, a primary subject-object confusion on the part of the infant is resolved into a subject-subject relation—an intersubjective relationship. Klein describes reparation as an act that encompasses a "variety of processes by which the ego feels it undoes harm done in phantasy, restores, preserves, and revives [dead] objects."[8]

How does this standard interpretation of loved and hated objects as a gendered narrative of the good and the bad mother assume its racial dimensions? In mourning her unacknowledged losses associated with Korea and her Korean birth mother, Mina deploys a psychic strategy of gender and racial segregation such that the white adoptive mother is unconditionally idealized while the Korean birth mother is unconditionally aggressed. In other words, for Mina, love and hate are racially polarized. From this perspective, the reparative position that Klein associates with the infant's reinstatement and restoration of the mother as a good and loved object—indeed, as a whole and separate subject—is inextricably a racialized position.

Mina's case history insists that we consider Klein's concepts of good and bad objects as theories about good and bad *racialized* objects, her concepts of the depressive and reparative positions as theories about *racial* reparation. Indeed, Mina's history broadly demands consideration of how racial difference is figured within primal fantasies of infantile development, fantasies that are usually analyzed solely in terms of a gendered developmentalism. Mina's "whole adoption thing" implicates an unresolved terrain of infantile growth and development—a primal territory of *racial* splitting and idealization, depression and guilt, reinstatement and reparation—that haunts and follows her into adulthood. It casts a long and profound psychic shadow over all her relations with others, romantic and otherwise, and it overdetermines her racial antipathies and prejudices.

In short, Mina's case history insists on a rethinking of Klein's concept of good and bad mothers through a more refined theory of good and bad *racialized* mothers. Psychic health and stability, therefore, would entail a reparative position for race accounting for the psychic possibility of two "good-enough" racialized mothers—not the white *or* Korean mother but the white *and* Korean mother. Put otherwise, it would require the desegregation of love and hate. Mina's continual negotiation between these two maternal figures—similar to our notions of mourning *and* melancholia as an everyday struggle for Asian Americans from Generation X in the prior chapter—constitutes one psychic locus of the racial melancholia with which the Asian transnational adoptee specifically struggles.

Mina's case history literalizes the psychic machinations of splitting and idealization we discussed earlier in relation to Nelson insofar as Mina, unlike Nelson, divides racial love and hate between *two* objects, two actual mothers. From a slightly different perspective, Mina's case history also illustrates a tortured mental gymnastics meant to preserve a "beautiful picture" of the Korean birth mother in the face of a "real object" felt to be wholly inadequate, feared, and debased.

The Korean birth mother—the "bitch" and "poor whore"—who abandoned Mina on a church doorstep without proper explanation or name comes to assume the status of this unattractive creature, this real object. She becomes "an injured, incurable, and therefore dreaded person."[9] Such dread opens on the affective terrain of hate and envy. It poisons Mina's relationship to Koreanness and accounts for her radical devaluation of all things associated with her birth mother and motherland— from her "slutty" Korean classmates at dance school to Korean/Korean Americans who are all "prejudiced against Korean adoptees," and from the other "screwed- up" Korean adoptees Mina encounters at adoption camp and in her local support group to the Koreans in Korea who will take advantage of "rich Americans" as they initiate the search for their birth mothers.

Mina's dread not only threatens her relationship to the Korean American therapist—whom Mina warns at their very first session not to be like these disparaged racial others—but also shapes her unbending bigotry toward numerous other people of color and subordinated groups. In her critical meditation on surviving racial hatred and being hated, Kathleen Pogue White proposes three ways of examining dilemmas of hatred as they derive from racism: first, being hated as a racial object; second, hating the self in which one internalizes and makes the self a repudiated racial object; and third, hating the other whereby malignant introjections and projections are reexternalized and directed toward the other.[10] Mina's racial melancholia and splitting embody all three psychic states at once.

If, as Klein insists, "the beautiful picture [of the birth mother] had been dissociated from the real object but had never been given up, and played a great part in the specific ways of their [the patient's] sublimations," then we witness in Mina's history the particular *racial* forms and defenses that these sublimations assume: Mina's idealization of whiteness and of the white adoptive mother, a figure of plenitude who would do "anything and everything" for her, coupled with her excessive devaluation of the Korean birth mother and racial others as a categorical whole. In short, Mina sublimates and displaces the beautiful picture of the Korean birth mother wholly into an idealized whiteness and an idealized white adoptive mother who possesses all the qualities— education, privilege, independence—that the Korean birth mother decidedly lacks.

The extreme nature of Mina's idealizations and de-idealizations—of her intense segregation of love and hate—suggests how race can function phantasmatically in primitive processes of splitting, introjection, and projection concerning the maternal figure. In addition, it indicates how for Mina good and bad objects become racially divided into white and Korean, and how this splitting forecloses the possibility that good and bad can simultaneously pertain to both maternal figures at once. Indeed, from a clinical perspective, as Peter Buckley notes, the foreclosure of "experiencing both goodness and badness in the same object and thus alternating between absolute extremes of perceiving others and the self as 'all good' or 'all bad'" underpins psychoanalytic theories on the etiology of borderline personality disorders.[11] Only by overcoming such an affective position—only by renegotiating a beautiful picture in relation to Korea and Koreanness as "good enough"—can Mina initiate the real work of racial reparation.

Mina seems prepared to undertake this task. Throughout all her various tirades against Korea and the Korean birth mother, we can nevertheless detect a beautiful picture—albeit repressed and unconscious—of the lost birth mother and motherland not fully circumscribed by an idealized whiteness. For instance, by describing the Korean birth mother as a "poor whore," Mina reveals a residue of ambivalence that opens onto the psychic terrain of not just hate but also love. As we have discussed, ambivalence is *the* psychic mark of melancholia, but it also contains unique ethical possibilities regarding the politics of loss.[12] Through this turn of phrase, Mina not only condemns the "whore" who abandoned her but also displays a degree of unacknowledged sympathy toward this devalued figure—the double meaning of *"poor* whore" assuming an economic as well as emotional valence in relation to the birth mother's imagined plight.

Indeed, throughout the course of her treatment as well as in her many primitive regressions into racial antipathy, Mina displays a remarkable psychic fidelity to the Korean birth mother. Mina's repeated failures with abusive and unavailable boyfriends; the imagined duplicities of her Korean classmates; her bonds with the mother duck, Suzette, who "pecked," "hurt," and finally "abandoned" her ugly ducklings; and the deep-seated fear that she ultimately instigated her own abandonment because of her lack of skills all underscore the ambivalent identifications that Mina preserves in relation to the lost Korean birth mother not only as a bad object but also as a good object. As Suzette stops abusing her ducklings and begins to care for them, the promise of forgiveness, love, and reparation as an open system emerges alongside Mina's abandonment.

Klein reminds us that extreme feelings of persecution and hate do not necessarily foreclose the possibility of love; indeed, they are its preconditions. Mina's racial tirades could simultaneously indicate a type of psychic desperation, a psychic defense against a feeling of imminent loss, the loss of the good object and of goodness itself. In this respect, Mina's racial persecution anxieties are psychically complex insofar as they indicate an attempt to preserve the ego as well as the "good internalized objects with whom the ego is identified as a whole."[13] Her excessive antipathy toward Koreanness can most certainly denote that persecution is "the main driving force" behind her polarizing and unyielding racist attitudes and affects, thereby rendering the possibility of love toward the racial other extremely tenuous.[14] Klein observes that infants "whose capacity for love is strong have less need for idealization than those in whom destructive impulses and persecutory anxiety are paramount."[15]

Mina's extreme affective polarities—her excessive love of whiteness and her excessive hatred of Koreanness—might, in fact, indicate a great psychic effort on her part to preserve unconsciously the goodness of the lost Korean birth mother, a figure whose existence is felt to be in crisis, if not entirely irrecoverable under the idealized palimpsest of the good white mother. Klein observes, "The stronger the anxiety is of losing the loved objects, the more the ego strives to save them, and the harder the task of restoration becomes the stricter will grow the demands which are associated with the super-ego."[16] Mina's case history thus raises the possibility of an ethical death drive at the heart of Klein's theories of infantile development. This ethical death drive preserves a space of goodness for the Korean birth mother precisely through sadistic hate and aggression, paradoxically mapping the twisted and arduous psychic conditions under which we might begin to theorize a process of racial reparation.

In the previous chapter on racial melancholia, we suggest that the melancholic's absolute refusal to relinquish the lost other—to forfeit alterity—at any cost delineates one psychic process of an ethical death drive in which the loved but lost racial object is so overwhelmingly important to the ego that it is willing to preserve it even at the cost of its own psychic health. In other words, racial melancholia indicates one way that lost and socially disparaged racial others live on unconsciously in the psychic realm. From this perspective, Mina's particular form of racial melancholia—of the segregation of racial love and hate—demands a more politicized understanding and interpretation of Kleinian processes of (racial) idealization and splitting outside theories of the drive and in terms of actual historical relations between subjects. Again, love and hate must be analyzed through the history of the (racial) subject in specific regard to the subject of (racial) history, the circulation of transnational adoptees in a global system of migration.

We have observed that Mina's affective quandaries might be said to underwrite a type of ethical fidelity to the Korean birth mother. Such an ethical hold on the part of the melancholic Korean transnational adoptee becomes the precondition for racial survival, a psychic strategy for living and for living on. In the transferential aspects of melancholic identifications, Freud reminds us, "is the expression of there being something in common which may signify love."[17] The redistribution of this love across a field of foreclosed, repressed, and unconscious objects—the desegregation of this love such that Mina can apportion to the devalued Korean birth mother some of the affect she reserves for the idealized white mother—constitutes one social and psychic project for what we describe as the ethics of racial reparation. In short, Mina's case history challenges us to rethink Kleinian object relations in order to imagine how we might come to repair what are socially and psychically constituted as not good but *bad* racial objects.

Klein is emphatic about the paradoxical connection between love and hate—of profound psychic violence, melancholia, the death drive, and suicide as the constitutive foundation for (racial) reparation: "But, while in committing suicide the ego intends to murder its bad objects, in my view at the same time it also always aims at saving its loved objects, internal or external. To put it shortly: in some cases the phantasies underlying suicide aim at preserving the internalized good objects and that part of the ego which is identified with good objects, and also at destroying the other part of the ego which is identified with the bad objects and the id. Thus the ego is enabled to become united with its loved objects."[18] According to Klein, successful psychic negotiation by patients who exhibit extreme anxieties of persecution or excessive mechanisms of idealization requires that the patients revise their relation to "their parents—whether they be dead or alive—and to rehabilitate them to some extent even if they have grounds for actual grievances."[19] Patients who fail in the work of mourning were "unable in early childhood to establish their internal 'good' objects and to feel secure in their inner world. They have never really overcome the infantile depressive position."[20] Perhaps the most crucial element in Mina's slow psychic evolution—her gradual shift toward a reparative position for her birth mother and motherland—is the transferential relationship that she builds with her Korean American therapist. She is a figure Mina has specifically sought out for treatment and one Mina ultimately constitutes as what we call a "racial transitional object."

RACIAL TRANSITIONAL OBJECTS

D. W. Winnicott's theory of transitional objects as well as transitional spaces proves especially useful in considering the racial dynamics of transference and countertransference between Mina and Dr. Han. Winnicott's concept of the "transitional object," that "first possession" of the infant (the thumb, the doll, the tattered blanket), opens up a "transitional space," an "intermediate area between the subjective and that which is objectively perceived."[21] Transitional space, according to Winnicott, exists between internal and external, between subjective and objective, between opposing realities. It is an intermediate area of creativity and play where strict divisions between self and other, fantasy and reality, are suspended. Winnicott explains, "It is not the object, of course, that is transitional. The object represents the infant's transition from a state of being merged with the mother to a state of being in relation to the mother as something outside and separate."[22] The transitional object is neither strictly internal nor strictly external: it "is never under magical control like the internal object, nor is it outside control as the real mother is."[23] On the whole, transitional phenomena "give[s] room [to the infant] for the process of becoming able to accept difference and similarity," and thus they become the "root of symbolism in time."[24]

Commenting on Winnicott's ideas of transition, Carol Long points out that in transitional space difference "is held in a state of playful tension and can thereby be understood relationally rather than as fixed or divided into immutable categories."[25] To return to a point in our introduction, we understand from this important insight how the concept of transitional space allows us to approach race not as a fixed object, not as a fixed thing with an essential nature, or as an intractable and frozen binary of white-black, of good and bad. Rather, transitional space configures race as an ever-evolving, contingent *relation* of inside and outside, inclusion and exclusion, good and bad—in short, as varied and multiple rather than unchanging and static. From this perspective, we might consider race itself as a kind of transitional space, whereby race, in Kimberlyn Leary's words, "exists on a continuum comprised of multiple variables" rather than as something referring to a fixed disposition or essence.[26]

Seen from this perspective, "race does not in any meaningful sense speak for itself. It is instead a complex negotiation within persons as well as a complex negotiation between persons."[27] Insofar as race might be played with creatively—thought of as belonging both to the social world and to the individual imagination—we reinforce the concept of race as a relation. When approaching race as transitional space, rather than race as a static object or a fixed stereotype inhabiting the polarized world of black-white, racial meaning can be multiple and varied, and race can be imagined otherwise.[28] In this regard, Long offers a provocation: "What would it mean to inhabit transitional spaces where race was a question rather than a given? One way of thinking about this is to return to Winnicott's understanding of paradox as a key feature of transitional space. A paradox takes the form of both/and rather than either/or; its contradictions are what keep it alive and spontaneous."[29]

Transitional objects and spaces negotiate the invariable frustrations of the infant as it comes to terms with its compromised autonomy and dependency in a world of (racial) objects it cannot fully control. By providing a third space between inner and outer worlds, transitional phenomena permit the infant to negotiate what were previously felt to be mutually exclusive choices: inside-outside, subjectivity-objectivity, unity-separation, black-white. Indeed, we might say that transitional phenomena allow the infant the means to negotiate Freud's pleasure and reality principles, as well as Klein's states of love and hate, that must be resolved through the integration of the (m)other as a whole, separate, and good-enough object. Ultimately, the ability to suspend through creative play what seem to be intolerable (racial) differences allows the infant not only to negotiate but also *to appreciate* and *to connect* with others as different.[30]

The transitional object, Adam Phillips observes, "is always a combination, but one that provides by virtue of being more than the sum of its parts, a new, third alternative," opening up a space of thirdness.[31] This third space is not a dead-end space of obstacle but one of psychic triangulation, possibility, and potentiality, an intermediate area, a space of creative play. It is worth emphasizing that for Winnicott states of play are not trivial or frivolous, as Mina's case history so eloquently underscores. To the contrary, they sustain psychic mechanisms of creativity that ameliorate frozen binaries of love and hate. They underwrite the serious psychic business of feeling authentic and alive, of developing a sense of what Winnicott describes as a "true self"—a topic we develop in the subsequent chapter on parachute children and racial dissociation.

For Long, a South African psychologist who writes in the context of postapartheid South Africa, the metaphor of a transitional society marks the hope of transitional justice—a sustained history and culture of injustice under apartheid in the "process of coming alive, of apprehending difference as paradoxical, and of creating an in-between space not wholly defined by internal experience or external reality."[32] Long's observations, along with our case history of Mina, underscore how racism can and does foreclose creative play, how it "not only splits the world into categories of good and bad but also disrupts a sense of continuity of being."[33]

Significantly, the fate of the transitional object is a gradual decathexis outside the strictures of interminable or ungrievable loss. Winnicott observes that "in the course of years, it becomes not so much forgotten as relegated to limbo. . . . It is not forgotten and it is not mourned. It loses meaning, and this is because the transitional phenomena have become diffused, have become spread out over the whole intermediate territory between 'inner psychic reality' and the 'external world as perceived by two persons in common,' that is to say, over the whole cultural field."[34] Unlike the lost object in racial melancholia that is mourned only with the greatest of difficulty, the transitional object is never lost; it is neither forgotten nor mourned, and its fate is markedly different from that of the melancholic object. In this manner, our critical focus turns to race not as a fixed object idealized or scorned, loved or hated, retained or lost.

Rather, we approach race as a *continuous relation* mediating the entire cultural field, as a historical and cultural *process* in constant transition. Race opens onto a third space of creativity and play in which social relations between "inner psychic reality" and the "external world as perceived by two persons in common" are subject to continuous revision. To align these observations more closely with our discussion of Mina, we might consider specifically how a transitional space of race, of creativity and play, enable the racial reparation of the disparaged Korean birth mother not as excoriated object but as good-enough object.

For Winnicott, the domains of play, artistic activity, religious feeling, and dreaming become those privileged zones of transitional space wherein the recurring burdens of reality—of social and psychic conflict—are negotiated throughout a person's adult life. All too often, racism forces one to grow up prematurely and too quickly, the fixing of the racial object and racial meaning foreclosing the benefits of creative play, transitional space, and the developmental growth of the subject. (In Nelson's case from the last chapter, for example, the teacher's linguistic interdiction forces a psychic fixing of the Japanese mother as a melancholic rather than transitional object.) The task of reality acceptance, as Winnicott underscores, is never complete. Rather, it is an ongoing process, since no "human being is free from the strain of relating inner and outer reality, and that relief from this strain is provided by an intermediate area of experience which is not challenged (arts, religion, etc.). This intermediate area is in direct continuity with the play area of the small child who is 'lost' in play."[35]

Winnicott observes that in patients who were not started off well enough by their mothers, the fundamental task of the psychotherapy is to open up this transitional space for creative engagement: "Psychotherapy takes place in the overlap of two areas of playing, that of the patient and that of the therapist. Psychotherapy has to do with two people playing together. The corollary of this is that where playing is not possible then the work done by the therapist is directed toward bringing the patient from a state of not being able to play into a state of being able to play."[36]

While it is clear that Mina draws great sustenance from practicing her art—dancing—it is also evident that such a privileged realm of artistic creativity does not fully allow her successful negotiation of the conflicts between her "inner psychic reality" and the "external world." Her dance teachers repeatedly tell Mina that, although her technique is "superb," her "emotional expression" remains blocked. Becoming a member of a ballet company conforms to certain aspects of the model minority stereotype—expectations concerning technical perfection—but it also raises significant challenges of assimilating Asian American racial otherness into dominant notions of white feminine beauty and comportment. Moreover, Mina's enactment of her adoption and abandonment fantasies through the parable of her ducks—constituted by Mina as transitional objects that remain to be decathected—underscores the extent to which her capacity to play with her racial predicaments, her ability to negotiate productively her inner demons and outer realities, is circumscribed. Under such conditions, the role of the therapist is to bring her patient into a state of being able to play such that racial meaning can be adjusted, and race can ultimately be dispersed over the whole cultural field not as dreaded object but as an intersubjective and shifting relation.

Winnicott's (1969) distinction between "object relating" and "object use" between the patient and the therapist illuminates Mina's situation in the space of the clinic. Winnicott associates object relating with orthodox Freudian notions of transference—the analyst as blank screen on whom figures from the past (mother, father, siblings) are projected. In contrast, object use not only takes into account the question "Who am I representing?" but also raises the important question "What am I being used to do?" In other words, Winnicott emphasizes, it is not enough to say that the analyst stands in for the mother, unless we specify what particular aspects of the mother are being revived and worked through, and for what purposes.

For Mina, the dilemma of object relating and object use comes together in crucial ways that are mediated by the pregnancy of the Korean American therapist. Like her race, the visibility of the analyst's pregnancy, as the clinical literature on this topic broadly indicates, makes the pregnancy visible "public property" between analyst and patient while intensifying the transference and countertransference between them. Frequently pregnancies can also lead to resistance and reaction formations that place inordinate strain on the therapeutic relationship.[37] It is clear that Mina cannot initially use the lost Korean birth mother in any productive manner to negotiate her racial conflicts and antipathies. However, the return of this figure in the transferential guise of the pregnant Korean American therapist-mother initiates psychic movement, play, and a new social formation. It allows the therapist to become for Mina what we would describe as a "racial transitional object," one moving Mina from object relating into object use, and one ultimately allowing her to rework her excessive patterns of aggression and hate directed toward racial others and, ultimately, herself.

How is the Korean American therapist used by Mina? Mina uses her as a transitional object to resignify her vexed racial identifications with the lost Korean birth mother—not as a bundle of hated projections but as a whole person, a "thing in itself." From this perspective, Mina might also be seen as using her Korean transnational adoptee peers and the young Chinese transnational adoptees that she mentors as racial transitional objects, as well, using them to construct a reparative integration of her various racial objects. Through them, she opens up a network of once static racist associations and stereotypes, renegotiating her more complicated identifications with her Koreanness. This racial evolution marks a kind of psychic coalitional identity politics marked by play—by movement and change rather than intransigence and fixity. In other words, similarity does not collapse into sameness all the while difference does not automatically translate into opposition.[38] This is the space of the good enough.

How is this dynamic managed between Mina and her therapist? By disclosing her pregnancy to her patient, the Korean American therapist becomes the "good-enough" Korean mother. Dr. Han not only keeps her child but also, and most importantly, does not abandon her patient in the process, opening up a transitional space in which her patient might play with her perceptions of the racial other. In this regard, the Korean American therapist is both a good-enough mother and a good-enough analyst. She is an educated, privileged, and independent Korean woman with qualities similar to Mina's idealized adoptive white mother who, in Mina's estimation, planned her pregnancy and "wouldn't be so stupid and just get knocked up." As a racial transitional object, she introduces into Mina's psyche the notion of similarity *and* difference in regard to the figure of the dreaded Korean birth mother—again, to help her realize that similarity is not sameness and that difference does not invariably lead to opposition. Moreover, Dr. Han allows Mina a way to play with and integrate the hated qualities of the bad Korean birth mother and the good qualities of the loved white adoptive mother into one figure. "You're a professional," Mina avers to her therapist. "You'll come back to the office, and we will work together then."

Indeed, we might say that, rather than a racial enactment, the therapist enacts a racial *relation* with Mina both by providing a space for her to explore any potential feelings of abandonment and jealousy—"Oh, I wasn't asking or even thinking that you could go with me [to Korea]. Besides you have a baby to take care of"—and by suggesting that Mina's Korean birth mother might "currently be around my [Dr. Han's] age." In this manner, the therapist becomes a screen on which the Korean birth mother can take shape as a real, concretized living person rather than a set of excoriated fragments, fixed illusions, and hated projections. The Korean birth mother becomes, in short, a person, a subject, with a separate reality. In using the therapist in this manner, Mina is finally able to undo and to resignify her intransigent affective stance toward the Korean birth mother. "I just always imagined her [my birth mother] as a twenty-something-year-old girl like me," Mina admits. "But I guess she isn't anymore."

Mina uses the Korean American therapist as a racial transitional object facilitating a renegotiation of race relations with the Korean birth mother, Koreanness, and racial others and otherness. A significant psychic shift occurs with regard to her ducks: Suzette ceases to abuse her ugly ducklings and has instead "bathed and cleaned them up." Exhibiting renewed care toward her abandoned ducklings represents for Mina an altered identification with her lost Korean birth mother and the emergence of a different set of affective capacities based not on unwavering judgment toward the "poor whore" but on creative play—on psychic flexibility and resilience. Moreover, Mina opens the book of her past. She decides to share with the therapist her adoption file and thus her "unofficial" past prior to her "official" arrival and history in the United States. At the same time, Mina decides to begin a search for the lost Korean birth mother, a search that she does not initiate in social or psychic isolation but with the support of others, including her white adoptive mother. Thus Mina arrives at a psychic position in which her racial melancholia might be addressed and the lost Korean birth mother repaired, reinstated, and reintegrated into a world of loved objects. Mina sets the psychic stage for her Korean birth mother to emerge as good enough.

CONCLUSION: WHITENESS AND ENVY

The capacity to use the analyst, as Winnicott points out, cannot be said to be inborn. It is the task of the therapist to abet the transformation from object relating to object use, to "be concerned with the development and establishment of the capacity to use objects and to recognize a patient's inability to use objects, where this is a fact."[39] Analysts, like mothers, Winnicott observes, "can be good or not good enough."[40]

Dr. Han's transformation into a good-enough mother-analyst allows Mina to constitute her disparaged Korean birth mother and, in turn, her idealized white adoptive mother as good-enough mothers, too. How does this happen? Mina's transition into racial reparation hinges on several factors regarding the recognition of race and the analysis of racial difference in the space of the clinic, as well as the importance of the therapist's and patient's racialized bodies in the course of treatment. Her case history provides the occasion to acknowledge not only the centrality of race to fundamental theories of psychic growth and development but also the fact that race is a constant though often unrecognized dynamic between analyst and patient.

As one of the most undertheorized aspects of psychoanalytic theory and practice, race cannot be seen as merely additive or symptomatic of more primary or fundamental psychic structures and conditions. Mina's case history insists on an understanding of race not only gender as constitutive of the earliest forms of object relations—of subjective development and identity as well as the negotiation of difference. Her narrative underscores the ways in which transnational adoption as a contemporary social phenomenon opens onto a psychic terrain of intense splitting and idealization, primitive psychic processes that can be understood only through sustained attention to race and racial difference—to the subject of (racial) history.

Mina's case history forces us to revise in fundamental ways Freud's notions of melancholia as an everyday structure of feeling; Klein's idea of the paranoid, depressive, and reparative positions as racial positions; and Winnicott's concept of transitional objects and spaces as negotiating the pain of racial history and reality. For Winnicott, the cultural and creative domain is the privileged dominion of transitional space and play. We learn from Mina that cultural difference may also be the source of racial upheaval and unrest, not just the panacea for, but also the poison of, reality. Her case history also suggests that we must consider how hate and envy, Klein's most toxic of psychic positions unfolding on the sadistic terrain of aggression, may in fact represent to immigrants and people of color a form of mental gymnastics to which they must subject themselves to preserve and to protect their socially disparaged loved objects, objects felt to be lost or under imminent social erasure.[41]

How do hate and envy index a nascent ethical project of desegregating love? On the one hand, Mina's intense aversion toward the Korean nationals at her dance academy—unconsciously in her mind, young Korean women who are cherished rather than abandoned by their affluent families—might be analyzed in light of envy. As Klein reminds us, a "very deep and sharp division between loved and hated objects indicates that destructive impulses, envy and persecutory anxiety are very strong and serve as a defense against these emotions."[42] Klein defines envy as "the angry feeling that another person possesses and enjoys something desirable—the envious impulse being to take it away or to spoil it."[43]

For Klein, envy is the most poisonous of psychic states; it is pure psychic destruction. Unlike jealousy, in which the subject feels deprived by somebody else of an object he or she loves, envy focuses aggression not on rivals but on the object itself. Envy entails not only the desire to possess this loved object but also the desire to "spoil" the goodness of the object with "bad parts" of the self—in other words, to destroy it. In an infant, envy simultaneously involves robbing the good breast of its positive qualities while "putting badness, primarily bad excrements and bad parts of the self, into the mother . . . in order to spoil and destroy her."[44] For Klein, envy thwarts all attempts at reparation and creativity. Representing unrelenting aggression, envy threatens mental development itself for it impairs the infant's ability to build up the good object and, instead, threatens to kill off the object on which one depends. In short, it opens onto the psychic terrain of aggression and death.

On the other hand, to the extent that Mina's primitive psychic processes of splitting and idealization segregate "good" (white) and "bad" (Korean) along a strictly racialized divide, her case history allows us another way of perceiving how envy might not be entirely psychically destructive or socially debilitating. That is, her hate and envy might be said to encompass an ethical death drive insofar as they initiate a psychic process by which Mina can spoil just a little bit the "goodness" of whiteness and the white mother she idealizes.[45] Through this spoiling of whiteness, she can create some room in her psyche to begin to repair the "badness" of Koreanness and the Korean birth mother. In other words, through envy's spoilage, she can begin to undo and to redress the psychic displacements that configure whiteness as a kind of fixed racial palimpsest masking the lost and unconscious goodness of the Korean birth mother. Proving to be resourceful if not indeed creative, envy emerges as a kind of melancholic racial coping mechanism that preserves the goodness of the lost Korean birth mother by eroding the exalted status of the idealized white mother, while also undoing the frozen racial binary of white and black. In this manner, envy abets rather than hampers Mina's ability to enter a reparative position for race.

Mina begins to address and to repair her racial melancholia by returning to the light of consciousness the lost goodness that was encrypted in this dreaded maternal figure. She begins to come to terms with not only the lost Korean birth mother but also the goodness that she has lost in her. Thus, Mina unfolds in her psyche the lost Korean birth mother as a different type of racial and historical subject, one who can come to occupy the place of the good-enough: a fixed Korean object is transformed into a living racial subject. In the process, Mina simultaneously creates psychic room and possibility for the idealized white adoptive mother to emerge as good enough, too. Mina creates a reparative mechanism through which good and bad can exist in both mothers and keep moving across once segregated racial divides. Racial reparation as a social and psychic process thus loosens the polarizing dichotomy of love and hate, subject and object, white and Korean, dominating Mina's psychic projections and fantasies.

Admittedly, such an interpretation of Kleinian envy is unorthodox. The racial exigencies of Mina's case history, however, demand creative infidelity, a melancholic bridge between envy and an ethical death drive that preserves a space of goodness for the lost Korean birth mother. Ultimately, just as Mina comes to discover a reparative position for race that is productive rather than debilitating, psychoanalysis as a theoretical enterprise and a clinical practice also must address in more systematic ways the profound and difficult legacies of racial pain and loss.

PART II

RACIAL DISSOCIATION

CHAPTER 3

RACIAL DISSOCIATION

Parachute Children
and Psychic Nowhere

My patient to whose care I have referred has come near the end of a long analysis *to the beginning of her life.* She contains no true experience, she has no past. She starts with fifty years of wasted life, but at last she feels real, and therefore she now wants to live.

—D. W. WINNICOTT, "EGO DISTORTION
IN TERMS OF TRUE AND FALSE SELF"

As we noted earlier, over the past two decades, the classroom and the clinic have functioned as social barometers of the changing politics of immigration, exclusion, assimilation, and loss across two different generations of Asian American adolescents and young adults in elite universities—from Generation X to Generation Y. In this manner, these spaces have helped track the shifting history of the (racial) subject in relation to the subject of (racial) history. Over this period, we have moved historically from the era of civil rights to the age of colorblindness. Generation X—born between the years of 1960 and 1980—was the last cohort with a collective memory of Cold War politics and civil rights struggles against sanctioned, legalized racial discrimination.

This generation was the first to come of age in an integrated education system following the Supreme Court decision *Brown v. Board of Education* (1954) desegregating the public realm of schools. It was not until 1967, however, that US state would finally withdraw from sanctioned, legalized racial segregation in the private realm of marriage. With *Loving v. Virginia,* the Supreme Court declared Virginia's antimiscegenation laws unconstitutional. It thus legally ended nearly seventy years of the "separate but equal" doctrine of legalized segregation established by the *Plessy v. Ferguson* (1896) Supreme Court decision and symbolically inaugurated our "colorblind" era. Generation X also came of sexual age during the height of the AIDS pandemic, when an HIV diagnosis usually meant premature death, in a time of closeting and outing, and when consensual same-sex relations were still criminalized in many states.

In contrast, Generation Y—the millennial generation born between the years of 1980 and 2000—entered a national landscape in which issues of race and racism are said to be irrelevant to the law, artifacts of the past. The millennials came of age under the banner of diversity, gender equality, multicultural inclusion, equal opportunity, and with the fall of the Berlin Wall in 1989 the end of history. Indeed, as adolescents and young adults, millennials witnessed a series of historical events concerning sexuality and race that were largely unthinkable for previous generations: the decriminalization of homosexuality with the *Lawrence v. Texas* (2003) Supreme Court ruling declaring Texas's sodomy statute unconstitutional as well as the election of the nation's first black president, Barack Obama, in 2008. While millennials are cognizant of racial and sexual differences, and indeed often celebrate them, they view them as devoid of political significance. From this perspective, our contemporary ideology of colorblindness might be seen as the apotheosis of the idea of the (neo)liberal individual as a free agent, unmarked by group history or social distinctions.

President Obama's election reinforced the regnant political belief that we inhabit a postracial society, denying the continuing effects of whiteness as property—of the prison industrial complex and institutionalized racism and violence highlighted more recently by the "Black Lives Matter" campaign, for instance. In the process, colorblind discourses have also reconfigured the political field such that "gay is the new black," as the December 16, 2008 cover of the *Advocate*, an LGBT magazine, declared after the presidential election. Equating gay and lesbian struggles for civil rights in the present with black civil rights movements in the past, "gay is the new black" consigns racism to the dustbin of history—as a historical project complete and completed.[1] With the legalization of same-sex marriage by the *Obergefell v. Hodges* (2015) Supreme Court ruling, along with the widespread introduction of protease inhibitors in the early 1990s that transformed HIV from a death sentence into a manageable disease in the Global North, even as it continues unabated in the Global South, we are now said to be entering a postgay and postsexuality era as well. Generation Y is a cohort whose social and psychic relationship to histories of whiteness as property, and to intersectional structures of racism and homophobia, [in a postidentity age] has been altered in significant ways that demand sustained analysis. From this perspective, we might describe part II of this book as investigating the social and psychic structures of colorblindness for millennials today.

Most of the Asian American students and patients we referenced in part I of this volume are *second-generation* immigrants who labor under the psychic shadows of what we delineated as "racial melancholia." These US-born young adults from Generation X are largely the offspring of immigrants from Asia who arrived after the reformation of the Immigration and Nationality Act of 1965.[2] In contrast, we focus in part II largely on *first-generation* Asian American millennial immigrants we have encountered in the classroom and clinic in growing numbers over the past decade. With the rise and accumulation of capital in East Asia and South Asia over the past several decades, an ever-greater proportion of our students and patients from Generation Y are now international students who have come directly from Asia, where they were born and raised as children and young adults. Many are "parachute children," kids as young as eight who migrate to the West, often on their own, for educational opportunities while their parents and families remain far away in Asia. Outside the intimate structures of family and kinship, these newly arrived international students do not always have a clear sense of whether they will settle in the US, return home, or move elsewhere after graduation. For this reason, they might be better described as (im)migrants. Significantly, they have little understanding of the subject of US racial history; they harbor scant knowledge of these received histories and have few resources to negotiate the patterns of racialization and barriers to assimilation they now face in a new nation.

In part II we explore social and psychic structures of colorblindness among Generation Y in relation to what we describe as "racial dissociation." Both chapter 3, "Racial Dissociation: Parachute Children and Psychic Nowhere," originally composed in 2013 for "Racism and Othering," a plenary session of the American Psychological Association, and chapter 4, "(Gay) Panic Attack: Coming Out in a Colorblind Age," examine an emergent formation of first-generation millennials from Asia sent abroad on their own.[3] What does it mean socially and how does it feel psychically to be an adolescent or a young adult navigating the politics of immigration, assimilation, and racialization alone? How do conventional processes of exclusion and loss for these first-generation millennials provide new critical insights into enduring legacies of race and sexuality— of racism and homophobia—in a colorblind age? If colorblindness suggests that racism and homophobia are now dissociated from wider public consciousness, what does it mean to bring problems of immigration and diaspora to what has conventionally been a domestic and legal discourse of colorblindness? How are the politics of colorblindness reconfigured by this shift from second-generation to first-generation students and patients and, in turn, how is the history of the Asian American subject reconfigured in relation to the subject of colorblind history?

While some parachute children thrive in their new environments, others struggle with school, friendships, and dating without parental supervision and outside the social structures of family and community. In chapter 3, we examine two case histories of parachute children, Yuna and

Yung, who are "psychically nowhere." They have spent a decade shut-tling from Korea to Australia and from China to the Philippines before moving on to the United States in pursuit of educational advancement and a second chance at academic success. In chapter 4, "(Gay) Panic Attack," we investigate two further case histories of Christopher and Neel, academically accomplished gay parachute children from China and India, who narrate their movement to the West in part as a search for sexual freedom. Across both chapters, we argue that these first-genera-tion Asian American millennials use mechanisms of racial dissociation to negotiate losses associated with the politics of immigration, assimila-tion, and racialization and, in particular, to navigate opposing realities of colorblindness—enduring legacies of racism and homophobia that shape their daily lives but can appear only as disappearing if not entirely absent in today's social and political landscape.

PARACHUTE CHILDREN

The term "parachute children" first emerged in the early 1990s, a ne-ologism coined by the Hong Kong media.[4] It describes minors verging on adolescence but also as young as eight years old. The phenomenon was originally associated with diasporic children from the elites in Hong Kong, Taiwan, and Singapore, three of the first East and South-east Asian economies to industrialize (following Japan) in the postwar period of Cold War struggle. These offspring of well-to-do Chinese par-ents were "parachuted"—often by themselves, sometimes accompanied by their mothers, a relative, or a domestic servant—to the United States and other Western English-speaking nations for primary and secondary school education. In migrating, the goal was to gain eventual admis-sion to a reputable if not prestigious US college or university. While the presence of international graduate students in US universities was by no means an unfamiliar phenomenon in prior generations, the educational migration of unaccompanied minors is a decidedly new practice deserv-ing greater scholarly attention in the social sciences and immigration studies.

With the end of the Cold War and accelerated economic develop-ment in the transpacific region, the term "parachute children" has ex-panded over the past two decades to encompass other parts of East Asia and South Asia and to include the offspring of rapidly growing middle classes in South Korea, India, and the Peoples' Republic of China (China). Indeed, in 2006, these three countries parachuted the largest number of children to the United States.[5] For instance, in 2004, the number of Korean elementary and middle school students studying abroad as parachute children totaled 390,000.[6] In 2005 alone, approximately 67,000 more unaccompanied minors departed South Korea for early study abroad (ESA) programs in a number of Western destinations, largely the United States but also Canada, New Zealand, Australia, and the United Kingdom.[7] More recently, according to the Council on Standards for International Educational Travel, the number of American high school students on F-1 student visas (conventionally used by college and graduate students) has increased from 1,700 in 2009 to over 80,000 in 2014. Currently, more than half of foreign high school students in California are from China.[8] While exact numbers are difficult to determine, these figures are hardly inconsequential.

The practice of parachute children creates divided families, separate households residing on different continents, often in physical and psychic isolation. Young children live in dormitories within boarding schools or in homestays with paid caretakers or relatives, typically without sustained parental supervision or the crucial resources of community support and reassurance. In some cases, older children live on their own or with a domestic servant. Like any typical new (im)migrant, these children labor under the stress of acquiring a new language, customs, and community, often in ambiguous relation to, if not in complete isolation from, their peers.

As the practice has evolved into an increasingly middle-class phenomenon with the expansion of global capital in Asia, parachuting has also placed great financial strain on its participants. In Korean households with more than USD$100,000 in annual pay, families report spending on average 35 percent of their income on their children's overseas education.[9] Numerous consulting businesses on ESA programs exist on both US coasts, with headquarters in various Asian capitals and global cities. For a flat fee—sometimes described in similar terms to an all-inclusive vacation package—these companies facilitate all aspects of parachuting: from selection of the destination country and school to the application and admissions process to securing housing and applying for student visas, and even providing guardianship in loco parentis.

In some respects the phenomenon might be usefully considered in relation to a much longer history of Asian transnational labor practices motivated by economic pressures of globalization. In these older practices men and women rather than children migrated abroad as (indentured) laborers and domestic workers in order to support families and offspring left behind. Parachute children are not technically laborers but are instead sent abroad for costly educational opportunities. (Indeed, many US high schools and universities today are actively recruiting students from Asia precisely because they are full-tuition "customers" who help to balance strained educational budgets.[10]) From this perspective, parachute children, unlike most typical Asian immigrant workers, might be seen as laboring to accumulate cultural capital for families with an already considerable amount of financial capital. Nonetheless, in either scenario families are separated by a great physical and emotional distance.

The practice of sending children to Western countries for primary and secondary education has been discussed as a practical response to political instability (for instance, Hong Kong's retrocession to China in 1997) and mandatory military conscription of young males (in Taiwan and Singapore). Moreover, insofar as parachute children acquire valuable English language skills, educational certification, and cultural capital in the United States and other Western countries, the practice is also depicted as a method of flexible accumulation and citizenship in which a family divests part of its resources in order to expand its economic networks and mobility in diverse global regions.[11] Parachuting activates parental fantasies that children will learn English quickly and adapt socially in a new country without much trouble. The decision of many Asian parents to send their children abroad is frequently driven by word of mouth, media coverage of the phenomenon, and peer pressure rather than in-depth research and consideration.

It is important to underscore that parachuting is most often described as a transnational solution to an overly competitive Asian university system. Elite public universities in Asia are able to accommodate only a tiny fraction of students vying for admission, and acceptance is usually based on a single test score from a yearly national entrance exam.[12] As such, these schools are considered even more competitive than top-tier private higher education institutions in the West where family wealth, alumni networks, social connections, and other soft factors influence admissions decisions. In this regard, the phenomenon of parachuting is typically represented as providing underperforming Asian students with a "second chance" at success in the West—a reset option after academic disappointment at home.

The scholarly literature on parachute children remains limited. Other than occasional lurid media accounts of Asian elites gone wild—of wayward parachute children living alone in empty New York luxury condos or California mansions on exorbitant allowances—academic publications on parachute children come largely from the field of sociology. There are a small number of academic articles and dissertations documenting the historical rise of the practice and the social effects on its participants.[13] Notably, there is no widespread agreement on the long-term consequences of the parachuting. Some studies find no major differences in long-term outcomes between parachute children and second-generation Asian Americans, the group to which they are most typically compared. Other studies describe considerable disparities in levels of assimilation, academic success, self-esteem, social adjustment, and mental stability between these two populations, with parachute children suffering comparatively in all categories.[14] Our clinical experiences with parachute children reveal alarming rates of depression, anxiety, substance abuse, addiction, sexual promiscuity, and even legal troubles. The handful of studies that have been published on the practice emphasize that children who initiate the educational migration process themselves fare best in parachuting.[15]

These divergent accounts are likely the result of the limited number of parachute children interviewed and studied, many of whom are high achievers recruited from competitive universities in which they are enrolled. However, as we suggest below, it may well also be the consequence of unexplored problems of false self that inhibit many parachute children from presenting genuine self-reflections on their social and psychic predicaments—reflections often interpreted as transparent empirical evidence by interviewers. In the following two case histories of Yuna and Yung, which recount the complicated lives and migrations of two parachute children, one from South Korea and the other from China, we are presented with narratives not easily reconciled with conventional accounts of second chances and self-redemption overseas. Neither do we encounter stories of self-sacrificing parents who consistently act on behalf of their children's best interests.

As always, the two case histories presented here are constrained by their own specificities. Nonetheless, our analysis seeks to illuminate important social and psychic dimensions of this recent form of Asian (im)migration, diaspora, and racialization not yet analyzed in the few sociological accounts of the phenomenon or in mental health research on college undergraduates and graduate students. Largely overlooked and less present in the collective imagination today than transnational adoptees from Asia, for instance, parachute children have also remained largely invisible within immigration, Asian American, critical race, and psychoanalytic studies. Yet they are everywhere—in cities and suburbs, in boarding schools and private and public high schools, in small colleges and large universities.

Christy Ling Hom observes, "Parachute kids undoubtedly become *physically* autonomous and independent from their parents once they move to the U. S. It is less clear if they also become *emotionally* autonomous and independent."[16] Our two case histories in this chapter focus specifically on problems of emotional autonomy and independence leading to what we describe as "psychic nowhere," a condition often correlated with the absence of a clear geographic belonging or destination. Attention to the contemporary phenomenon of Asian youth displaced in the global system reveals how psychic nowhere ultimately manifests in psychic states of racial dissociation: unyielding problems of compliance associated with D. W. Winnicott's concept of "True and False Self," the phenomenon of multiple selves and "standing in the spaces" connected with Philip M. Bromberg's ideas on dissociation, and problems of bonding and security linked to John Bowlby's theories of attachment. Using these critical resources, we seek to rework psychoanalytic theory in general and dissociation in particular in the context of race and the transnational displacement of "failed" young children from Asia seeking a second chance in the West. We ask: for these struggling parachute children, how does it feel *not* to be a model minority in a colorblind age?

Yuna is a twenty-three-year-old international student from Korea study-ing fine art at a design school in New York City. She was referred to me (Dr. Han) in 2011 by her academic advisor who sent her to the school's counseling and psychological services after Yuna admitted to a lengthy history of eating disorders and alcoholism. Initially, Yuna appeared withdrawn, her pretty face hidden behind long straight black hair and thick black eyeglass frames. Dressed in black from head to toe and wear-ing three-inch spiked heels, in one hand she held on tightly to an over-sized designer bag; in the other, she grasped a canvas tote filled with paint bottles and rolled-up canvases.

After Yuna sat down on the sofa, I asked her if she wanted to speak Korean or English, or a mixture of both. She glanced up slowly and whispered that she would prefer to speak Korean. It took some time get-ting used to Yuna's broken Korean as well as her heavy southern accent, with its fast staccato beat, but after a number of sessions I grew fond of its rhythms. At times, Yuna's face revealed glimpses of a young girl of about twelve; at others, a mature woman of about thirty.

In her singsong voice, Yuna recounted a complicated migration his-tory in a rather matter-of-fact style. She was born in a southern prov-ince in South Korea. As a result of her father's business success, her family moved north to Seoul as she began elementary school. She is the eldest of three children, and her parents have lived together on and off over the years. Her two younger brothers are ages ten and eight. In addition, Yuna's father has another family with a longtime mistress; together, they are raising a daughter who is eight years old in a separate household.

After Yuna's mother gave birth to the third child, she suffered from postpartum depression. When Yuna was thirteen, her parents separated because of her father's infidelities. With chaos engulfing her family, Yu-na's parents decided to send her away to Australia under the pretense of her getting a head start on acquiring English. They emphasized the privilege of studying abroad, and they promised that during her time away they would sort out their marital problems. Yuna was not part of this decision. She felt that she became the "most disposable" of her parents' children as their domestic troubles unfolded. She stated flatly,

"I was erased from my family because I wasn't as needy as my younger siblings who were babies."

Yuna traveled alone from Seoul to Sydney, Australia. Her parents rented a room for her from a distant uncle's family, and she attended a private middle school. At this uncle's house, Yuna lived in constant fear of the family's psychological and verbal abuse. In particular, she described the uncle's wife as a greedy and controlling woman who monitored Yuna's every phone conversation with her parents. The uncle's wife threatened to hurt Yuna if she complained about being mistreated. After enduring these conditions for six months, Yuna ran away.

Initially Yuna just walked around town and slept on the beach. She thought of suicide as a "practical solution" to her problems, but said she really didn't know how to go about it. The police found her two days later. Even after police and school officials notified her parents about their daughter's crisis, neither mother nor father rushed to Sydney to care for Yuna. To the contrary, Yuna's parents expressed in no uncertain terms that she was to remain in Australia and to go back to school, even though Yuna communicated a strong desire to return to Korea.

Through the ESA consulting company that her family had originally employed, Yuna's father arranged for her to transfer to a boarding school in Sydney. At this school, Yuna met several other parachute children from Korea. She described them as spoiled rich kids—displaced like she—who were lonely and lost. It was during this period in boarding school that Yuna acquired several self-destructive habits: binge drinking, a binge-and-purge eating disorder, and chain-smoking cigarettes. In her worst periods, Yuna purged up to five times a day over periods that lasted as long as two months. Yuna reflected that all she remembers about boarding school in Sydney was bonding with other Korean parachute children over cigarettes, alcohol, purging, and speaking in their mother tongue—activities allowing them periodic respite from the isolation of living abroad as well as the difficulties of speaking English.

Having spent two school years in Australia, and as she approached her sixteenth birthday, Yuna parachuted once again. From Australia, she traveled to the United States to attend high school in Los Angeles. Yuna's decision to move to the United States was motivated by the fact that the majority of her boarding school friends—all Korean parachute children—were moving on to American high schools. In Los Angeles, she reunited with a number of old friends and spent most of her time smoking, drinking, and purging at her new boarding school. She also began dating older men, reporting that unprotected sex resulted in two unwanted pregnancies and abortions. Moreover, because of poor attendance and grades, Yuna was forced to change high schools every year. Each time, her father arranged these transfers through ESA consultancies while both parents remained in Korea.

Although her parents never visited Yuna in Sydney or Los Angeles, Yuna did regularly return to Seoul during winter and summer recesses. During these visits home, Yuna's father began to invite her out to dinner and then to clubs for drinks. Yuna reported feeling privileged by the special attention her father showed her. She said she wanted to prove to him that she was "grown up" and that she could "hold her liquor." Father and daughter would drink all night, getting progressively inebriated. At times, he would ask Yuna to sit on his lap. With an amused smile, Yuna admitted that these invitations made her feel like "a whore and daddy's girl, at once."

During one of these drunken escapades, Yuna's father introduced his mistress to her. Yuna recalled feeling jealousy toward her father's girlfriend, who "was not as pretty as my mother." Nevertheless, witnessing her father's loving attention toward his mistress, Yuna made a practical decision to get along with her in order to prove her maturity. To her regret, her parents' initial promise to work out their marital difficulties never came to pass, and Yuna's father continued to vacillate between his wife and mistress. At the same time, Yuna's mother became obsessed with healthy eating and various beauty regimes. She devoted all her waking hours to these self-care activities, and she neglected not just Yuna during her visits but even the younger siblings who continued to reside with her.

It took Yuna two extra years to graduate high school and gain admission to an art college in New York City. Yuna chose art school because she felt her academic skills were not up to par for admission to a competitive liberal arts college. She quietly admitted, "It was the only major I could think of where I would not be required to speak or write in English." While Yuna admits to having chosen art school to avoid academic demands, she nonetheless felt a sense of optimism upon enrolling in college. Despite the momentary surge of hope and excitement accompanying this new beginning, Yuna continued to live her life at age twenty carelessly and without self-regard. In college, as in high school, she bonded with other Korean international students, especially older male peers, who took her out drinking every night. After one dismal semester, Yuna was suspended for poor grades and was forced to take a semester leave from school. She returned to Seoul, where she continued her self-destructive habits.

I met Yuna the following fall semester after she returned to New York. Besides her complicated personal narrative, one underpinned by solitary migrations from one global city to another, Yuna explained to me that her heart was currently being broken by an older married man. Yuna met Hyun when she first arrived in New York, and they dated on and off. Like Yuna, he too was an international student from Korea, studying for an LLM (Masters of Law) in graduate school. When they first met, Hyun's wife was in Korea preparing to join him in New York. However, Hyun told Yuna that he was single, and she did not suspect he was lying. Yuna discovered that Hyun was married when she began to receive harassing phone calls from Hyun's wife, who demanded that Yuna cut off relations with her husband. Yuna felt overwhelmed by her love for Hyun, but she also felt betrayed and ashamed. Despite knowing it was the proper thing to do, Yuna could not bring herself to separate from Hyun. Even after Hyun's wife joined him in the United States, the two continued to see each other intermittently for months.

Hyun broke up with Yuna after a year and a half of this turbulent dynamic—a little after she had begun therapy with me. At this point, her self-destructive behavior spun out of control. By midspring semester of her second year in college, Yuna had missed the majority of her classes as well as counseling appointments; her days and nights reversed. Whenever she did show up for sessions, I refrained from offering too much interpretation and focused instead on crisis management. However, one interpretation that "woke her up" resulted in her understanding of how she was the other woman for Hyun, just as her father's mistress had been for him. Upon realizing this similarity, Yuna appeared physically shaken. Her eyes widened in disbelief, and she stated, "I was her. My father's whore I hated and envied." As Yuna's alcohol abuse and eating disorder accelerated, we were not able to explore this unexpected identification with the "fallen" woman any further.

With my repeated exhortations, Yuna finally consented to entering an inpatient treatment center in New York for bulimia and alcoholism. She stayed there for nearly three months. After completing her addiction treatment, she took an extended medical leave from school and returned to Seoul.

What is most poignant about Yuna to me is her sense of what I would describe as being psychically "nowhere." At a young age, she parachuted alone to Sydney and then to Los Angeles and New York. In each location, Yuna falls, but the parachute fails to open. In none of these places does Yuna learn how to cultivate attachments or grow roots. This inability is the result of Yuna not having firmly rooted herself in Korea, either. From an early age, Yuna's parents neglected to include her in any of the critical discussions directly affecting her life. Yuna was never given a chance to develop what we explicate below as a sense of a "true self"—to learn to play, to devise creative solutions, and to make authentic decisions that might affect her life positively.

Just before Yuna returned to Korea, she called me. She spoke in her timid, singsong voice and told me that at first she was angry at me for "sending her away," as her parents had done all her life. Yuna said that, under the pretense of care, she felt abandoned all over again. She added that the major theme in her life was feeling "unwanted" because she was at best a "second-class citizen"—at home, in foreign lands, to her parents, and to her lover. However, while she was in the hospital, Yuna realized that my intervention was the first time that someone cared enough to help her confront the significant problems she created in order to avoid her deep feelings of loss and abandonment. She told me that she was returning to Korea not to escape or to take a break, as before, but to engage in a sober examination of herself in the context of family, home, and nation. Yuna said she would call me at some point if she came back to New York, but I have not heard from her as of yet.

HOW DOES IT FEEL *NOT* TO BE A MODEL MINORITY?

Let us return to 1903 and W. E. B. Du Bois's provocative question to African Americans in *The Souls of Black Folk*: "How does it feel to be a problem?"[17] Asian American model minority discourse emerged nearly seven decades later in the wake of Cold War conflict, US civil rights movements, and the reformation of the Immigration and Nationality Act of 1965. As we point out in chapter 1, the model minority stereotype developed in the historical context of new immigrants and refugees from Asia under communist threat, working to sort out "good" Asian capitalists from "bad" Asian communist subjects. More specifically, it identified the academic success of second-generation Asian Americans (Generation X) and their upward economic mobility as proof positive of the United States as a land of equal opportunity and free markets liberated from racial discrimination and distress. In this particular deployment of the stereotype, the unequal status of African Americans in US society was viewed as a self-inflicted injury. Inequality was seen as an issue of individual responsibility rather than a problem of institutional racism or enduring legacies of whiteness as property, of group discrimination and structural bias.

Resisting the invidious political juxtaposition of Asian American "success" against African American "failure," comparative race scholars have sought to reformulate this regulatory dialectic. They have revised Du Bois's earlier inquiry, asking Asian Americans, in the words of Vijay Prashad, "How does it feel to be a solution?"[18] The question of how it feels to be a solution underscores the ways in which Asian Americans are politically exploited as "middle men minorities" in order to discipline other people of color while still suffering themselves from various forms of social exclusion and advancement. At the same time, the question also emphasizes the fact that race relations in the United States are triangulated, although they largely continue to be seen in binary terms of black and white. Like the Asian transnational adoptee who is more easily assimilated into the imaginary of the white nuclear family than the domestic black adoptee, the figure of the meritorious, compliant, and upwardly mobile model minority serves here as a political wedge between black and white. It serves as both an alibi for and a buffer between white privilege and black disenfranchisement, reinforcing in the process historical legacies of whiteness as property.

Chapter 1's focus on depression and suicide explored in effect various psychic dimensions of how it feels to be a solution—to be a model minority in a society that continues to exclude Asian Americans from full participation and social belonging in national life. The predicament of racial melancholia indexes the considerable social as well as psychic pressures associated with successfully approximating the model minority stereotype of the hard working, self-effacing, and perpetually agreeable Asian American immigrant child. Yuna's case history allows us to extend our prior analyses of the model minority stereotype and racial melancholia by revealing also how it feels *not* to be a solution, how it feels *not* to be a model minority. It does so through the psychic paradigm of racial dissociation, which we continue to explore in the remainder of part 2.

As a parachute child and first-generation (im)migrant, Yuna's peripatetic movements across Australia and the United States illustrate the formidable psychic costs linked with the everyday difficulties of immigration, racialization, and assimilation for a young (im)migrant on her own and with the *inability* to approximate the dominant racial stereotypes of the model minority in any way, shape, or form. Indeed, as we elaborate below, newly arrived first-generation international students such as Yuna cannot situate themselves within any racial discourse at all. Equally so, as her case history so poignantly underscores, Yuna's parachuting to the West is driven as much by structural problems of higher education in Asia and the idea of second chances as by parental dysfunction. Together, these factors underscore the need to consider the shifting history of the racial subject in relation to the subject of racial history— that is, personal family histories in the larger historical context of shifting political economies in Asia and the West under neoliberalism and globalization.

What is immediately apparent in Yuna's case history are the heterogeneous reasons for which parachute children are sent away. The sustained marital difficulties of Yuna's parents as well as their general neglect of their eldest daughter exposes a family drama leading to Yuna's displacement and diaspora to the West under the pretense of care and concern. As their marriage dissolves, Yuna is sent away to get a "head start" on acquiring English. She becomes the "most disposable" of her parents' children as they promise to sort out their marital difficulties, an inconvenience to both a depressive mother obsessed with self-care and an unavailable father who would rather spend time with his mistress and second family. Like many competitive school systems in the East and West, the Korean education system demands continuous parental involvement, in addition to a battery of after-school clinics and tutoring. Because of their various personal conflicts, Yuna's parents simply would not commit themselves to these time-consuming responsibilities. Although their decision to send Yuna away was justified as both a protective measure and an invaluable educational opportunity, on reflection her parents' actions struck Yuna as hasty and selfish.

To approach the situation from a different angle, in the private sphere of family and kinship relations, the idea of parental concern and economic sacrifice in the practice of parachuting often effaces turbulent family dynamics and negligence frequently motivating the sending away of children as a convenient solution to the abnegation of parental responsibility. In the public sphere, insofar as discourses of parachuting configure the practice as a transnational substitute for an inflexible and stringent Asian education system, the displacement of Asian youth into the diaspora implicitly reinscribes the East as "problem" while reconstituting the West as "solution." In the process, it implicitly aligns on a more encompassing scale the problem of Asia with the problem of Africa, returning us to Du Bois's query from a different, global perspective. In this manner American exceptionalism is reinvented in the age of globalization under ideals of neoliberalism and multiculturalism: the fantasy of the United States as an accommodating land of equal opportunity, a "level playing field" where individualism, self-determination, and merit can lead to success unavailable at home (the capital costs of US higher education notwithstanding).

It is these two histories—of turbulent family psychodynamics and structural conditions of education and competition under global capitalism—that reconfigure enduring problems of immigration and race at the heart of parachuting. Insofar as Yuna's case history does not easily fit with conventional narratives of parental benevolence as well as achievement and success associated with the model minority stereotype, it reveals in the process an intransigent psychic negativity at the heart of parachuting. It discloses how it feels to be psychically nowhere in terms of what we describe as true and false self as well as racial dissociation.

Not unlike Winnicott's fifty-year-old patient of our epigraph, Yuna does not yet feel she has started to exist. She contains little "true experience." She has "no past," and she does not feel "real."[19] In "Ego Distortion in Terms of True and False Self" (1960), Winnicott outlines the psychic process by which the infant adapts to the growing demands of a world of objects it cannot control—indeed objects (most notably the mother) on which it is dependent. For the infant, spontaneous gestures of omnipotence felt to be emanating from within are met with environmental impingements from without. Winnicott associates these spontaneous impulses with the beginnings of id satisfaction, with the strengthening of the infantile ego, and with the emergence of what he describes as "True Self." Crucially, how these expressions of omnipotence are met and mediated by the mother's actions determine the eventual trajectory of the infant's ego organization and development. Winnicott writes,

> The good-enough mother meets the omnipotence of the infant and to some extent makes sense of it. She does this repeatedly. A True Self begins to have life, through the strength given to the infant's weak ego by the mother's implementation of the infant's omnipotent expressions.
>
> The mother who is not good enough is not able to implement the infant's omnipotence, and so she repeatedly fails to meet the infant gesture; instead she substitutes her own gesture which is to be given sense by the compliance of the infant. This compliance on the part of the infant is the earliest stage of the False Self, and belongs to the mother's inability to sense her infant's needs.[20]

On the one hand, spontaneous gestures of omnipotence are met with good-enough mothering and satisfaction on the part of the infant's fragile ego. This process creates a shared transitional space between mother and child that allows the infant to "gradually abrogate omnipotence" and to move from "object relating" to "object usage," as discussed in the previous chapter.[21]

The former concept describes the infant's apprehension of the object in isolation, as a projection of the infant having no independent existence—the infant as absolute creator. The latter concept indicates a "shared reality," the ability of the infant to "use" the object, to appreciate the object as a separate entity in its own right, and to develop the capacity for concern. In moving from relating to usage, the infant learns to mediate its omnipotent impulses and to modulate its narcissism—to play; to be creative; to symbolize; to negotiate borders between inside and outside, self and other; and, most importantly, to experience feelings of authenticity and aliveness that signal psychic health and growth. In this manner, a true self develops. "The True Self has a spontaneity, and this has been joined up with the world's events," writes Winnicott. "The infant can now begin to enjoy the *illusion* of omnipotent creating and controlling, and then can gradually come to recognize the illusory element, the fact of playing and imagining."[22]

On the other hand, spontaneous expressions of omnipotence thwarted by the unyielding gestures of the mother force the infant to retreat, stimulating the development of false self. The false self marks an affective state in which creativity and play become diminished if not altogether impossible. Overshadowed by the mother's will, the infant's spontaneous feelings of authenticity and aliveness become secreted and hidden. The infant begins to apprehend reality through the mother's eyes and to distrust its own experiences. The false self comes to cover over a true self, and a true self fails to appear. Ultimately, false self leads to states of compliance, feelings of fraudulence, and detachment as a way of guarding the infantile ego's fragile existence. "In the extreme examples of False Self development," Winnicott writes, "the True Self is so well hidden that spontaneity is not a feature in the infant's living experiences. Compliance is then the main feature, with imitation as a specialty."[23]

Turning to the personal dynamics of her dysfunctional family, Yuna's case history reads like an elaborate disquisition on problems of false self. For Yuna, compliance manifests in notably destructive and perverse ways. Like Freud's spindle in the famous *fort-da* episode of *Beyond the Pleasure Principle,* Yuna is continually tossed away into the global system by her parents. As she parachutes from country to country, they do not pull her back—there is no return, no miraculous "da." Unsurprisingly, Yuna feels like a "second-class citizen"—in Korea, in foreign lands, to her parents, and to her lover. In her own words, she is both "erased" and "unwanted"; unwanted, Yuna cannot want. Indeed, throughout the academic literature investigating the phenomenon of parachute children, participants report distressing levels of isolation and loneliness. To reformulate Hom's earlier query, while parachute children are *physically* autonomous, their ability to be *emotionally* autonomous—to be spontaneous and alive—is often acutely constrained.

Yuna states that she is the "most disposable" of her parents' children. Perversely, she meets this parental gesture of abandonment by disposing of herself. Yuna's bulimia and alcoholism constitute a repetition compulsion written under the sign of the death drive as well as a twisted compliance, a distorted anger and agency destructively turned against the self that returns us to the territory of racial melancholia and suicide. Conventional explanations of bulimia characterize this condition as a somatic variant of false self and compliance.[24] Bulimia underscores the will to "dispose of" and "to expel" but also "to feel" something—ideas we might usefully align with the conflicts between true and false self and the will to feel something spontaneous and real.

Moreover, by drinking excessively with her father at seedy nightclubs in Seoul, Yuna exacerbates her self-annihilation by transforming herself from a vulnerable daughter into a sophisticated mistress. That is, being a "whore and a daddy's girl" at once functions not only as a method of stealing emotional attention away from the whore Yuna hates and envies but also as a mode of perverse compliance with her father's particular erotic dispositions and desires. (Notably, Yuna's father himself is literally dissociated from his own family and, in particular, his role as father to Yuna through his sexually tinged interactions with his eldest child. He exerts a powerful psychic effect on Yuna who functions as a kind of dissociated secondary other to his desires.)

Through this repeated gesture of identifying with the fallen woman, Yuna also contributes to the destruction of her family romance, a pattern that Yuna replicates across the various diasporic spaces in which she finds herself. In the United States, Yuna consorts with older men, resulting in two unwanted pregnancies and abortions, mimicking a repetition compulsion of infidelity not dissimilar to that defining her parents' relationship and the split formation of her father's two families. With Hyun, Yuna literalizes this pattern of perverse compliance, occupying the structural position of mistress and fallen woman to his wife who, like Yuna's mother, remains elsewhere.

Yuna's life narrative might be described as an elaborate narrative of compliance with the demands of others—her parents, her peers, and her lovers. She is unable to create a healthy illusion of a unified self, becoming at once a docile and self-destructive subject. To return for a moment to our earlier discussion of race and the clinic, the required compliance and docility of the Asian American model minority subject—his or her seeming lack of resistance to and acceptance of the therapist's interpretations and interventions—makes the therapeutic address to false self especially fraught and difficult to treat. "In analysis of a False Self personality," Winnicott reminds us, "the fact must be recognized that the analyst can only talk to the False Self of the patient about the patient's True Self."[25] In Yuna's case history, the only self to whom either the therapist or Yuna herself had any access was the self-annihilating Yuna. As such, when working with false self personalities—when grappling with the problem of Asian Americans in the space of the clinic—the analyst (and the sociologist) needs to be cognizant of this dynamic. The analyst cannot necessarily take the information, responses, and answers being offered at face value, rendering the work of interpretation especially vexed and difficult.[26] In this manner compliance and imitation as manifesting conditions of a (racial) false self thus contribute an added layer of difficulty to the enigmatic kernel of the symptom, to its interpretation and to the formulation of an appropriate therapeutic response.

RACIAL DISSOCIATION AND PSYCHIC NOWHERE

Bromberg takes up Winnicott's notions of compliance and detachment in his writings on dissociation. He defines dissociation as the loss of capacity for self-reflection, the inability to process emotionally charged mental conflicts, and the disconnection of the mind from the psyche-soma as a (paradoxical) defense to preserve a sense of selfhood and self-continuity. Extending Winnicott's conceptions of healthy and defensive negotiations between true and false self, Bromberg introduces the notion of "adaptive" (healthy) and "pathological" (defensive) forms of dissociation shaped by the earliest of infantile experiences. "Dissociation becomes pathological," he notes, "to the degree that it proactively limits and often forecloses one's ability to hold and reflect upon different states of mind with a single experience of 'me-ness.'"[27]

For Bromberg, psychic health and stability is marked by adaptive dissociation, the ability to "feel like one self while being many," and the psychic capacity to "stand in the spaces."[28] Adaptive dissociation allows our various self-states to function as if they were a single, coherent reality and to facilitate the "illusion of cohesive personal identity."[29] Since multiplicity is the basic condition of human existence, we do not start as an integrated whole but rather as fractured subjects. We are continuously subject to a range of competing social realities and pressures. In turn, "'standing in the spaces' is a shorthand way of describing a person's relative capacity to make room at any given moment for subjective reality that is not readily containable by the self he experiences as 'me' at that moment. It is what distinguishes creative imagination from both fantasy and concreteness, and distinguishes playfulness from facetiousness. Some people can 'stand in the spaces' better than others."[30]

Bromberg stresses that psychic health is not predicated on seamless integration but rather on the adaptive *illusion* of one's unity. That is, psychic stability is marked by the capacity to "stand in the spaces between [opposing] realities without losing any of them."[31] In most people, he observes, "the adaptive illusion of one's 'sameness' is taken for granted. In other individuals, the experience of continuity and integrity of the sense of self is never taken for granted; it is absent either partially or totally, and it often involves a lifelong struggle to deal with the existence of relatively or totally dissociated self-states."[32]

Patterns of false self and compliance established in infancy continue to manifest themselves in the everyday habits and patterns of adulthood—shaping subjectivities marked by defensive and pathological, or alternately adaptive and healthy, forms of dissociation. If a patient cannot play—cannot mediate competing social realities in a healthy and adaptive manner—then it is the goal of therapy to enable this basic, creative skill, to facilitate a transitional space of creative imagination consensually constructed between patient and therapist. To reprise a passage from Winnicott analyzed earlier, "Psychotherapy has to do with two people playing together."[33] As the patient shifts from defensive to adaptive dissociation, conflict can emerge and repression can be loosened such that trauma becomes available for the patient to negotiate and work through. Only by doing so can the patient develop a true self, feel spontaneous and alive, and, like Winnicott's patient, desire to live. In sum, the ability to connect disparate realities into a healthy illusion of "me-ness" defines genuine and authentic *relationality* between two subjects.

If the promise of true self and adaptive dissociation yields the possibility of authentic relationality among subjects, then how do competing *racial* realities—disparate racial demands and pressures that define everyday conflicts—reconfigure dissociation specifically in regard to race and racism? Furthermore, insofar as race continues to be an especially fraught and overdetermined social category, how does it constrain the illusion of unified (racial) self? How does it interrupt the emergence of a true (racial) self?

Winnicott and Bromberg focus their psychic accounts of true and false self and dissociation on the problem of "good-enough" mothering—that is, exclusively on the private dynamics of family history rather than the public dynamics of group histories. However, Yuna's displacement into the diaspora accompanied by her inexorable predicament of being psychically nowhere demands a more comprehensive accounting of how to think race in relation to dissociation—that is, a larger *social* account of racial dissociation. How do we begin to socialize and to historicize dissociation?

To start, just as Bromberg stresses healthy and adaptive forms of dissociation, Winnicott is careful not to pathologize the false self, emphasizing its productive capacities and protective role in relation to a true self. The false self, that is, can serve the critical function of shielding the ego in potentially hazardous environments and threatening social conditions. In health, Winnicott writes, "the False self "is represented by the whole organization of the polite and mannered social attitude . . . the gain being the place in society which can never be attained or maintained by the True Self alone."[34] In pathology, on the other hand, the false self marks a defensive position whose purpose is "to hide and protect the True Self, whatever that may be."[35] Unmodulated, pathological manifestations of false self ultimately hide the True Self even from one's *own* self, resulting in feelings of fraudulence and phoniness, the absence of "true experience," and the affective incapacity to feel real, spontaneous, authentic, or alive.[36] Sensations of wasted life—of emptiness, futility, and hopelessness—overshadow all social interactions and relations.

Importantly, Winnicott observes that patients with a highly developed sense of unhealthy false self can nonetheless be high-functioning and accomplished individuals. They exhibit not only great intelligence and professional success but also the ability to cooperate and work well—in short, to comply and to be compliant—with others.[37] "The world may observe academic success of a high degree," Winnicott writes, "and may find it hard to believe in the very real distress of the individual concerned, who feels 'phoney' the more he or she is successful. When such individuals destroy themselves in one way or another, instead of fulfilling promise, this invariably produces a sense of shock in those who have developed high hopes of the individual."[38]

For us, Winnicott's description of high-functioning academic success—accompanied by phony or deadened feelings of accomplishment—is strikingly resonant with pathological manifestations of the Asian American model minority stereotype explored in our theories of racial melancholia. Winnicott describes defensive and unhealthy versions of the false self in terms of performance: "There are those who can be themselves and who also can act, whereas there are others who can only act, and who are completely at a loss when not in a role, and when not being appreciated or applauded (acknowledged as existing)."[39] To mimic a stereotype without self-reflection or the ability to step out of that role returns us to Antonio Viego's provocative account of "dead subjects": a racial subject incessantly driven by imperatives of need but dead to his or her own spontaneous desires, his or her own spontaneous feelings.[40]

Indeed, compliance and cooperation, as well as deference and agreeability, as strategies for acceptance and survival quite accurately describe the social contract of Asian American model minority citizenship in the United States. Simultaneously, the social contract for Asian Americans demands acquiescence to the ideology of colorblindness—to the idea of a level playing field, to a narrative of individualism and merit outside of history, and to the absence of racism and interdependence in the liberal project. This contract is especially applicable to new immigrants, and it is especially fraught for refugees upon whom the "gift of freedom" has been bestowed.[41]

In short, Asian American model minority subjectivity can be described as predicated on the compliant achievement of academic success and upward economic mobility, even at the cost of a true self—of great psychic distress as well as personal sacrifice and, in Winnicott's estimation, "a dissociation between intellectual activity and psycho-somatic existence."[42] (We will return to this splitting of mind and body in our next chapter.) In turn, such unhealthy forms of dissociation for the racial subject come to determine whether racial melancholia and loss will assume self-annihilating and suicidal proportions.

To approach racial dissociation and the stereotype from another angle, we might consider Bromberg's concept of "standing in the spaces" in light of Du Bois's notion of "double consciousness." While the stereotype has been analyzed in critical race studies largely in terms of mimicry and performance—that is, in terms of imitations of whiteness or routines of passing that Winnicott relates to acting—"double consciousness" also carries with it an implicit spatial metaphor we can connect to Bromberg's theories of dissociation. "Double consciousness" as multiple and conflicting spaces in which the racial subject must stand underscores how race and racism make "standing in the spaces" socially and psychically easier for some and more difficult for others.

Frantz Fanon's *Black Skin, White Masks* (1952) contains a famous description of feelings of dread while he sits in a darkened movie theater waiting for repugnant images of himself to appear on the silver screen. Often interpreted in terms of a racialized Lacanian mirror stage, Fanon's critique of the racial stereotype in this parable of race relations underscores how the black male subject, rather than joyfully tipping into and identifying with the mirror image of this scene, would work hard to keep as much distance as possible between himself and these de-idealized images, between his bodily ego and these racially disparaged imagoes. "In the white world the man of color encounters difficulties in the development of his bodily schema," Fanon writes. "Consciousness of the body is solely a negating activity."[43]

Here, tensions between looking at an image and the feeling of dread return us to Du Bois's question "How does it *feel* to be a problem?," Prashad's query "How does it *feel* to be a solution?" or, alternately, our inquiry "How does it *feel* not to be a model minority?" Collectively, these questions force us to consider more systematically different emotional registers of race that constrain the emergence of a (racial) true self, while emphasizing the affective dimensions of racism in our theories of dissociation—as Michelle Stephens suggests, the gaps between "*being* black, i.e., identity, and *feeling* black, which has more to do with a broad array of embodied experiences, including but not exclusive to the emotional."[44] Stephens's observations encourage us to consider the differences between being and feeling—the problem of race as looking versus feeling, skin versus flesh, and epistemology versus phenomenology. In so doing, it allows us to reconsider the social and psychic parameters of true and false self, the gaps and fissures between racial meaning and feeling that lead to self-protective or, alternately, self-destructive behavior in psychic processes of racial dissociation.

Bromberg narrates the ability to stand in the spaces as a shorthand method for describing the capacity of an abstract individual "to make room at any given moment for subjective reality that is not readily containable by the self he experiences as 'me' at that moment." Du Bois's and Fanon's accounts of double consciousness and the stereotype extend Bromberg's theory by rendering explicit the *intersubjective* dissonance by which racial dissociation functions as an everyday social and psychic mechanism in a society in which it is often difficult, if not impossible, to reconcile the ways in which others see you with the ways in which you see yourself. That is, they illustrate how race as an intersubjective relation continually constrains the ability of some to "stand in the spaces" and thus to shape a healthy illusion and cohesive sense of "me-ness." Indeed, we might consider in this context how the fixity of the racial stereotype—its antirelational refusal of spontaneity, creativity, and play—becomes the hallmark of an intractable if not impossible intersubjective relation among competing racial realities and subject positions. In short, the fixity of the racial stereotype—the impingements of its polarizing social roles and demands—renders any possibility of "good-enough" race relations tenuous, the topic of our concluding remarks.

Returning to Yuna's psychic predicaments provides us with an additional number of critical insights on the history of the (racial) subject in regard to the subject of (racial) history. Like her record of unhealthy false self and perverse compliance, Yuna's problems of racial dissociation reveal that she cannot easily "stand in the spaces" of Seoul, Sydney, Los Angeles, or New York. This inability is compounded by a racial history of how it feels to be a problem (or, for that matter, a solution) connected to the structural difficulties of immigration and assimilation as an adolescent on her own. Considering the dynamics of healthy and pathological forms of racial dissociation, Yuna can neither turn to nor seek shelter in the model minority myth as a self-protective shield. She cannot "use" (in Winnicotts's sense) the model minority stereotype to negotiate her conflicting racial self-states in US society or to seek cover in the racial stereotype's self-protective and ostensibly positive dimensions as academic achievement and success. In short, Yuna displays all the debilitating aspects of the false self and defensive dissociation but none of its self-protective or adaptive dimensions. In this regard, for Yuna, racial dissociation describes a psychic state of being nowhere that results from the decided cleaving of compliance from social defense.

Yuna is in the perpetual psychic limbo of an unhealthy false self and unproductive compliance. Her state of psychic suspension is mirrored by her linguistic dislocation—her inability, like that of many other parachute children we have encountered, to function competently in either English or Korean. She has no "native tongue." Such a state of psychic dislocation and detachment is also exacerbated by the ambiguous legal status of parachute children. To the extent that some parachute children are undocumented, there is an extra social burden of compliance—the imperative not to draw the attention of the police or other disciplining authorities—in Roberto Gonzales's words, "learning to be illegal."[45] Finally, as sociological studies of the phenomenon emphasize, when living alone, parachute children are typically in the closet about their status as unaccompanied minors. Certainly, this information rarely comes up in the public space of the classroom, although more so in the private space of the clinic. In all these different ways, parachute children are placed in a similar structural situation to undocumented immigrants who never willingly disclose their legal status.

Here, we might compare the social and psychic pressures on parachute children under the cloud of racial dissociation to those of transnational adoptees under the shadows of racial melancholia whose parents do not share a common history of immigration and loss with their adopted children. Unlike transnational adoptees or second-generation children of Asian immigrants "over here," the status of parachute children as "immigrants who have settled" or as "sojourners who will return" is indeterminate; they are in geographic limbo. With parents and family remaining in Asia—or often scattered among various global locations—there is no clear sense among parachute children whether they are immigrants or sojourners, whether they are coming or going, and where they might physically or psychically locate themselves. In this sense, they are also nowhere.

From another perspective, being psychically nowhere also connects the history of the (racial) subject to the subject of different racial as well as national and cultural histories. Yuna lacks the ability to shift among states of racial consciousness that would allow her to stand successfully in the competing geographical spaces—the different national histories, racial discourses, and cultural practices—of Korea, Australia, or the United States. Here, we might consider how modes of compliance and expected social behavior manifest in historically specific ways on both sides of the transpacific: the demands of Confucian social norms and filial piety emphasizing collective over individual desires and the imperative to "save face," and dominant US and Western societies requiring of their Asian immigrants continuous displays of compliance, gratitude, docility, and self-effacement. Yuna does not feel at ease in US society, but she does not feel that she can return to Korea either.[46] Her narrative and treatment end abruptly with an ostensible return to Korea and the hope of a genuine and authentic confrontation with the self—a true self—in the context of family, home, and nation. Certain transnational accounts laud cosmopolitanism and globalization as "being at home in the world," being "psychically everywhere." However, it is quite clear that Yuna does not feel at home anywhere.[47] In all these different ways, Yuna cannot stand in the spaces. She is psychically nowhere.

As we have noted, removed from the context of family, home, and nation, parachute children negotiate the trauma of relocation on their own. They do not experience the security of negotiating problems of immigration, assimilation, and racialization in the context of intergenerational family conflicts. Put otherwise, they do not mourn the loss of language, culture, customs, and community in the context of kinship relations— between first-generation parents and their second-generation offspring, as was typical with Generation X—but in faraway isolation. (In contrast, the stereotype of Asian immigrant families and "tiger mothers" in the United States is often characterized by excessive parental supervision and involvement.)

Moreover, to the extent that middle-class Asian parents are making considerable financial sacrifices to send their children abroad, many parachute children report great reluctance to burden their parents with the extra worry of their social adjustment or mental distress. Hence, losses that should be negotiated as an *intersubjective* relation between parent and child become again a profoundly *intrasubjective* affair—returning us to the psychic dynamics of racial melancholia and loss from our previous chapters. Suicide, transnational adoption, and the contemporary phenomenon of parachute children each demand a different historical account and narrative of loss across the shift from Generation X to Generation Y, and from second-generation structures of family and kinship to first-generation structures of isolation and solitude under globalization.

Relatedly, the issue of being a first- rather than a second-generation (im)migrant configures the problem of racial dissociation and the contemporary politics of colorblindness in notable ways. Parachute children enter the country largely colorblind to the patterns of racialization to which they are subjected and which frame their everyday interactions and experiences. Put otherwise, often they do not comprehend themselves as racialized subjects, thereby bringing a history of immigration and diaspora to the politics of colorblindness. At the young age of thirteen, Yuna is parachuted to the West. As a teenager, she moves from being part of the racial majority in Korea to being part of a racial minority in both Australia and the United States without family or community support to help her navigate this significant transition. We might say that parachute children are racially interpellated in their new Western countries at a moment in their lives when racial discourses and critiques of those discourses have, in a sense, already passed them by. Yuna arrives both too early and too late in racial discourse.

It is notable that during therapy Yuna spoke neither about race nor racism. She did not have a critical vocabulary for discussing the vicissitudes of immigration, assimilation, or racialization—similar to many of the parachute children we have encountered in the clinic. The absence of any overt discussion of race or racism is a striking departure from second-generation Asian American adolescents and transnational adoptees explored in our previous two chapters. (For second-generation immigrants in Generation X, these topics were central points of conflict and discussion in the classroom and in treatment.) In short, for Yuna, psychic nowhere is also racial nowhere.

Yuna's case history underscores how racial dissociation adaptively functions, or fails to function, as a psychic paradigm for racial consciousness and survival—indeed, how dissociation can be a profoundly racialized affair in US society. For first-generation millennials who cannot locate themselves in any racial discourse or identity, the politics of racial dissociation and colorblindness assume a specific historical dimension. That is, dominant historical accounts of colorblindness are narrated as part of a changing landscape of US constitutional law and struggles for civil rights in the name of liberal citizenship and belonging. However, Yuna's racial dissociation and colorblindness trace their genealogy to the contemporary politics of diaspora and globalization—to parachuting and to the politics of race and assimilation as an isolated intrasubjective process disconnected from these conventional legal accounts. Her psychic predicament thus brings an alternative history of (im)migration to the politics of colorblindness under the contemporary mandates of neoliberalism and multicultural inclusion.

Yuna's case history compels us to rethink the politics of colorblindness and race in terms of the changing history of the Asian American subject in relation to the subject of a changing Asian and Asian American history. Written under the sign of social failure, Yuna's state of psychic nowhere is an extreme example of unhealthy false self and what we have outlined as the various social aspects and psychic processes of racial dissociation. Poignantly, Yuna exhibits none of dissociation's protective or adaptive qualities—a thick skin, mannered social behavior, the illusion of accomplishment and success that might mime the high-functioning even if psychically distressed profile of the Asian American model minority.

If racial dissociation can result in either healthy or pathological forms of psychic survival or self-annihilation, we must continue to rethink the racial stereotype, the model minority myth, double consciousness, and the gaps between racial meaning and feeling in both Winnicott's and Bromberg's theories. We must contextualize problems of racial dissociation in regard to private family dynamics as well as evolving socioeconomic histories across the transpacific. The transnational displacement of young children into the global system encompasses both traumatic forfeitures of family, home, and nation "over there" and the realities of immigration, assimilation, and racialization "over here." For Yuna, psychic nowhere outlines a mental state of racial dissociation in which parachute children not only fail to be a racial solution but also fail to create any protective version of selfhood at all. Yuna is literally defenseless.

In outlining these symptoms of unhealthy racial dissociation and perverse compliance, we are wary of pathologizing Yuna in particular and parachute children in general. Admittedly, Yuna's case is extreme, but it nonetheless illustrates some of the larger social and psychic issues in an age of colorblindness with which all parachute children struggle. As we have seen, Winnicott and Bromberg are careful to emphasize the healthy and adaptive dimensions of the false self and dissociation. Notably, "homeless" youth, whether wealthy like some parachute children or impoverished like most transnational adoptees, often exhibit great self-possession and survival skills—deep resources of psychic wherewithal. To be sure, many parachute children, too, are high-functioning, accomplished, and successful individuals; they are model minorities more in the sense of solution than problem. Those who have learned to cultivate a healthy sense of self-reflection and creative play—to learn to stand in the multiple spaces that parachuting and the model minority stereotype engender—fare considerably better under the inevitable pressures and stresses of loss connected to immigration, assimilation, and racialization.

Yung, a twenty-year-old Chinese male raised in Shanghai, began treatment with me (Dr. Han) in 2012 at the school's counseling and psychological services because of severe panic attacks; a central topic to which we will return in our final chapter on gay parachute kids. Yung resembled a big teddy bear—tall, broad-shouldered, a bit overweight with a protruding belly that he hid behind his schoolbag. Appearing considerably younger than twenty, he had large, sad eyes, which were cast down during the majority of our intake session. Yung's voice cracked when he spoke, as though he had not been in a conversation with anyone for a long time.

Yung is an only child whose father was absent from much of his youth for months at a time because of business ventures in the Philippines. Yung's mother is a depressive who does not work and stays at home. In fourth grade, Yung was tapped as one of the country's up-and-coming soccer players. He recalled learning soccer from his father; the two played together whenever his father was visiting from the Philippines. Yung stated, "My father was so proud of me when I was selected by the national soccer program, and he took me to the soccer academy to help me get settled. I wanted to succeed for him."

At the state boarding school, Yung attended classes and practiced exclusively with other elite soccer recruits. In sixth grade, Yung hurt his knee and was told that he could no longer compete. Because the sports academy did not emphasize academics, Yung would have lagged behind in the Shanghai school system. At this point, his parents decided to parachute Yung to the Philippines so that he could attend an international school. Yung recalled that after his injury he had very limited choices regarding his future: he could either enroll in a regular Shanghai school and fall academically behind his peers or move to the Philippines and try to start over. He felt strongly that living with his father, whom he admired and wanted to please, was a preferable option to living with his depressive mother and performing poorly in school. Both Yung and his parents hoped he would acquire English rapidly in the Philippines and ultimately gain admission to a US university upon graduation.

Yung moved to the Philippines. Although he lived together with his father in Manila, Yung rarely saw or spent time with him as his father was constantly at work. Yung's mother did not visit. As a result, Yung spent most of the time alone in the apartment. He had difficulty adjusting to the Philippines, meeting friends, and learning English. He became depressed, even suicidal, although he did not attempt to kill himself. Despite the fact that Yung did not want to stay in the Philippines, he felt that returning to Shanghai was really not an option.

In tenth grade, Yung asked his father if he could go to the United States for high school. His father agreed, and Yung was parachuted to Los Angeles, where he lived as a boarder with a Chinese family while attending a local public school. Yung thought he could start a new life in the United States but, as in the Philippines, he once again faced social isolation and academic difficulties. Yung recalled that he began experiencing panic attacks in eleventh grade. He described his panic attacks as his heart racing so fast that he thought it would explode and kill him. He felt like these attacks lasted for hours, and he described being terrified, crying himself to sleep after they finally dissipated.

Yung lived in fear of more panic attacks and, indeed, he endured many more, especially during times of high stress such as exams. However, Yung did not seek help or disclose his mental state to anyone, including his parents. Yung feared his parents would become overly worried and that that would only stress him out further. He stated that he did not want to carry the "extra burden" of their worries on top of the financial sacrifices they were already making for him to study abroad. Yung remained silent about his condition to everyone, and upon graduation from high school, he once again moved alone from Los Angeles to New York City for college.

In our sessions, Yung spoke slowly, sometimes trying to think of the right word or phrase in English to describe his thoughts and emotions. Often he appeared frustrated, in a linguistic jumble, messing up his hair with his hands and looking up from the floor helplessly. He explained his frustration in this way: "I can't remember simple words in Chinese but know them in English. But then when I want to speak English, Chinese words jump out instead. Everything is mixed up, and I forget what I want to say." (Yung's linguistic jumble is a contemporary revision of Nelson's problem of accent and a metaphor of multiple selves that remain to be integrated.) Yung said that he felt he did not belong anywhere—not in China, the Philippines, or the United States. There was nothing in his life that could motivate him through college and onto a future career. He recalled feeling his best and most confident when he played soccer as a youngster, picturing himself representing China at the World Cup. However, since his injury, Yung lost his confidence and did not feel secure in anything he attempted. Yung remarked that panic attacks were a chronic reminder of his "failures," of his "wasted life," and how "time was running out" for a second chance.

Initially, Yung was treated with antidepressants. Within a month or so, his panic attacks subsided and his mood improved markedly. He started to exhibit more energy, concentration, and motivation. Yung stated, "I can get up in the morning and take a shower now. It's not as hard now. I'm not so scared to go to classes because I might have a panic attack." At that point, our sessions turned from crisis management to a space of mourning—mourning for the loss of Yung's early identity as a star soccer player and for his childhood in the sports academy. We spoke about the need for a new identity and for other objects of interest to emerge and replace the ones he had lost. As we explored various possibilities, Yung responded enthusiastically to any suggestion I made. Like a dry sponge, he soaked up any encouragement I had to offer, working hard to win my approval and to demonstrate his engagement with our discussions and plans. This was a dramatic and striking reversal from our initial meetings.

I asked Yung if he had ever blossomed like this before. He recalled that when he lived in the dormitory with the other soccer players he thrived, receiving praise and support from his coaches and teammates alike. Yung spent several sessions mourning the loss of his former days as a soccer star loved by his mentors and peers. He brought in an old team photograph to show me, recounting each person's name and their positions on the field. In the photograph, Yung appeared happy and healthy. He had a broad smile and radiated confidence.

Although Yung thought he had lost himself permanently, I explained that because he was able to ground himself in China early on, he could rebuild himself with renewed passion in the United States. Yung decided to join a social soccer league at school, and he met new friends on the field who introduced him to a new cultural language and political vocabulary. He immersed himself in schoolwork and started dating a Chinese American art student. Yung, like Yuna, never developed a critical vocabulary to speak about race or racism during our sessions together. However, it seemed that his relationship with his Asian American girlfriend might provide for a transitional object as well as collective, transitional space for negotiating the vicissitudes of his immigration, assimilation, and racialization in the United States that he was hitherto experiencing only on his own—that is, to move from being racially nowhere to racially somewhere. Yung's relationship to his girlfriend marked not only a demonstrable shift in his attitude but also, and more importantly, a change in his self-understanding and self-representation as a potentially successful person rather than as a social failure. Yung was beginning to learn to stand in the various spaces of his adopted home.

In the end, Yung discovered that being connected to sports gave him the greatest emotional satisfaction and sense of accomplishment. No longer defenseless or feeling "erased," he exhibited a genuine confidence that should be described less as "psychic nowhere" and more as "psychic somewhere," as "psychic wherewithal." As Yung's self-understanding began to expand, he decided to focus on sports management as a major. At this point, and with these formative reorganizations of self, Yung's sessions ended with our mutual understanding that mourning his previous passion allowed Yung to feel passionate again for life.

THE POLITICS OF ATTACHMENT

As Yung's case history underscores, with proper social support and guidance, the act of parachuting can provide a tremendous opportunity for self-reinvention and self-discovery, orienting the subject toward healthy and adaptive forms of racial dissociation. Diaspora can function as a wide transitional space for creative play and self-reinvention, for the renegotiating of racial borders and social identities as one restarts life elsewhere. Alternately, as Yuna's case history illustrates, it can be an empty psychic nowhere.

Yung and Yuna reveal the social and psychic difficulties that must be surmounted when children are alone in the diaspora, unaccompanied minors displaced from home and detached from homeland under the cloud of failure, negotiating burdens of separation and loss on their own. Their case histories also highlight how conventional psychoanalytic understandings of the false self and dissociation must be rethought in terms of not only early family dynamics but also the politics of immigration, assimilation, and racialization, and specifically in relation to evolving racial stereotypes and ideals through which Asian Americans are interpellated in mainstream culture and society across space and time.

As a psychic concept, racial dissociation provides an opportunity to broaden our exploration of race in a colorblind age. As Stephens points out, unlike repression in Freud or the symbolic in Lacan, both of which emphasize unconscious, internal structures of the psyche, dissociation "assumes that there is an outside to the Self, that there is a Real Other outside the self, and that what is constitutive of the self has quite a bit to do with external, Self-Other relations."[48] Body and world, subject and object, self and other are the privileged actors in racial dissociation as a psychic and social process. In contrast to depth psychology, which is predicated on overcoming of conflict and repression, dissociation as a psychic process highlights the need to learn how to relate *intersubjectively* between and among social subjects.

Heightened attention to the ways in which intersubjective relations enable or disable the different racial self-states we inhabit—different meanings of our racial identities, different experiences and feelings of our racial selves—lends immediate political and theoretical urgency to the analysis of psychoanalysis and race from this critical perspective. Such consideration lends substance to the social and psychic predicament of how we might "accept the vision of the [racial] self seen in the eyes of the other while simultaneously holding one's own vision of oneself."[49] Only by renegotiating these impasses can we develop authentic racial intersubjectivity and new modes of social relation outside the dominant master-slave, self-other, white-black polarities of liberal society.

In the final analysis, Yung's and Yuna's case histories are moving examples of what Bowlby describes as the politics of attachment: "a way of conceptualizing the propensity of human beings to make strong affectional bonds to particular others and of explaining the many forms of emotional distress and personality disturbance, including anxiety, anger, depression and emotional detachment, to which unwilling separation and loss give rise."[50] Unwilling separation and loss across great physical and psychic distance lie at the heart of the parachute child's dilemma. False self, perverse compliance, and defensive dissociation become symptoms of failed adjustment, of what we have been describing in this chapter as pathological and defensive forms of racial dissociation for these diasporic millennial (im)migrants.

Yuna could not reinvent herself—to learn to stand in the spaces of Australia and the United States—because she was never quite able to root herself in Korea first, to establish a secure base of attachments with family, home, and nation so that a true self might hold and take shape. After his life-changing injury and dismissal from the soccer academy, Yung parachutes from the Philippines to the United States, such that school can no longer provide the formative and secure attachments that it did before. Yung cannot make good on his second chances in either country, and his panic attacks are a continual reminder of his "wasted life."

Yet, unlike Yuna, Yung had once built a stable and enriching set of attachments to people—his father, coach, and peers—and to place—the soccer academy in China where communication goes beyond language to physical, visceral, and affective forms of social interactions. In leaving, he lost these ideals and eventually himself, the happy and healthy young boy of his childhood. However, because Yung had once learned to play—literally—with great success, he can rekindle this passion with the support of the analyst as an intersubjective, relational, and transitional reminder of his ability to play well with others. In his later sessions, after his panic attacks had subsided, Yung regresses to these earlier experiences, recreating feelings of gratitude and appreciation for his earlier life and indexing his capacity for concern and authentic relationality. "At the point of transition," Winnicott observes, "when the analyst begins to get into contact with the patient's True Self, there must be a period of extreme dependence."[51]

By holding these moments of extreme dependence, especially during Yung's regressions to his lost childhood in China, the analyst helps Yung to renegotiate the transnational—and transitional—spaces of racial dissociation, of diaspora and displacement in the West and their accompanying problems of immigration, assimilation, and racialization. Yung is able to bring the past into the present; he is able to bring the affective passion he once felt as a child to give new meaning to an unfamiliar set of (racial) objects, people, and places, such as his new Chinese American girlfriend. He is able to create the psychic wherewithal to stand in the spaces, the psychic illusion of a unified me-ness, because of earlier experiences of attachment and the ability to play well with others. However, we should emphasize, this renegotiation and creative play also required a certain level of historical and cultural literacy—a critical vocabulary—concerning the politics of immigration, histories of parachuting, and the predicaments of Asian American subjectivity in an age of colorblindness. His case history emphasizes once more the pressing need to consider not only the racial dynamics of the clinic but the racial relations of the larger world outside as well.

When Yuna returned to Korea after completing her inpatient treatment, she went back with at least a cognitive if not affective knowledge that being sent away by the therapist may not constitute a repetition compulsion of disposal that overshadows her young life thus far but perhaps the chance for an authentic confrontation with her deep feelings of loss, displacement, and abandonment. "To assist such a person to discover [her] 'true self,'" Bowlby observes, "entails helping [her] recognize and become possessed of [her] yearnings for love and care and [her] anger at those who earlier failed to give it."[52] Yuna's treatment was cut short, and it was unclear whether she would come to a point of emotional self-recognition that would allow her to abandon, in Bromberg's words, "the instant and absolute 'truth' of dissociative reality in favor of internal conflict and human relatedness."[53] The possibility of an authentic encounter with her past—an affective encounter with her true self and a more healthy form of racial dissociation—remains an open question for the future.

Bowlby wrote about the politics of attachment in the context of his own traumatic childhood exile to English boarding school at the age of seven. Subsequently, he refined his theories of attachment disorder in relation to the experiences of young war orphans violently separated from their parents in war-torn Europe. Through these experiences, Bowlby insisted that real-life events and social histories were as determining of our psychic lives and maladies as internal fantasies and structures. The two cases presented here expand Bowlby's insights on the role of the social and the psychic in diaspora and displacement, and in relation to the politics of immigration, assimilation, and racialization. They expand our discussion of the history of the subject and subject of history in a colorblind era of neoliberalism and globalization. By considering the transnational dilemmas of racial dissociation and attachment for parachute children, we tried to present how it feels to grow up on your own as a minor without a language for the everyday traumas of immigration and race. We have explored how it feels to be a problem under the shadows of a shifting model minority stereotype of Asian American success as well as failure.

Yet, at the same time, we have also tried to be attentive to the particular family dynamics of Yuna and Yung, as well as the fact that, because they were first-generation parachute children relocating on their own, they had no critical language to analyze problems of race, racism, immigration, or assimilation in relation to their psychic dilemmas. As a social problem and political discourse, race is an ever-present phenomenon in US society, but these problems and discourses have passed Yuna and Yung by. Yuna and Yung thus present an alternative genealogy of colorblindness that demands greater critical attention and historical consideration. While we believe that racial dissociation as a relational dynamic provides a critical account for understanding the contemporary politics of colorblindness, we might also start to develop, along the lines of Winnicott's notions of mothering and (racial) true and false self, the concept of good-enough analyses of race.

GOOD-ENOUGH RACE

What is a good-enough interpretation of race under the social and political mandates of colorblindness today? First, a concept of the good-enough would seek to mediate the extreme dialectics of love and hate, self and other, white and black that we have been exploring throughout this book. We might pause to consider how racial stereotypes such as the model minority myth illustrate such extremes. Stereotypes vitiate relationality precisely by denying creative play and negotiation, by fixing the self and the other in static positions. That is, by privileging race as a fixed difference—Asian American "success" versus African American "failure," for example—rather than as ever-changing forms of relationality, the racial stereotype renders authenticity, attachment, and psychic growth tenuous. The stereotype forecloses the illusion of a unified me-ness. It obviates the different racial self-states, feelings, and experiences we inhabit, forcing instead frozen and intransigent states of racial division and dissonance. As we discussed in the previous chapter, the ability to play and to (re)negotiate borders is fundamental to an ethics that does not fix or polarize race into static and oppositional categories but rather approaches it as a relational and shifting concept.

At the same time, in the face of debilitating family dynamics such as those of Yuna, a good-enough interpretation of race would also shift our focus to psychic pain and misery away from analyses that would configure the subject of racial history as an all-encompassing explanatory narrative. In effect, a good-enough interpretation of race would avoid asserting structural racism as the universal key to understanding the source of all psychic dissonance. While the history of the racial subject needs to be systematically thought in relation to the subject of racial history, these are finally not one and the same thing. The good-enough would acknowledge the incomplete overlap between these two categories.

Lastly, a good-enough interpretation of race would avoid creating a binary of absolute victims and perpetrators that render individual agency and responsibility of the racial subject moot in the face of larger historical and political shifts. As Kathleen Pogue White observes, "If one can't find a kernel of self-operation in a victimized condition, then despair is the correct response."[54] Discovering such agency would open up a sorely needed space of play in which difference might be held in creative tension for the reinvention of race and racial politics in our colorblind moment. In the final analysis, the space of the Asian diaspora, exemplified here by the transnational movement of parachute children, constitutes a wide terrain of multiple spaces and theoretical opportunities to explore these various issues in order to assemble the illusion—a good-enough illusion—of a unified self and society. It constitutes a wide transitional space, a potential space, in which, as Bowlby suggests, the "unchallenged maintenance of a bond is experienced as a source of security and the renewal of a bond as a source of joy."[55]

CHAPTER 4

(GAY) PANIC ATTACK

*Coming Out in
a Colorblind Age*

How are we to arrive at a knowledge of the unconscious? It is of course only as something conscious that
we know it, after it has undergone transformation or
translation into something conscious.

—SIGMUND FREUD, "THE UNCONSCIOUS"

This final chapter extends our analyses of racial dissociation developed in the previous chapter. It draws from our experiences in the classroom and clinic with a number of academically accomplished Asian parachute children, all of whom identify as gay men. While they are not a homogenous group, overall these young men are smart, ambitious, and even worldly in their globetrotting pursuits of elite education and upward mobility. In particular, we focus on case histories of two millennials, one from China (Christopher) and the other from India (Neel). In contrast to Yuna's story, what is striking about Christopher's and Neel's life narratives is not just the self-determination that motivates their transnational movements but also their common goal of living freely—however they define it—as gay people in the United States.[1] Similar to Yung—and indeed to most millennials in general—many of these gay young men sought therapy because of debilitating panic attacks: high levels of anxiety and distress that rendered them dissociated, incapacitated, depressed, and in some cases suicidal, suffering inexplicable bodily and psychic pain.

Yet, what remains perplexing in almost every case history of these driven undergraduate and graduate students is the fact that sexuality remains largely tangential to their self-understandings of their psychic predicaments. That is, although sexual orientation often constituted a key factor in their desires to (im)migrate, it is never posited as a significant site of conflict or cause for their debilitating panic attacks. Unlike gays and lesbians from Generation X, the distress and pain these millennials suffer are seldom attributed to problems of "coming out," or to issues of racism, for that matter. For these reasons, we have placed parentheses around the word "gay" in our chapter title. What exactly, then, is all the panic about?

This final chapter on "(gay) panic attack" continues our exploration of the contemporary social and psychic structures of colorblindness and racial dissociation in terms of coming out today for gay parachute children. These cases provide a critical opportunity for us to reflect on the shifting politics of sexuality and race—and on intersectional structures of homophobia and racism—from Generation X to Generation Y, from civil rights to a colorblind age, and from racial exclusion and protest to multiculturalism and inclusion. Our analysis in this chapter also represents the closing of a political and intellectual circle for us. We both conducted our doctoral research on Asian American male subjectivity and the politics of race and (homo)sexuality in psychoanalysis and psychotherapy.[2] This common research interest first brought us together, and it facilitated what has now been a twenty-year relationship coauthoring the case histories and commentaries comprising this book.

We turn to these topics at the end of our project with a series of further inquiries. In moving from Generation X to Generation Y, and from second-generation to first-generation immigrants, how do we explain this significant shift in the history of coming out and panic? What do (gay) panic attacks reveal about contemporary legacies of whiteness as property as well as structures of racial inclusion and exclusion that we have been investigating throughout this book? How does the emergence of what we have described elsewhere as "queer liberalism"—the inclusion of gays and lesbians in liberal rights and recognitions—affect structures of parachuting and race in a colorblind age?[3] And, lastly, how does the rise and accumulation of capital in Asia reconfigure the politics of sexuality and race under neoliberalism and globalization?

This chapter begins with a discussion of the changing politics of coming out for Generation X and Generation Y. It then moves to an examination of the psychic structures of coming out and colorblindness for Christopher by exploring Freud's concepts of the unconscious in terms of racial dissociation. The problem of the unconscious as opaque—a series of symptoms that can be analyzed only through their transformations and translations into consciousness—provides a number of insights on how contemporary losses associated with immigration, assimilation, and racialization are metabolized for gay Asian millennials through psychic mechanisms of dissociation and the repression of both race and sexuality from political consciousness. We end with an analysis of Neel as well as an exploration of paranoia and dispersion, which structure racial dissociation, repression, exclusion, and loss for Generation Y, in contrast to racial melancholia for Generation X. Racial dissociation provides one way to rethink intersectional yet displaced relations among homophobia, racism, and economic precarity today.

In our prior research, we found that the majority of gay Asian American men in Generation X (those born between 1960 and 1980) came out of the closet to friends during college, postponing such disclosures to their parents until they were financially independent, involved in a long-term relationship, or could no longer bear to be silent about their sexuality.[4] While for most gay Asian American males their parents were the last to be told about their homosexuality, for many gay white males their parents were often one of the first to be informed. These mostly second-generation Asian American men largely believed that coming out made sense in a Western context, but they often considered such a concept incomprehensible or untranslatable to their first-generation immigrant parents. The act of coming out of the closet—indeed, the performative declaration itself—was often conveyed in English.

As we have emphasized earlier, Generation X came of age in the wake of civil rights, feminist, and gay liberation movements, and under the shadows of the AIDS pandemic, in an atmosphere of stigma and shame when there was no one actively involved in the gay community who did not know someone who had died of the disease. Some common reactions from Asian immigrant parents to their sons' coming out included the equation of being gay with a death sentence from AIDS; the rejection of their sexual identity as a permanent condition; the idea that attending university and the upward social mobility it afforded enabled sexual self-indulgence and irresponsibility; and the belief that their sons could nevertheless get married to women and create families regardless of their sexual orientation. Indeed, these various responses largely outline the plot of Ang Lee's breakout film *The Wedding Banquet* (1993), in which a gay Asian landlord from Taiwan concocts a fake green-card marriage with his tenant, a starving female artist from mainland China, comes out of the closet to his mother after his father's sudden hospitalization, and inadvertently sires a son, to his parents' unmitigated delight.[5]

The film's happy resolution is the stuff of cinematic fantasy. Nonetheless, those gay Asian men who had intimate, loving relationships with their mothers could create a mutual holding environment after coming out, eventually working through the initial shock and fears accompanying their disclosure. After a period of collective adjustment, their bonds with their mothers were ultimately strengthened.[6] Predictably, those men who had a tumultuous history with their mothers prior to coming out experienced heightened conflict after disclosing their sexual orientation. For these men, their fathers (or siblings) frequently facilitated as mediators between mothers and sons, becoming the more understanding and accepting parent. Often gay men with longtime partners offered some relief to their Asian parents' fears that their sons were fated to perish from AIDS or destined for a life of loneliness outside structures of family and kinship. In turn, their coming out often put parents in the closet about their sons' homosexuality. For them, support organizations such as Parents and Friends of Lesbian and Gays (PFLAG) were an unthinkable "white" concept.

In addition to such individual family dynamics, gay Asian American men in Generation X struggled with larger institutional structures of homophobia and racism, which remained prevalent in public discourse in the wake of civil rights and gay liberation movements as well as the cultural wars and sex panics of the 1990s. In this social and political climate, gay Asian men were continually forced to contend with assumptions that Asian immigrant communities were especially homophobic while white mainstream gay communities were especially racist. In reality, dominant stereotypes in both mainstream and gay communities alike characterizing Asian men (heterosexual or homosexual) as emasculated and feminized underscore the complex and intersectional relationships between sex and race and the inextricable ways in which sexuality and race are constituted, articulated, and expressed through one another.[7]

Kimberlé Crenshaw's groundbreaking work in critical race theory on the concept of intersectionality—the idea that US antidiscrimination law privileges one axis of oppression while occluding another—highlights the ways in which the law cannot fully account for the multiple and overlapping origins of social violence and subordination. Crenshaw observes,

> Racism as experienced by people of color who are of a particular gender—male—tends to determine the parameters of antiracist strategies, just as sexism as experienced by women who are of a particular race—white—tends to ground the women's movement. The prob-

lem is not simply that both discourses fail women of color by not acknowledging the "additional" issue of race or of patriarchy but that the discourses are often inadequate even to the discrete tasks of articulating the full dimensions of racism and sexism. Because women of color experience racism in ways not always the same as those experienced by men of color and sexism in ways not always parallel to experiences of white women, antiracism and feminism are limited, even on their own terms.[8]

Crenshaw proposes an intersectional, legal analysis from the perspective of "women of color" to interrogate more thoroughly the multiple and overlapping dimensions of racism and sexism, and to articulate more adequate antiracist and feminist political agendas and collective responses. Similarly, we propose an intersectional investigation of coming out in a colorblind age from the perspective of gay Asian men. Such a perspective would allow us to analyze the shifting history of the Asian American subject in relation to the subject of racial history in terms of dominant as well as emergent structures of racism and homophobia that contemporary colorblind society would seek to deny. In other words, both Christopher's and Neel's case histories challenge us to think new relations of sex and race together in our contemporary moment while reformulating the boundaries of Asian American identity.

Historically, the past two decades have witnessed enormous social and political change in the United States regarding the depathologizing of gay and lesbian life, its recasting as "virtually normal," and the liberal acceptance of same-sex relations and marriage. The AIDS pandemic of the 1980s and 1990s unleashed enormous social and political violence against gays and lesbians, but it also brought issues of homosexuality and homophobia into widespread public debate. Since then, increasing visibility of gays and lesbians in US public life and popular culture, coupled with heightened political activism on the national stage, local level, and in the corporate domain for rights and representation, laid the legal foundation for the landmark Supreme Court decision *Lawrence v. Texas* (2003). As we noted earlier, this 5–4 ruling declared Texas's statute against same-sex sodomy unconstitutional and thus decriminalized same-sex relations in the United States. *Lawrence* was a surprising reversal of *Bowers v. Hardwick*, a Supreme Court decision that only seventeen years earlier, in 1986, had upheld the constitutionality of a Georgia statute criminalizing same-sex relations in private between consenting adults.

In 2015, twelve years after *Lawrence,* and with popular support for same-sex marriage reaching a majority in 2011, the legal right for same-sex couples to marry nationwide was affirmed in yet another landmark 5–4 Supreme Court ruling, *Obergefell v. Hodges.* Importantly, this narrative of liberal progress characterized gay marriage as the "final frontier" of social struggle and liberation in US society, putting the nails in the coffin, as it were, of civil rights movements for racial and now sexual equality and justice (trans civil rights notwithstanding). In short, the achievement of marriage equality for gays and lesbians has consigned racism to the dustbin of history—as a historical project complete and completed.

This brief synopsis of the historical emergence of queer liberalism in the evolution of a colorblind liberal society raises important questions about how the political reordering of same-sex relations in contemporary US life has rearticulated psychic norms of sexuality while reshaping the history of the Asian American subject in relation to the subject of colorblind history. To begin, we must first recognize how regnant discourses of colorblindness are in effect anti-intersectional political mandates. Put otherwise, discourses of colorblindness that refuse to acknowledge race or racism as structuring conditions today are simultaneously discourses that all too often refuse to acknowledge sexism or homophobia as well.

Extending Crenshaw's legal observations in order to explore the psychic structures of colorblindness, we might return to our earlier analysis of how incest and antimiscegenation taboos order conventional structures of Oedipalization. How have sexual and racial norms and prohibitions shifted in the age of colorblindness with the US state's official withdrawal from racial and now (homo)sexual regulation and discrimination? More specifically, how have these historical shifts affected both the social lives and psychic structures of a growing number of first-generation gay Asian parachute children in the diaspora?

For one thing, processes of coming out for gay Asian parachute children today underscore the historical contingency of psychic ideals and taboos. For Generation X, difficulties related to coming out, intertwined issues of homophobia and racism, and problems in dating and (inter)racial desire were all fundamental topics for exploration in therapy. For gay Asian millennials today, sexual orientation and dilemmas of coming out are rarely proffered as presenting problems. Notably, for many gay Asian parachute children racial discrimination is not a presenting problem either: neither sexual orientation nor racial identity—neither homophobia nor racism—manifest as conscious sources for their panic attacks and psychic distress. Instead, like many millennials in general, these young gay Asian men seek therapy to help manage psychic distress and acute feelings of anxiety—high levels of stress, insecurity, depression, and family as well as work problems that often lead to emergency room visits and even hospitalization. Although sexual orientation and race are important aspects of their social identities, they are not constituted as part of their psychic predicaments. Put otherwise, both sex and race are dissociated from their conscious psychic lives. In their place, pervasive feelings of social insecurity and economic precarity prevail.

Like millennials in general, gay Asian parachute children have largely abandoned the phrase "coming out" when discussing their sexual orientations. Queer liberalism's mainstreaming of gay and lesbian life has configured coming out for comparatively privileged gay millennials as a somewhat commonplace or even passé event. Admittedly, for many middle-class gay adolescents in progressive communities coming out today is not as socially or psychically fraught as for past generations. For example, when in therapy, Christopher first mentioned his boyfriend in passing during a conversation that had little to do with same-sex issues. Subsequently, his boyfriend would come up incidentally from time to time in whatever topic he happened to be exploring at the moment.

This restructuring of coming out and the politics of the closet is, in part, the result of the technological restructuring of the closet through the rapid expansion of the worldwide web, social media, and new technologies rendering public and private space, "over there" and "over here," in the closet and out of the closet, virtual and indistinct. Notably, this shift might be considered a technological expansion of both D. W. Winnicott's notions of the false self and Philip M. Bromberg's ideas of standing in the spaces. That is, the Internet has proliferated the multiple (virtual) spaces in which a person might stand, act, pass, and perform at any given moment. Technological innovation has led to new forms of adaptive as well as pathological dissociation that warrant further investigation. As the worldwide web has facilitated same-sex identity formation and blurred the line between inside and outside, it has simultaneously created new forms of social exclusion, false intimacy, flaming, cyber bullying, and virtual trolling, swatting, and stalking. This technological paradox, along with our earlier discussion in chapter 3 of the ways in which racial discourse is both too early and too late for first-generation parachute children from Asia, frames our understanding of (gay) panic attacks and the politics of coming out for gay Asian millennials.

This scenario has become a common experience for us in both the classroom and the clinic: gay and lesbian millennials as a group do not place great significance on their sexual orientation. In comparison to Generation X, they exhibit fewer feelings of stigma and shame concerning their homosexuality. For many gay parachute kids who were openly dating in high school, coming out of the closet is often consigned to a distant past. When Neel first told his mother that he was attracted to his best friend in high school (another boy), she responded by asking him to think seriously about the impact this disclosure might have on his girlfriend. She also encouraged Neel to share these feelings with his best friend, who was flattered by Neel's affections but could not reciprocate in the same manner.

While sexual and racial violence have far from disappeared, Neel's experiences nonetheless underscore increasing parental acceptance of, as well as peer support for, same-sex relations in certain global spaces and locales. At the same time, Neel's narrative also underscores the error of positing the United States "over here" as a site of sexual freedom and progress and the homeland "over there" as a site of benighted homophobia and conservatism, however much the idealization of educational and economic success was associated with gayness and whiteness in the West for these young men. (Indeed, there are numerous countries that legalized gay marriage many years before the *Obergefell* decision in the United States.) In the context of gay parachute children, we are especially wary of turning sexuality into a developmental narrative of civilization and progress, in which an intolerant Asia, Africa, or Latin America is required to play catchup with an enlightened Euro-America. Instead, we are more concerned with exploring how homophobia, racism, sexism, religious, and other cultural and political fundamentalisms manifest themselves *differently* in different places. Consequently, we need to consider how evolving structures of homophobia and racism might manifest themselves in a colorblind US society precisely as a dissociative structure.

If many gay parachute children from Asia describe the search for sexual freedom as a significant impetus for their migration, as we have suggested—often devising ingenious methods to leave their home country to pursue primary, secondary, and higher education abroad—how exactly do the politics of sexuality and race play out once they arrive in their chosen destinations? Again, what is the panic all about?

CASE HISTORY: CHRISTOPHER

Christopher's case history is emblematic of the experiences of many gay parachute kids that I (Dr. Han) have encountered over this past decade. Raised in Beijing, Christopher is a tall, lanky, floppy-haired, boyish-looking undergraduate, who has a tinge of a British accent when speaking English. He introduced himself as "Christopher," a name he chose in eighth grade after reading A. A. Milne's *Winnie the Pooh* during his first year at boarding school in Singapore. Upon our first meeting in 2013, he greeted me with a firm handshake and stated, "My name is Christopher. I'm a senior in college, double majoring in mechanical engineering and math."

Christopher was referred to my private practice by his college counseling center because of severe panic attacks. In the prior two months, Christopher had rushed to the emergency room four times, only to be told repeatedly that he was having a panic attack. Unconvinced, he was certain that he had a rare neurological or cardiological disorder that would lead to premature death. He spent countless hours obsessively searching the Internet for a medical explanation that would explain his "illness." Sure that he had an inoperable brain tumor or incurable heart disease, he could not accept the idea that he had a "mental condition." During these two months, Christopher was wracked with insomnia, endured considerable weight loss, and lacked concentration and motivation in his studies. Although he suffered tremendously from the anxiety associated with his panic attacks, Christopher did not share his pain and fears with anyone, including his boyfriend, Matt—this is how his sexual orientation entered the conversation—and their close circle of mutual friends, all of whom were high-achieving Chinese parachute children.

Christopher is an only child who was raised with abundant support from a loving mother who taught him the joy of reading literature and philosophy. When Christopher was eight, his mother was diagnosed with cancer. To his great relief, after a number of years of treatment, she went into remission. In sixth grade, Christopher realized he was different from most of his schoolmates: he liked boys. He researched homosexuality on the internet and began to chat frequently online with other gay-identified adolescents and adults. These online discussions offered an outlet for Christopher's budding sexuality, and they helped to influence his decision to leave China as a parachute child. Although he had few conflicts with his parents, Christopher did not see coming out to them as a viable option, similar to second-generation gay Asian men in Generation X. He did not see staying in China as a possibility, either. As such, Christopher worked hard and won a scholarship to a prestigious boarding school in Singapore beginning in eighth grade. His father, a small business owner, was especially proud of Christopher and supported his decision to pursue overseas education.

Boarding school proved to be a wonderful social environment and positive intellectual experience for Christopher. He belonged to a tight-knit group of parachute kids primarily from China but also from India, Korea, the Philippines, and Vietnam. He came out to them in ninth grade without much difficulty. At this point, Christopher began to date boys openly and did not fear any backlash or negative consequences from his sexual orientation. He applied to colleges only in the United States and was accepted to several prestigious universities, choosing a school in the city where he thought he would live after graduation. Unlike many parachute children who were unsure where they would settle, Christopher was certain that he would remain in the United States after completing his undergraduate degree.

Repeating his school experiences in Singapore, Christopher quickly assembled in college a group of Chinese international students who became his friends and support community. Many of them had lived abroad as parachute children in the United States, Canada, and Australia before starting university, and some of them were gay. During freshman year, Christopher fell in love with Matt, also a first-year student, who grew up in Shanghai and attended high school in Toronto. Christopher and Matt shared a common dream of succeeding in college and, thereafter, pursuing careers in finance. They became roommates and lovers but continued to spend time socializing with their larger cohort.

In college, Christopher studied nonstop. He conformed to a rigid daily schedule, and every semester he packed his classes with an overload of credits. He reported that he slept no more than four to five hours a night, limited eating to two meals a day, and devoted the rest of his waking hours to studying and planning his future. During winter and spring recess, while some of his friends traveled back to China to see family or went on vacations, he stayed in the dorms to continue studying. Each summer, instead of returning home to visit his parents, Christopher interned at prestigious financial firms. He studied the habitus of white bankers as if he were a graduate student in anthropology, absorbing their mannerisms, dispositions, interests in sports teams, and use of language. He compiled an extensive list of the sociocultural differences between "self" and "other."

As I learned more about Christopher's personal history, I offered an interpretation of his panic attacks as an acute warning for him to slow down and take care of himself emotionally, physically, and spiritually. Christopher had channeled all of his energy and efforts toward intellectual development, at the expense of his emotional well-being and mental health. Indeed, this fact was quite obvious in Christopher's physical appearance: his head resembled a large boulder on top of a long skinny stick. When I asked Christopher how easy it was to hold a large stone on a stick, he chuckled and replied, "I guess my head was about to fall off." He then added, "Whenever I felt a panic attack coming on, it started with a killer headache. I felt like my head could explode. I was so scared that it would blow up. Kaboom."

Christopher began to assess his numerous sacrifices over the years since leaving China as an eighth grader. He admitted to poor dietary habits, skipping meals and eating cheap instant ramen several times per week so as to lessen the financial burden on his parents. He had not seen his parents in person (only virtually) for many years. He became quite saddened when he realized that in college he had stopped feeding his mind and spirit with literature and philosophy, his mother's gift to him, replacing them instead with a quantitative double major in science and math. Equally devastating, in his relationship with Matt, both had made a pact to work together as a collective team, consciously suppressing their sexual appetites and scheduling their romantic encounters for rare special occasions.

While there was a bounty of anxiety in Christopher's life, there was a deficit of spontaneity. He was an automaton; like many high-achieving millennials, his was an inordinately planned and scheduled life. At the beginning of his treatment, Christopher believed that every question and problem could be solved rationally and intellectually. With this technocratic attitude, he rejected his feelings—all feelings—as unreliable and unnecessary. As his treatment progressed and his reflections deepened, Christopher realized that he had firmly believed from a very young age that he was doing "the right thing" and that "constant sacrifice" was necessary in order to become "successful in life." I asked him what he meant by a successful life. Poignantly, Christopher responded, "I guess I meant financial success, but I forgot my goal of living a free life in the United States as a gay person. It all just became work and more work. What's the point of living here if I'm a robot?" He added, "Robots don't have a sexual orientation. I'm basically asexual."

The emergence of this self-awareness led to several bouts of crying and the recollection of earlier dreams of living a happy life with a good partner in New York, while not burdening his parents in Beijing with the possible embarrassment of his sexual orientation. "I used to care about being happy. I didn't even realize that I was unhappy until the panic attacks told me so." It struck me that Christopher was an updated, neoliberal version of the model minority stereotype under globalization. Unlike many stressed-out model minorities with overbearing helicopter parents, Christopher's stress was largely self-imposed. However, like all stereotypes, this one, too, was unsustainable.

From the beginning of therapy, and despite advice from his psychiatrist, Christopher refused medication to treat his panic attacks. What is interesting to note is that, from his first session until the end of his five-month treatment, Christopher never experienced another panic attack. He said putting his feelings into language and identifying his problems felt very empowering to him. As his talking cure progressed, Christopher's language noticeably shifted from "I think" to "I feel." With his fears of premature death dissipating, Christopher became more open to my suggestion to learn some basic restorative yoga poses. He began attending yoga classes to learn more breathing, stretching, and meditative techniques. After his first official yoga session, Christopher reported that it was the hardest class he has ever taken in his life because he had to use his mind, body, and spirit together rather than compartmentalize them as he had done before.

About a month and half into therapy, Christopher told Matt as well as some other close friends about his panic attacks and his decision to seek therapy. While Christopher felt somewhat self-conscious though not embarrassed about his condition, he also felt compelled to suggest that his friends might benefit from therapy, as well. Christopher was pleasantly surprised by his friends' curiosity and openness toward mental health support. Some began to open up and share their own experiences with panic attacks. He felt that these admissions of collective pain, anxiety, and fear brought their social group closer together, leading to deeper, more meaningful relations and a more supportive environment for emotional well-being. Unlike many immigrants and students of color, Christopher's willingness to avail himself of mental health services is notable.

As employment season rolled around, Christopher and I met less frequently. At his job interviews, Christopher felt confident, presenting himself not only as a very smart young person but also as a well-rounded colleague who could engage in conversations ranging from quantitative derivatives to football and baseball. Christopher deliberately chose not to disclose his sexual orientation at these firms. Like many millennials, he exhibited little shame about his homosexuality, but he perceived corporate culture in finance to be overtly heterosexual. While many of these firms had gay social groups, he stated that the majority of their members worked in noninvestment banking positions and not in the high-profile work groups he hoped to join. Before Christopher graduated from college, he secured a position in a firm that was his sixth choice. Christopher admitted that he was disappointed, but he also stated that he was okay with the situation for the time being.

Psychoanalysis teaches us that we are decentered subjects, not unified beings. Rather, to return to our discussion of Bromberg, we are composed of multiple selves. The phenomenon of multiple personality is present in everyone. As we have observed, while in most well-functioning individuals normal personality structure is shaped by psychic processes of dissociation, as well as by repression and intrapsychic conflict, some individuals are able to create a healthy illusion of a cohesive personal identity—that is, to stand in the spaces—much better than others.

Christopher leads an extraordinarily compartmentalized and dissociated existence, and he cannot easily stand in the multiple spaces of his life. Christopher is academically accomplished—a model minority by all outward appearances—but his body is in pieces. He is not compliant in the ways that define Yuna's life history. Nonetheless, he is a classic illustration of Winnicott's model of unhealthy false self insofar as he is an individual with "high intellectual potential" who has developed "a dissociation between intellectual activity and psycho-somatic being." For those who have learned to dissociate productively, Winnicott writes, "the mind is not something for the individual to exploit in escape from psycho-somatic being."[9] This splitting of mind from body is what organizes Christopher's unhealthy estrangement from embodiment—his feelings of panic—and his fears concerning premature death. Christopher's panic attacks always started with a "killer headache" and the anxiety that his head, which resembled a large stone on a stick, was going to explode: "Kaboom."

The true self, Winnicott observes, emanates from the spontaneous gesture, and it "comes from the aliveness of the body tissues and the working of body-functions, including the heart's action and breathing."[10] Oriented only toward studying and future success, and organized by bodily deprivation and insufficient contact with his lover, family, and friends, Christopher's life is marked by a deficit of spontaneity. He has an inordinately planned and scheduled existence. It is no surprise that, when he began to attend yoga classes in an attempt to reassemble his body—to learn how to breathe, stretch, meditate, and be present to himself—he described it as the hardest class he has ever taken in his life because he had to use his mind, body, and spirit together rather than compartmentalize them as he had done before." What is the source of Christopher's disembodiment and dissociation, of his panic and pain?

Throughout this book, we have investigated the shifting history of the racial subject in regard to the evolving subject of racial history. We have consistently investigated psychoanalysis not only as a theory of intergenerational family dynamics and the intergenerational transmission of trauma but also as a critical tool for interpreting the historical forces of the social and cultural order that shape and form racial subjectivity. To the extent that psychoanalysis functions as a hermeneutic for analyzing how subjectivity is constituted through the internalization of social norms and ideals, it also emphasizes that no subject develops as a simple repetition of these norms and ideals either. In their repetition, psychic prohibitions and taboos continually misfire and go awry.

As our discussion of coming out in Generation X and Generation Y underscores, racial and sexual norms and prohibitions are historically contingent. The legal expansion of marriage to include same-sex couples, shifting definitions of family and kinship, the loosening of traditional gender roles, and the invention of new language and terminology around sex and sexuality all highlight the shifting boundaries of sexual ideals and taboos. In the gap between the ideal and its (distorted) repetition lies the kernel of social change and transformation. This gap, to return to our discussion of racial melancholia from chapter 1, is often inhabited by the politics of psychic loss and refusal. For example, the subject's slavish mimicry of or, alternately, refusal to idealize whiteness at the expense of the disparaged racial (or sexual) others constitutes one aspect of racial melancholia's psychic and social protest.

The historical emergence of colorblindness and queer liberalism provides an opportunity to explore how the public reordering of contemporary racial and sexual life has affected the psychic-symbolic order, and vice versa, reconfiguring processes of psychic loss and social protest in terms of what we describe as racial dissociation. Christopher's case history provides a detailed example of how neoliberal anxieties concerning financial (in)security, work, and employment organize discourses of race and sex today. Christopher comes to the United States to live "a free life" as a gay man. He has a nice Chinese boyfriend, Matt, but they don't have sex. On the face of it, his psychic struggles seem not to concern issues of sexuality, or race, much at all. Like many other millennials, homophobia is not a significant aspect of Christopher's self-narrative.

Nonetheless, Christopher (like prior generations of Asian immigrants before him) seems quite aware of not only his sexual but also his racial otherness, especially in his Wall Street environment. Indeed, his actions at work suggest that, in order to stand in the space of his high-powered Wall Street firm, he must disavow both his (homo)sexuality and his race. Christopher studies the habitus of the white male investment banking world—his colleagues' mannerisms, dispositions, interests in sports teams, and use of language—as if he were a graduate student in anthropology. We might approach this dynamic in terms of our prior discussions of race as relation—as processes of social inclusion and exclusion. While Christopher is a part of this Wall Street world, he is also apart from it, an Asian alien from the outside looking in. Similarly, although Christopher seems somewhat nonchalant about his homosexuality, he deliberately keeps his sexual orientation separate from both his high-profile work group and his parents.

"I forgot my goal of living a free life in the US as a gay person," he states. "It all just became work and more work. What's the point of living here if I'm a robot? . . . Robots don't have a sexual orientation. I'm basically asexual." In a colorblind and multicultural world, and with the steady rise of capital accumulation in Asia, one is no longer *required* to pass as white or as straight in order to partake in the benefits of global capitalism. Melanie Abeygunawardana observes that Christopher is not "passing as a white person, a straight person, or even a *human* person. Christopher's unhealthy version of racial dissociation takes the form of passing as a robot, valued only for his productive capacity for 'work and more work.'"[11]

The automaton marks the dream of a neoliberal world order: a paragon of economic productivity and efficiency for global capital and, tellingly, a figure devoid of race or sex, devoid of racial difference or sexual desire. Moreover, the automaton, like the replicants of Ridley Scott's *Blade Runner*, is a figure without history. With no past, present, or future, the robot is not only about efficiency without sex but also outside lived histories of oppression—that is, outside histories of institutionalized

racism and homophobia and without the sticky liabilities of social difference and demands. As such, the automaton is a made-to-order witness for a neoliberal economic world order, marking a new form of racial
and sexual exclusion in a colorblind and multicultural world precisely by
having no relation whatsoever to these formative categories of history.

Importantly for our discussion, Christopher as automaton is a *self-
regulating subject*. For Generation X, the concept of "panic attacks" and
"panic defenses" were conventionally associated with unwarranted and
projected violence that homophobes directed *against* homosexuals. In
contrast, as we witness here, panic attacks indexes a very different psychic phenomenon for Christopher and his generation. Rather than sig-
naling *external* physical assaults directed against gays and lesbians, these
are *internal* psychic assaults experienced by gay millennials as a form of
self-discipline. This neoliberal regulation of the self begins to explain
how panic attacks against gays in a prior generation have transformed
today into "(gay) panic attacks"—attacks by the self *against* the self in
an age of colorblindness and queer liberalism.

As financial (in)security and entrepreneurial self-cultivation—work
and more work—come to eclipse all other social concerns and emotional needs, Christopher's life is drained of spontaneity but also
marked by an excess of affect without a proper object, returning us to
Michelle Stephen's distinctions between skin and flesh, between racial
meaning and feeling. Bracketing the fact of his feelings, Christopher
believes every question and problem could be solved rationally and intellectually. He separates mind from body, science from literature, self
from history, thought from feeling. With the technocratic flourish of an
automaton, he rejects all feelings as unreliable and unnecessary, sacrificing in the process his true self, sex with his boyfriend, and the ability to
stand in the spaces. Ultimately, his unhealthy dissociation of the disparate aspects of his life is a self-disciplining project that proves unsustainable. He cannot create a healthy illusion of a unified me-ness, and the
repeated panic attacks that send Christopher to the emergency room on
multiple occasions underscore his untenable psychic predicament. We
might describe Christopher's condition of racial and sexual dissociation as one fundamental psychic structure of colorblindness today—
especially in relation to conventional stereotypes of Asian American
model minorities as technocratic and emotionless automatons.

What does Christopher's panic tell us about continuing legacies of whiteness as property in a colorblind world? Christopher's inability to reconcile his aspirations to become a *homo economicus* with his racial and sexual selves extends in provocative ways Neil Gotanda's observations on the legal structure of colorblindness today. In "A Critique of 'Our Constitution Is Color-Blind,'" Gotanda points out that the official withdrawal of the US state from racial (and now homosexual) regulation does not mean that discrimination has disappeared. While *public* discrimination has been outlawed, *private* discrimination is "constitutionally permissible. Absent legislative action, no barrier exists to private considerations of race or to private action based on such consideration. Race discrimination is unconstitutional only in the realm marked out by the doctrine of state action."[12]

Gotanda not only emphasizes that discrimination remains constitutionally protected for private actors but also stresses that the very distinction between public and private, the state and the individual, is a normative effect of the law. Here, we need to connect Gotanda's observations with our analysis of Christopher's case history by highlighting that neoliberalism is predicated on the principle that an ever-greater number of state functions and responsibilities should be outsourced to the private sphere. As the public sphere continues to shrink under neoliberal demands for economic rationality and efficiency, and as the private sphere continues to grow and overshadow every aspect of human life, private discrimination also expands and intensifies through the privileged language of individual choice.

For example, as legal scholar Rachel Moran points out in her analysis of intimacy, kinship, and dating, just because it is no longer illegal to marry someone of a different race in the United States, there is certainly little social support or encouragement to do so.[13] Though we can customize the requirements for a potential partner on a dating website from factors of race, gender, sexuality, class, education, politics, and religion to physical attributes down to the pound and inch, we do not usually characterize these "preferences" as racist, sexist, or homophobic. Indeed, under the banner of colorblindness and multiculturalism, discrimination in social life and continuing legacies of whiteness as property are reinvented for everyone as a matter of individual choice and personal preference outside history. From this perspective, *everyone* in a colorblind and multicultural age is now dissociated. Today, a legal ideology of colorblindness has been transformed into a psychic state of racial dissociation. What Christopher's (gay) panic attack teaches us, however, is that racial dissociation affects different racialized subjects unequally. "Asians are the loneliest Americans," Jay Caspian Kang observes in an article about fraternity hazing and the search for Asian American identity. "The collective political consciousness of the '80s has been replaced by the quiet, unaddressed isolation that comes with knowing that you can be born in this country, excel in its schools and find a comfortable place in its economy and still feel no stake in the national conversation."[14]

Let us end our discussion of Christopher's case history by returning to the topic of racial feeling—to the excess of affect that marks his panic attacks—in order to reassess this emergent history of gay Asian millennials in relation to the subject of colorblind history. Freud posits that repressed ideas can emerge in the conscious as inexplicable affects. In this regard, we might consider Christopher's panic attacks as the affective form in which repressed ideas of homophobia and racism are transformed and translated into conscious forms for him. Christopher's (gay) panic attacks raise the problem of conscious and unconscious knowledge, of how to read his affective pain symptomatically. Similar to hysteria in Freud's fin de siècle Vienna, in panic attacks among millennials today the body speaks because the unconscious cannot. Hence, we might think of panic attacks as the contemporary (neoliberal) form of hysteria in our contemporary colorblind age.

In his essays on "Repression" and "The Unconscious," Freud posits that repressed ideas in the unconscious (Ucs.) can emerge into consciousness (Cs.) as inexplicable affects. He calls this psychic process "double inscription," noting that

> an idea may exist simultaneously in two places in the mental apparatus—indeed, that if it is not inhibited by the censorship, it regularly advances from the one position to the other, possibly without losing its first location or registration.
>
> This view may seem odd, but it can be supported by observations from psycho–analytic practice. If we communicate to a patient some idea which he has at one time repressed but which we have discovered

in him, our telling him makes at first no change in his mental condition. Above all, it does not remove the repression nor undo its effects, as might perhaps be expected from the fact that the previously unconscious idea has now become conscious. On the contrary, all that we shall achieve at first will be a fresh rejection of the repressed idea.... Actually there is no lifting of the repression until the conscious idea, after the resistances have been overcome, has entered into connection with the unconscious memory-trace. It is only through the making conscious of the latter itself that success is achieved. On superficial consideration this would seem to show that conscious and unconscious ideas are distinct registrations, topographically separated, of the same content. But a moment's reflection shows that the identity of the information given to the patient with his repressed memory is only apparent. To have heard something and to have experienced something are in their psychological nature two quite different things, even though the content of both is the same.[15]

Freud outlines what he describes as "double inscription"—the fact that the same idea might appear in two forms and in two different places of the mental apparatus, in the conscious and unconscious. Freud associates the conscious manifestation of the prohibited idea with the auditory representation of the analyst (with what the patient *hears* or knows of the analyst's suggestions) and he attributes the unconscious manifestation of the forbidden idea in its earlier forms with affect (what the patient *feels* of the forbidden memory). In double inscription, we witness a cleaving between what we might describe as the epistemological and phenomenological manifestations—the knowing versus the feeling— of a prohibited idea.

Conscious thoughts (word-presentations) and unconscious affects (thing-presentations), as Freud admits, may seem to be "distinct registrations... of the same content." However, the correspondence is hardly straightforward. After passing through the unconscious, memory traces come together with linguistic signifiers that can never fully define them. As Freud emphasizes, to "have heard something and to have experienced something are in their psychological nature two quite different things, even though the content of both is the same." Representations, as Jean Laplanche puts it, are "fixed beyond the meaning that may inhabit them, beyond the multiple meanings that may be assigned to them."[16] In a larger sense, the limits of these representations are constituted by the limits of history.

For example, Kenji, a gay Asian male from Generation X who was raised in a small midwestern town, recounts the awakening of his racial consciousness in this manner: "For me, homosexuality was a constant source of anxiety while growing up. It wasn't until I started college and met other Asian Americans that I began to realize that my discomfort with my sexuality had something to do with my discomfort with my race. I was the only Japanese kid in a high school class of one hundred. This fact is—was—obvious, but it took me years to realize it. As an unapologetic potato queen [a gay Asian man attracted to white men], I still struggle with the revelation." Whether the "feel good" affects of queer liberalism or the "bad feelings" connected to Kenji's being closeted in high school and, indeed, well into graduate school, both examples mark the evolving ways in which a conscious discourse of (homo)sexuality is linked to and expresses an unconscious discourse of racial prohibition and loss. Indeed, as Gotanda points out, legal discourses of colorblindness require the subject first to recognize and then disavow racial difference. In this regard, double inscription and the displacement of an unconscious racism into a conscious queer liberalism outlines one key psychic mechanism of racial dissociation and colorblindness today.

In reality, as both Freud and Kenji suggest, the analyst's suggestions are usually met with skepticism on the part of the patient and with "a fresh rejection of the repressed idea." It is only by working through the patient's affective resistances that the bar of repression can be lifted, and it is only after this lifting of censorship that the conscious idea can be narrated and connected to the unconscious memory such that the patient might recognize the content of what is heard and what is felt as related to one another. The unconscious, as Freud concludes in "The Unconscious," can only be known "after it has undergone transformation or translation into something conscious." Transformation and translation facilitate a psychic link and connection between what is initially thought to be two entirely disparate and disconnected ideas. However, there is always an enigmatic remainder, an elusive and receding meaning, demanding to be captured and renarrated.

As Freud emphasizes, the patient's tendency to reject the analyst's suggestions reveals the intransigence of the subject to alter his or her psychic attitudes and commitments. Indeed, double inscription exposes the power and persistence of censorship to reinforce social norms and prohibition precisely through the segregating of affect from repressed idea or the displacement of the repressed idea as inexplicable affect. From one perspective, in the age of queer liberalism, sexuality may be the *conscious* form in which *unconscious* structures of race and racism appear today: gay is the new black. Put otherwise, processes of double inscription under queer liberalism posit progressive politics and good feelings about same-sex relations as disconnected from unconscious, unacknowledged, and persistent structures of institutional racism and legacies of whiteness as property. In this scenario, progressive attitudes toward homosexuality exhibited by gay millennials might be the *conscious* transformation and translation of a political *unconscious* of race that a colorblind US society refuses to acknowledge or to recognize as connected to one another. As race continues to slip into the unconscious in a colorblind society, psychoanalysis becomes increasingly important for analyzing this secreting of race.

From another perspective, for gay millennials like Christopher, we might also observe how economic precarity functions as the conscious inscription of both unconscious homophobia and racism. In this particular psychic incarnation, homophobia and racial violence are repressed, disavowed, and denied precisely because they have been reinscribed by a neoliberal language of individual choice and personal preference. Put otherwise, conscious, overt sexism and racism have been replaced by more subtle, unconscious forms of homophobia and racial hostility—psychically effective and politically charged precisely because they proliferate without conscious acknowledgment. In effect, homophobia and racism have gone underground—they remain unconscious—neither directly translated nor transformed into consciousness. Christopher's case history and (gay) panic attacks thus outline how racial dissociation functions in the psychic reproduction of structural racism and homophobia in a colorblind age. It suggests that the unprocessed anxieties of millennials today are indeed affects searching for a political form.

Neel, an international student from Delhi, provides a stark contrast to Christopher in several respects. Neel did not initially seek treatment for panic attacks per se. Rather, similar to many gays and lesbians from Generation X, he began counseling (with Dr. Han) in 2016 after being rejected by his first white boyfriend, whom he met in law school. A class-mate with Nordic good looks, this boyfriend had initially pursued Neel hard. In an early session, Neel wondered aloud, "No white man ever pursued me, and when he wanted me, I felt a surge of self-esteem . . . it was so weird. Intellectually, I wanted to reject it . . . but, still, I wanted it, and I liked it." With a tinge of shame, Neel admitted, "I felt proud to be with him in public and even wondered if people thought better of me when they saw us together."

In our sessions, Neel obsessed about his failed relationship, ruminating over every detail of what went wrong and wondering if its unraveling had anything to do with his race and skin color. Neel admitted to feeling extremely conscious about his dark skin, and he speculated as to whether his ex-boyfriend did not find him attractive enough because of it. Although he constantly sought physical approval from him, Neel remarked that his ex rarely complimented him on his appearance. Throughout their brief relationship, Neel constantly felt that "I was in the lower caste between the two of us. I would have to do more for the relationship because he was white. I think we both knew this, although we never spoke of it. But we were each clear about our divided status based on race and color."

Neel associated these ruminations with his dark-skinned father. Neel's father often complained of his own dark skin color as a central problem affecting his professional advancement in India. After marrying Neel's mother, who is very light-skinned, his father was disappointed when Neel was born darker than he had hoped or expected. Neel confessed with a chuckle that he is relieved he is not as dark as his father. He perceived his father as always having to put more effort into their marriage than his lighter-skinned mother. Neel remarked that the color line was not only pervasive in his family but also throughout Indian society. He recalled going home for summer break after first year of college; his father and other family members "congratulated me for getting lighter in America."

Following their tumultuous breakup, Neel admitted, "I'm scared of white men. I know I shouldn't generalize and feel this way, but I can't help it." At the same time, Neel reluctantly acknowledged his wish to be desired by white men, a conflict he has been struggling to navigate. In essence, Neel's initial break up has transformed into a full-blown psychic crisis concerning the problem of desiring and being desired by whiteness. The issue frequently sends him into near panic attacks— extreme states of anxiety and agitation.

Neel comes from a wealthy and well-educated family in India with loving parents and several siblings, all of whom are educated abroad, scattered across Asia and Europe. He is the only person in his immediate family to have parachuted to the United States for college. Both his immediate and his extended family live near each other in what Neel refers to as "the family compound." In middle school, Neel was sent to an exclusive boarding school, not abroad but in a distant region of India. An institution attracting a student body from diverse racial, ethnic, caste, cultural, religious, and national backgrounds, the school is known to send many of its graduates to prestigious colleges and universities in Europe and the United States. Neel made many friends in his boarding school, and they keep close ties via social media and frequent visits. Indeed, when one of the group members fell into a suicidal crisis at his university, Neel and his cohort rushed to the United Kingdom to support him, waiting until their friend's parents arrived to take their son home.

During Neel's boarding school days, he dated girls while secretly harboring a crush on his best friend, a boy from Singapore who was also of Indian descent. During his last year of high school, Neel came out to his mother first, confessing to her that he was in love with his best friend. To Neel's great surprise, his mother's immediate reaction was one of support. She encouraged Neel to work through his feelings for both his girlfriend and best friend and to be especially considerate of their feelings, as well. She remained the consistent and loving figure he knew her to be even after the disclosure of his sexual orientation.

Neel's ambition to attend a university in the United States was, as with Christopher, connected to his sexual orientation. Similarly, he planned on remaining abroad after graduating. His family's wish, however, was for Neel to earn his degree and to return home to India, something Neel did not believe he could do after coming out. Despite this belief, after a recent summer break at home, Neel reported being surprised by how open and engaged his immediate and extended family had been in relation to his sexuality. His mother, father, siblings, and cousins all took interest in not only his academic life but also his love life, inquiring whether he had a boyfriend and what it's like to date in the United States.

For the first time, Neel started to contemplate whether it might be possible for him to return home upon graduation. He began to wonder what life would be like to live and work as a gay man in India with his family's support. He fell into depression at this point, confused about his initial goals of living a free life in the United States as a gay man. He also began to reassess the numerous sacrifices he made along the way, including being separated from his family at a young age and the various insecurities and anxieties he had developed abroad as a minority.

In his final year of law school, Neel's depression worsened. As graduation drew closer, Neel became increasingly confused about his career and the personal plans he had mapped out long ago to settle in the United States. This confusion was exacerbated by the unexpected behavior of Neel's ex-boyfriend, who started contacting him again, flirting and asking Neel to hang out together and to share meals. During one difficult session, Neel expressed with great distress, "I'm so messed up. I don't know what I want to do, where I want to live, who I want to date, and how to be me. . . . I'm still scared of 'him,' and I just want to get away from here." He tried to avoid his ex-boyfriend's texts and calls, but he succumbed to getting together on a number of occasions, only to feel jilted all over again. In tears, Neel confessed, "I'm still really afraid of him. I feel like he has so much power over me." Again, he related this imbalance and anxiety to race and skin color—and to leftover colonial ideals that he and his family have internalized.

As Neel dragged his feet (and heart) through this identity crisis, the US election results of Donald Trump's presidential victory knocked him flat out. His depressive mood quickly flipped into mania. The day after the presidential election, Neel was the victim of a hate crime in broad daylight outside the gates of his school campus. He was shoved down by a young white man, who yelled, "I hate Muslims!" at him. (Neel is in fact part of the Hindu majority.) This incident has stricken Neel, throwing him into an utter panic about his personal security and, even more, how the election has jeopardized his meticulously cultivated plans for a future in the United States. While he has received an attractive job offer at a prestigious law firm in New York, Neel is terrified that the offer may be rescinded. He is worried that his visa status could suddenly change under the new administration and that he will be "forced to leave the country and have to start all over again."

Increasingly, Neel feels angry that the sacrifices he has made and the hard work he has directed toward academic success could become wasted. For him, the possibility of returning to India, which initially sparked his curiosity during the summer recess, now feels more like a coerced inevitability than one of several possible choices for him to consider. Exploring and sorting through Neel's psychic tumult in the face of current political events feels like the blind leading the blind for both patient and therapist alike.

RACIAL DISSOCIATION AND THE MECHANISM OF PARANOIA

In several key ways, Neel's case history provides an important contrast to that of Christopher. To begin, Christopher grew up as part of the dominant racial majority in China, a country with little public discourse on race, though, like all empires, with an abundance of race problems.[17] (It might be said that Christopher also re-creates a version of Chinese Han nationalism with his social groups in both Singapore and the United States.) In contrast, Neel was raised in an Indian society in which long histories of colonialism, caste, and color provide a critical foundation and vocabulary for Neel to evaluate his sexual encounters and racial experiences in the United States. For Neel, these intersectional experiences of race and sex cannot be dissociated from one another. Indeed, unlike Christopher, Neel cannot be described as racially dissociated. Equally so, for Neel, neither can private and public forms of discrimination be dissociated from one another: caste and skin color structure his parents' relationship and everyday interactions with one another in apparent ways, even as they continue to affect his father's career and employment opportunities.

The history of caste in postcolonial India after British colonization is radically different from the history of race in the postcolonial United States after indigenous dispossession and slavery. These warrant independent studies altogether. Nonetheless, it is his personal experiences with collective histories of social hierarchy and subordination in India through which Neel comes to narrate his failed relationship with his ex-boyfriend in the United States. Unlike Christopher and many Asian American millennials of his generation, Neel has developed a critical vocabulary and analysis concerning caste and skin color through which he frames and interprets his sexuality and sexual encounters in India and the United States, transforming and translating them into the language of race and racial difference. Notably, with the rise of Asia globally and the shift of economic and political power to the East, we must factor into the history of the Asian American subject a more expansive account of the subject of racial history connected to different empires (the United States, China, India) and their organizations of race and caste into social hierarchy and subordination. Indeed, we must begin to account how the enfranchised subjects of these countries have their own particular histories of race and property—their own national versions of whiteness (of Han or Hindu nationalism) as property.

Moreover, unlike Christopher and most millennials today, Neel also does not suffer the same degree of panic as many of his peers. Rather, like those in Generation X, his psychic predicaments are more connected to depression. Neel is a racial melancholic: he knows the object he has lost (his white ex-boyfriend). He continues to suffer as he tries to come to terms with the multiple meanings and implications of this formative loss of whiteness on both a personal and collective level. In the aftermath of the recent presidential election, his meticulous plans of settling in the United States upon graduating from law school have been unmoored in and through this loss.

Both Christopher's and Neel's life stories are marked by parachuting and multiple diasporas, first in Asia and then in the United States. (Unlike Yuna, who goes immediately to the West—Australia and then the United States—Christopher and Neel start their parachuting in India and Singapore before moving west. Here, we might speculate on the ways in which Asia functions as a transitional space for their migration and academic success.) Both come out in high school with relative ease. However, the differences in their psychic dilemmas—panic and depression—and as well as the disparate ways in which they narrate problems of race and sex, raise crucial questions of how mechanisms of racial dissociation and racial melancholia configure repression, exclusion, and loss for these two young men.

Let us turn to Freud's essay "Psycho-Analytic Notes on an Autobiographical Account of a Case of Paranoia" (1911) to explore their differing psychic mechanisms. Freud's thoughts on paranoia seem especially appropriate to (gay) panic attacks as they originally ground his understandings of homosexuality in psychoanalytic theory. Here, the autobiography that Freud explores is the poignant case history of Dr. Daniel Paul Schreber, the distinguished German judge and once chief justice of the Saxony Supreme Court, who becomes for Freud the premier illustration of repressed homosexual desire.

Freud reads Schreber's paranoid psychoses as the effect of repressed homosexual desires—wish fantasies with which Schreber cannot come to terms. The mechanism of paranoia delineates the ways in which Schreber disavows these forbidden desires and projects them outward. In her reading of the "Psycho-Analytic Notes," Eve Kosofsky Sedgwick supplements Freud's analysis of Schreber with the observation that the case history needs to be investigated in terms of repressed homosexual wish fantasies but, even more, in relation to homophobia and its schizogenic force—the psychopathological effects that the repression of homosexual desire produces in the putatively heterosexual albeit tortured Schreber.[18]

Freud's case history interests us here because of the ways in which it connects homosexuality with a self-punishing homophobic regulation. In our colorblind age, Christopher's self-regulation and dissociation of sexuality and race under the mandates of neoliberalism and its principles of economic rationality and efficiency is an uncanny echo of Schreber's prior self-denials and self-punishments. If homosexual desire today is no longer repressed and disavowed to the same degree as during Schreber's tortured era, nonetheless a kind of self-regulating and self-punishing homophobia emerges under the political banner of liberal equality, progress, rights, and reason.

More specifically, Freud's model of paranoia helps us understand how the psychic mechanisms of racial dissociation for Generation Y differ from those of racial melancholia for Generation X. Halfway through his case history, Freud observes that "Paranoia decomposes just as hysteria condenses."[19] He continues in a subsequent passage:

> The delusional formation [of paranoia], which we take to be the pathological product, is in reality an attempt at recovery, a process of reconstruction. Such a reconstruction after the catastrophe is successful to a greater or lesser extent, but never wholly so; in Schreber's words, there has been a "profound internal change" in the world. But the human subject has recaptured a relation, and often a very intense one, to the people and things in the world, even though the relation is a hostile one now, where formerly it was hopefully affectionate. We may say, then, that the process of repression proper consists in a detachment of the libido from people—and things—that were previously loved.[20]

That is to say, in hysteria, repressed and forbidden identifications and desires are condensed into a symptom, into a lost object to be interpreted and named. Our theory of racial melancholia—losses associated with immigration, assimilation, and racialization that cannot be easily mourned—follows this hysteric model of condensation. In racial melancholia, you can name the lost object, although, as Freud reminds us, it often remains quite difficult to identify exactly what it is in that object that you have lost. Put otherwise, in racial melancholia, you lift the rock of repression and you discover something underneath—a lost object, one demanding to be analyzed and interpreted.[21] Indeed, it is the naming of this object of loss that creates identity from difference; it is the naming and narrating of the social exclusions compelling its foreclosure that creates a racial identity and racial politics in its wake. In this regard, to paraphrase Angela Davis, identity emerges from politics rather than politics emerging from identity.[22]

In contrast, in racial dissociation, we are faced not with condensation but rather with a paranoid structure of decomposition, of dispersion. In Freud's paranoid model of homosexual repression, what is "abolished internally returns from without."[23] That is, what is repressed and abolished internally is first disavowed and projected outward into multiple and dispersed spaces across a wide social terrain. In the process, feelings of love and affection are transformed and return as sensations of hostility and aggression—or the refusal of feeling altogether, as Christopher's case history underscores. The attempt at recovery—the will to reconstruct the origins for psychic pain—and the desire to name the loss and to narrate social exclusion become extremely difficult precisely because the origins are diffuse, dispersed, and dissociated. On the one hand, Christopher's panic attacks and anxiety have no proper object. On the other hand, Christopher's body in pieces illustrates how in racial dissociation there is no coherent (racial) subject, only a series of scattered and disconnected objects. Put otherwise, in racial dissociation, when you lift the rock of repression, there is nothing underneath to discover.

In a colorblind age, the politics of race and sex therefore remain exceedingly obscure, and it has become increasingly difficult to narrate personal and collective loss in conscious political terms. Racial dissociation is the emergent psychic paradigm underwriting evolving histories of race as relation and whiteness as property, of changing structures of racial exclusion and violence under the directives of neoliberalism and globalization. From this perspective, (gay) panic attacks and coming out today are less markers of liberal advancement and progress for race and sex; rather, they are the latest installment of what Toni Morrison describes in *The Bluest Eye* as "adjustment without improvement."[24]

WE ARE ALL MODEL MINORITIES

Returning to the discussion of psychoanalysis and critical race theory with which we began this book, rather than accepting queer liberalism's teleological narrative of colorblindness and liberal progress, we might consider how queer liberalism is only the latest historical installment of whiteness as property and race as relation.[25] Over the course of US constitutional history, the law has not delegitimated whiteness as property or dismantled the continuing social exclusions of race and racism. Rather, it has adapted and readapted them in a changing historical landscape whereby white privilege remains "a legitimate and natural baseline," in Cheryl Harris's words.[26] Though social norms and ideals may have changed, and homophobic and racist attitudes may have shifted, the right to exclude remains a historical and legal constant. It has been the purpose of this book to trace these changing modes of exclusion and inclusion in the history of the Asian American subject in relation to the subject of racial history among our students in institutions of higher education. Notably, for gay Asian men in Generation Y, racial dissociation continues to mediate evolving forms of social inclusion and exclusion precisely through a psychic mechanism of self-enforcement and self-regulation.

In the final analysis, neoliberal multiculturalism portrays racism as nonracialism in a postracist world order of individual freedom, opportunity, discrimination, and choice. Under its mandates, as Jodi Melamed observes, "racism constantly appears as disappearing . . . even as it takes on new forms that can signify as nonracial or even antiracist."[27] It is a new form of colorblindness. The shift to an ever-more-integrated global economy has created vast disparities of wealth in every society, First World and Third World, while wreaking environmental degradation across the planet. At the same time, it has been able to accommodate and include select minority populations who can advance the interests of global capital and, in turn, have become the beneficiaries of it. This economy of globalization and neoliberal multiculturalism is the world Christopher, Neel, and other high-achieving gay parachute children seek to join.

From another perspective we might observe that, under the tenets of neoliberal multiculturalism, everyone must become an Asian American model minority. Everyone must work incessantly, buy into the system, not rock the boat, embody economic efficiency, display technocratic expertise, and enroll in a major that will immediately translate instrumental knowledge into economic capital and power. Today, we are bombarded by discourses of multiculturalism and diversity, by facts and figures relating to race and racial violence, but we have few critical resources to explore what they mean in a colorblind world—their history, how we got here, and what we can do about it. Instead, we have become entrenched in the polarized positions that a winner-take-all world demands of us. We have an abundance of racial grievance but no critical resources to process racial grief and loss.[28] In this race for time, as these case histories underscore, there is no time for race or, for that matter, sex. *That* is what all the panic is about.

Perhaps Freud was ahead of himself when he described the transformation and translation of the unconscious into a seemingly organized and contradiction-free consciousness in the specific terms of race and the problem of miscegenation:

Among the derivatives of the *Ucs.* instinctual impulses, of the sort we have described, there are some which unite in themselves characters of an opposite kind. On the one hand, they are highly organized, free from self-contradiction, have made use of every acquisition of the system *Cs.* and would hardly be distinguished in our judgement from the formations of that system. On the other hand they are unconscious and are incapable of becoming conscious. Thus *qualitatively* they belong to the system *Pcs.*, but *factually* to the *Ucs.* Their origin is what decides their fate. We may compare them with individuals of mixed race who, taken all round, resemble white men, but who betray their coloured descent by some striking feature or other, and on that account are excluded from society and enjoy none of the privileges of white people.[29]

For us, as for Freud, psychoanalysis provides a critical vocabulary, one important framework to evaluate and account for a qualitative whiteness that is not one. Together with these case histories on parachute children, a renewed psychoanalytic theory helps us to rethink legacies of whiteness as property in a global frame. Under the shadows of neoliberalism and globalization, they teach us that race as relation, sex as relation, are increasingly impossible in a multicultural and colorblind age. They are lost, they are dissociated, there is no relation. That is the problem.

EPILOGUE

The subject of history affects the history of the racial subject often in immediate, apprehensible, and debilitating ways. We completed this book just after the presidential election of 2016—an event that, as we recount in our last chapter and case history, framed Neel's unnerving experience of a racial hate crime outside the gates of his university campus the day after voting. Already in his brief tenure as the forty-fifth US president, Mr. Trump has enacted, or attempted to enact, a slew of racist, homophobic, and transphobic policies against immigrants, people of color, and sexual minorities. These are accompanied by an all-out assault on health care and the environment, coupled with a personal history of unapologetic misogyny, that are finally notable only insofar as they expose a level of utter disregard and contempt for much of human life that hitherto affirmed remained unstated, at least publicly so, by most of his ilk. Unsurprisingly, these acts are carried out in the language of colorblindness and racial dissociation. Mr. Trump proclaims of himself, "I'm the least racist person I know."

Mr. Trump's rhetoric of white nationalism—his divisive calls to make America great again by returning the nation to its glorious past—may seem exceptional. They may be unique in their bombast. However, they are less so in their deleterious effects insofar as they lay bare a long history of whiteness as property, while exposing a racial unconscious and provoking a racial violence that emboldens and renews legacies of white supremacy. How does the racial subject survive this moment in history? In our turbulent state of colorblind politics, and in the face of an ever-shrinking public sphere in which racism and discrimination are transformed into the neoliberal language of individual choice, how can our students and patients create social and psychic spaces in which spontaneity, creativity, and paradox are possible and racial reparation might emerge?

Throughout this book, we have investigated the ways in which our students and patients have survived individual and collective experiences of exclusion and loss across histories of race as relation and whiteness as property. The history of the racial subject and the subject of racial history continue to shift, especially under the current administration and with the rise of competing nationalisms and fundamentalisms across the globe, most notably (for the purposes of our study) China and India. Exploring such challenges is an ongoing project. There is no easy solution, no easy cure, for the racial subject. Any possible response must be a collective endeavor, for there is no likelihood of individual healing outside of social healing, outside of structural reforms for a more just society and sustainable world.

The liberal university that Mr. Trump and his administration delight in attacking is no exception to this state of affairs. It is no different from—it is in fact a reflection of—the larger society in which it is situated. The university is a fraught public space, and the existence of a token Asian American therapist in counseling and psychological services or a token scholar of Asian American studies not only parallels the isolation that many students of color feel on college campuses but also underscores the dynamic relationship between racial segregation in physical and psychic space. Nonetheless, the university still harbors certain possibilities—to reformulate Toni Morrison—for adjustment *with* improvement, insofar as it remains a fugitive space for critical thinking and racial exchange.[1]

Toward that end, we conclude with a few words on strategies for community-building on college campuses. Within the space of the university, the clinic is a particularly overdetermined and understudied racialized space. Theoretically, it offers its mental health services to all students in varying degrees of distress. The multitude of issues students bring to the clinic range from depression and anxiety such as panic attacks to self-injurious behaviors such as eating disorders and substance abuse to sexual assault to more severe forms of mental illness and psychoses. Today, increasing numbers of students arrive on campus with ongoing needs for counseling and psychiatric medication follow-ups.

What is being treated less and less are students with normal developmental issues such as separation and individuation processes including homesickness, loneliness, and adjustment difficulties.[2]

The demographic makeup of the university clinic in terms of therapists as well as patients reveals a segregated space no different from that of the larger university and, indeed, larger society.[3] As a case in point, Dr. Han was the first person of color to be hired as staff member at the five university clinics with which she has been affiliated over the past twenty-five years in the Midwest and the Northeast. Given the comparatively homogenous racial, sexual, and class backgrounds of the clinical staff, it is not surprising that middle-class white students with moderate levels of distress utilize counseling and psychological services in disproportionate numbers compared to students of color who may experience the space as socially and psychically alienating. For them, the clinic is not a transitional space of play, or a neutral space for development, but a fraught and *unsafe* space of premature growth and fixity, to return to a concept from Carol Long's work on South Africa.[4]

It is telling that there is little in-depth research on the clinic and race, only anecdotal evidence. In our own experience, the majority of Asian American students do not self-refer to the university clinic. To the contrary, professors, academic advisors, residential assistants, and deans often refer Asian American students and, at times, involuntarily escort them there. Like most other racial groups, the highest numbers of Asian American students seek counseling and psychological services during exam periods when stress levels are particularly acute among the entire student body. At that point, however, much of their psychic distress extends beyond normal crises to panic attacks, suicidal behavior, and psychoses requiring hospitalization and demanding medical leave from the university under the threat of legal liability.

In short, Asian American students are often brought to the attention of counseling and psychological services when it is too late, when they are beyond manageable levels of crisis, and when there is little to be done to reverse their situations. In comparison to Asian American populations, African American and Latina/o students rarely seek counseling at all. Often, they do not feel entitled or welcome to the space of the clinic. Once more, the history of the racial subject must be considered in relation to the subject of racial history, including cultural stigmas against psychotherapy, and to the everyday processes of inclusion and exclusion on college campuses.

Students of color are at a distinct remove from institutional resources and support to which they are all entitled as abstract members of the university community. Even after a person of color manages to enter the space of the clinic, race continues to create difficult if not insurmountable obstacles for the therapist-patient relationship. Racial misrecognitions and racial enactments on the part of the therapist or patient are occasions for "narcissistic exposure" and "narcissistic disruption," often provoking reactions of discomfort or shame ruinous to the therapeutic relationship and quickly replacing trust with fear.[5] Ironically, race as relation—as social inclusion and exclusion—becomes especially fraught in the space of the clinic that is supposed to address and to repair these formative social foreclosures.

At the same time, in terms of academic programming on university campuses, establishing and growing Asian American and ethnic studies programs as spaces for critical thinking and racial exchange has been a contested demand since the late 1960s, when student and faculty activists protested for structural change to academic institutions and curricula in order to study histories of race and racism. We continue to live in the shadows of these unrequited demands.

Today, with the neoliberal reordering of the university—its promotion of instrumental knowledge and its reinforcing of social inequality and privilege—the model minority stereotype continues to be marshaled by detractors of such programs as proof that Asian Americans are neither in want of any special recognition nor have any particular needs as a group. Indeed, few research universities outside of the West Coast have more than a handful of scholars of Asian American studies, while the student body is often more than twenty percent (and higher on the West Coast) Asian and Asian American. In no liberal democratic system would such stark imbalances in representation be tolerated. However, this state of affairs is a unique and recurrent aspect of racialization for Asian Americans. Indeed, the social contract of model minority citizenship demands colorblindness.

Furthermore, with the rapid accumulation of capital in East and

South Asia under globalization, university administrations today are especially eager to recruit international students from Asia as an important source of revenue to balance stretched school budgets. Yet the same administrators are unwilling to recognize any obligation to attend to the particular social and psychic needs of these transnational and diasporic student populations, as we discussed in part II of this book. Psychic nowhere and racial dissociation are the symptoms of such institutional disregard.

The mainstream vision of Asian Americans as model minorities having the best of both worlds—two cultures, two languages—is a multicultural fantasy in the neoliberal age of diversity management. Our investigation of immigration, assimilation, and racialization as conflicted and unresolved processes of mourning and racial melancholia for first-generation students in Generation X, as well as our exploration of colorblindness and racial dissociation organizing the transnational world of first-generation Asian parachute children in Generation Y, reveal the links between East and West as less than fluid. For these Asian and Asian American students, the addressing and redressing of racial melancholia and racial dissociation requires a public language. It requires a public space in which these conflicts can be acknowledged, analyzed, and negotiated.

Ideally, Asian American and ethnic studies programs provide the social and psychic space to bring together various fragmented parts (social, psychic, intellectual, affective, political, economic, religious, and cultural) to compose, borrowing from D. W. Winnicott, a "holding environment," a "whole" environment for critical analysis and thinking.[6] Ideally, these programs are public spaces in which the history of race as relation and whiteness as property can be interrogated—a project of critical race studies that is important for *all* students to explore in our insistently colorblind age. Ultimately, these programs ought to facilitate the collective creation of new representations and narratives for communities entangled with histories of exclusion and loss. These emergent formations not only contest the conventional ways in which Asians and Asian Americans have been apprehended in mainstream culture across generations but also, we hope, maintain an open space for new ideas and for new racial politics and coalitions to take hold. In this sense, Asian American and ethnic studies programs can function as "good-enough" spaces for the discussion and development of psychoanalysis and critical race studies in tandem—for the investigation of the shifting history of the racial subject in relation to the changing subject of racial history.

A good-enough analysis of race entails an understanding that any adequate response to racism emerges, as Long suggests, from an ability to tolerate paradoxes—an ability to listen, to play, and to (be)hold multiple narratives not only for their similarities but also their contradictions. Any new understandings of race must emerge from the overlapping spaces of the classroom and the clinic, as well as from community-based organizations and social groups, which collectively provide a holding environment for the critical examination of race and racial difference. As we emphasize, it is the naming of loss and the narrating of exclusion that transforms difference into identity and, in this way, identity emerges from politics rather than politics from identity.

We would like to believe that such ideal (not idealized) spaces are within reach—that we might begin to address and ameliorate the social and psychic pain of our students and patients more adequately and with greater responsibility and care. However, we must also acknowledge that a cure is yet to come. As long as the history of the racial subject continues to be configured by the evolving histories of race as relation and whiteness as property, cure remains a verb rather than a noun, in process, in constant movement and flux. By investigating both Generation X and Generation Y, second-generation and first-generation (im)migrants, as well as racial melancholia and racial dissociation, we hope to have offered a deeper understanding of the social possibilities and psychic limits of the lives of our students and patients across different historical spaces and times. Their social and psychic pain has lent us a particular insight into US society and an important critique of legacies of race and racism.

In the final analysis, this project has also been an exercise for us to mourn the various passings of Asian American students who no longer felt tied to our world, such as it is. As long as social and racial injustice persists, there invariably will be new and shifting accounts of loss to be analyzed, new strategies of social and psychic survival to be examined. This book should not be taken as a summary moment. Instead, it should be understood as an initial assessment of the continuing transformations of mourning and racial melancholia, the continuing translations of colorblindness and racial dissociation, for the purpose of building new communities. We offer these evolving paradigms with the hope that others will continue to explore their possibilities and limits with us.

NOTES

INTRODUCTION

1 "Some Good News on Asian-American Poverty in New York City," published by The Mayor's Office for Economic Opportunity, New York City, June 1, 2017. Accessed on April 7, 2018: http://www1.nyc.gov/site/opportunity/news/004 /some-good-news-asian-american-poverty-new-york-city.

2 Sigmund Freud, "Mourning and Melancholia" (1917), in *The Standard Edition of the Complete Psychological Works of Sigmund Freud*, vol. 14, trans. and ed. James Strachey et al. (London: Hogarth, 1957), 245; emphasis in original.

3 Freud, "Mourning and Melancholia," 245; emphasis in original.

4 Kimberlyn Leary, "Race as an Adaptive Challenge: Working with Diversity in the Clinical Consulting Room," *Psychoanalytic Psychology* 29, no. 3 (2012): 283.

5 See Farhad Dalal, "Racism: Processes of Detachment, Dehumanization, and Hatred," *Psychoanalytic Quarterly* 75 (2006): 131–61. Dalal writes, "Interestingly, much of psychoanalytic thinking has been reluctant to allow the external social world to play a *causal* role in the structuring of internal distress, and, instead, is more likely to explain difficulties in the external social world as due to, and driven by, distress in the internal world" (138); emphasis in original. See also Lynne Layton, "Racial Identities, Racial Enactments, and Normative Unconscious Processes," *Psychoanalytic Quarterly* 75 (2006): 237–69. Paraphrasing Dalal, Layton writes, "Culture is considered external to internal psychic functions. Further, Dalal found that the actual fact of cultural racism was just about never taken into account as a cause of problems in the clinical psychoanalytic encounter. The patient is frequently assumed to be acting out infantile fantasies; at best, race becomes intertwined with those fantasies, but it is never determinant. Racism is conceptualized as an effect of individual prejudice, never as a cause of it" (244).

6 See Kwame Ture (aka Stokely Carmichael) and Charles V. Hamilton, *Black Power: The Politics of Liberation* (New York: Vintage, 1992).

7 See, for instance, Patricia Williams, *The Alchemy of Race and Rights: Diary of a Law Professor* (Cambridge, MA: Harvard University Press, 1992).

8 See Raymond Williams, *Marxism and Literature* (Oxford: Oxford University Press, 1977), 128–35.

9 Dalal, "Racism," 148.

10 In the humanities, see, for example, Gwen Bergner, *Taboo Subjects: Race, Sex, and Psychoanalysis* (Minneapolis: University of Minnesota Press, 1997); Anne Anlin Cheng, *The Melancholy of Race: Psychoanalysis, Assimilation, and Hidden Grief* (New York: Oxford University Press, 2001); David L. Eng, *Racial Castration: Managing Masculinity in Asian America* (Durham, NC: Duke University Press, 2001); Christopher J. Lane, ed., *The Psychoanalysis of Race* (New York: Columbia University Press, 1998); Amber Jamilla Musser, *Sensational Flesh: Race, Power, and Masochism* (New York: New York University Press, 2014); Michelle Anne Stephens, *Skin Acts: Race, Psychoanalysis, and the Black Male Performer* (Durham, NC: Duke University Press, 2014); Antonio Viego, *Dead Subjects: Toward a Politics of Loss in Latino Studies* (Durham: Duke University Press, 2007); and Jean Walton, *Fair Sex, Savage Dreams: Race, Psychoanalysis, Sexual Difference* (Durham, NC: Duke University Press, 2001).

In the clinical arena, in addition to Dalal and Layton, for example, see Neil Altman, "Black and White Thinking: A Psychoanalyst Reconsiders Race," *Psychoanalytic Dialogues* 10 (2000): 589–605; Leary, "Race as an Adaptive Challenge," 279–91; Carol Long, "Transitioning Racialized Spaces," *Psychoanalysis, Culture and Society* 16, no. 1 (2011): 49–70; Melanie Suchet, "A Relational Encounter with Race," *Psychoanalytic Dialogues* 14 (2004): 423–38; Pratyusha Tummala-Narra, "Skin Color and the Therapeutic Relationship," *Psychoanalytic Psychology* 24 (2007): 255–70; Kate White, ed., *Unmasking Race, Culture, and Attachment in the Psychoanalytic Space* (London: Karnac Books, 2006); and Kathleen P. White, "Surviving Hating and Being Hated: Some Personal Thoughts about Racism from a Psychoanalytic Perspective," *Contemporary Psychoanalysis* 38 (2002): 401–22.

11 See Charles R. Lawrence, III, "The Id, the Ego, and Equal Protection," *Stanford Law Review* 39, no. 2 (January 1987): 317–88; and Neil Gotanda, "A Critique of 'Our Constitution Is Color-Blind,'" *Stanford Law Review* 44, no. 1 (November 1991): 1–68.

12 In recent years, there has also been a group of postcolonial scholars who have investigated the global history of psychoanalysis and its (non)relation to European colonial violence. See, for example, Stef Craps, *Postcolonial Witnessing: Trauma Out of Bounds* (London: Palgrave Macmillan, 2013); Ranjana Khanna, *Dark Continents: Psychoanalysis and Colonialism* (Durham, NC: Duke University Press, 2003); Michael Rothberg, *Multidirectional Memory: Remembering the Holocaust in the Age of Decolonization* (Stanford, CA: Stanford University Press, 2009); Kalpana Seshadri-Crooks, *Desiring Whiteness: A Lacanian Analysis of Race* (New York: Routledge, 2000).

13 See Peter Buckley, ed., introduction to *Essential Papers on Object Relations,* (New York: New York University Press, 1986), xi–xxv. Among other things, the debate fundamentally concerns whether objects upon which the drives are focused are people and things with no inherent connection to the internal fantasies and the psychic development of the infant or whether these objects are

reflections of real experiences with actual people in an infant's life, that is, that these people and things are of primary, not secondary, importance.

14 Gunnar Myrdal, assisted by Richard Sterner and Arnold Rose, *An American Dilemma: The Negro Problem and Modern Democracy* (New York: Harper and Brothers, 1944).

15 Dorothy E. Holmes, "The Wrecking Effects of Race and Social Class on Self and Success," *Psychoanalytic Quarterly* 75 (2006): 221.

16 On this dynamic of affirmation and forgetting, see Lisa Lowe, "The Intimacies of Four Continents," in *Haunted by Empire: Geographies of Intimacy in North American History*, ed. Ann Laura Stoler (Durham, NC: Duke University Press, 2006), 191–212. More recently, scholars in numerous fields, historical periods, and geographical areas of specialty have taken up this intellectual mandate to investigate global histories of race. See, for instance, Jack D. Forbes, *Africans and Native Americans: The Language of Race and the Evolution of Red-Black Peoples* (Urbana: University of Illinois, 1993); Takashi Fujitani, *Race for Empire: Koreans as Japanese and Japanese as Americans during World War II* (Berkeley: University of California Press, 2013); Dru C. Gladney, *Dislocating China: Muslims, Minorities, and Other Subaltern Subjects* (Chicago, IL: University of Chicago Press, 2004); Ania Loomba, "Race and the Possibilities of Comparative Critique," *New Literary History* 40 (2009): 501–22; María Elena Martínez, "The Language, Genealogy, and Classification of 'Race' in Colonial Mexico," in *Race and Classification: The Case of Mexican America*, ed. Ilona Katzew and Susan Deans-Smith (Stanford, CA: Stanford University Press, 2009), 25–42.

17 See Ian Baucom, *Specters of the Atlantic: Finance Capital, Slavery, and the Philosophy of History* (Durham, NC: Duke University Press, 2005).

18 See Loomba, "Race and the Possibilities," 503–16.

19 Daniel Patrick Moynihan, *The Negro Family: The Case For National Action* (Washington, DC: Office of Policy Planning and Research, United States Department of Labor, 1965); and Samuel P. Huntington, *The Clash of Civilizations and the Remaking of World Order* (New York: Simon and Schuster, 1996).

20 See Karl Marx, *Capital*, vol. 1, *A Critique of Political Economy* (New York: Penguin, 1992), part I, chap., sect. 4.

21 Cedric J. Robinson, *Black Marxism: The Making of the Black Radical Tradition* (Chapel Hill: University of North Carolina Press, 2000).

22 See, for example, Alexander Saxton, "Introduction: Historical Explanations of Racial Inequality," in *The Rise and Fall of the White Republic: Class Politics and Mass Culture in Nineteenth-Century America* (New York: Verso, 1990), 1–20; and Alden T. Vaughan, "The Origins Debate: Slavery and Racism in Seventeenth-Century Virginia," in *The Roots of American Racism: Essays on the Colonial Experience* (New York: Oxford University Press, 1989), 136–74.

23 David Kazanjian, "'When They Come Here They Feal So Free': Race and Early American Studies." *Early American Literature* 41, no. 2 (June 2006): 331.

24 Lowe, "Intimacies of Four Continents," 206.

25 William Blackstone, *Commentaries on the Laws of England, Book II: Of the Rights of Things* (Oxford: Oxford University Press, 2016), 1.

26 See Wesley Hohfeld, "Faulty Analysis in Easement and License Cases," *Yale Law Journal* 27 (1917): 66–101; Wesley Hohfeld, "Fundamental Legal Conceptions as Applied in Judicial Reasoning," *Yale Law Journal* 26 (1917): 710–770; and Wesley Hohfeld, "Some Fundamental Legal Conceptions as Applied in Judicial Reasoning," *Yale Law Journal* 23 (1913): 16–59.

27 See John S. Harbison, "Hohfeld and Herefords: The Concept of Property and the Law of the Range," *New Mexico Law Review* 22 (1992): 459–99.

28 Thomas C. Grey, "The Disintegration of Property," *Nomos XII* (1980): 69–85.

29 Cheryl I. Harris, "Whiteness as Property," *Harvard Law Review* 106, no. 8 (June 1993): 1709–91.

30 Harris, "Whiteness as Property," 1714.

31 Altman, "Black and White Thinking," 589.

32 See Moon-Ho Jung, *Coolies and Cane: Race, Labor, and Sugar in the Age of Emancipation* (Baltimore, MD: Johns Hopkins University Press, 2006).

33 See Mae Ngai, *Impossible Subjects: Illegal Aliens and the Making of Modern America* (Princeton, NJ: Princeton University Press, 2004).

34 See Ann Anlin Cheng, "Passing, Natural Selection, and Love's Failure: Ethics of Survival from Chang-rae Lee to Jacques Lacan," *American Literary History* 17, no. 3 (fall 2005): 553–74. Writing on Lacan, Cheng puts the dynamic of lack (or relation) in these terms: "The Gaze as that elusive thing beyond both vision and representation offers an uncanny insight into the political and ethical implications of racial visibility as unveiled by the phenomenon of passing. Racial passing depends on a visual world, but it also lays bare the *objet a* around which racial ideology circles. I do not offer this connection by way of some simple analogy (such as race equals the Gaze or the *objet a*) but rather in order to help us grasp *the logic of lack* operating within both racial and subjective legibility. And it is precisely the collusion between 'lack' as the precondition for subjectivity and 'loss' as the material condition of racial abjection that requires acknowledgment. There is no political 'remedy' for this complicity between psychic and material impoverishment. There is only the ethical injunction to acknowledge this imbricated relationship" (568–69); emphasis in original.

35 For a discussion of the Oedipus complex in the context of colonial Senegal and its history of decolonization, see Alice Bullard, *"L'Oedipe Africain:* A Retrospective," *Transcultural Psychiatry* 42, no. 2 (2005): 171–203.

36 See Frantz Fanon, *Black Skin, White Mask,* trans. Charles Lam Markmann (1952; repr., New York: Grove, 1963); and Albert Memmi, *The Colonizer and the Colonized* (1957; repr., New York: Orion Press, 1965); and Albert Memmi, *Dependence: A Sketch for a Portrait of the Dependent,* trans. Philip A. Facey (1979; repr., Boston: Beacon Press, 1984).

37 For an analysis of the intergenerational transfer of white wealth and privilege in the antebellum United States, see Adrienne D. Davis's "The Private Law of

Race and Sex: An Antebellum Perspective," *Stanford Law Review* 51 (1998–99): 221–88.

38 See W. E. B. Du Bois, *The Souls of Black Folk* (Chicago: A. C. McClurg, 1903).

39 Sigmund Freud, "The Unconscious" (1915), in *The Standard Edition of the Complete Psychological Works of Sigmund Freud*, vol. 14, trans. and ed. James Strachey et al. (London: Hogarth, 1957), 159–215. Freud writes, "If we communicate to a patient some idea which he has at one time repressed but which we have discovered in him, our telling him makes at first no change in his mental condition. Above all, it does not remove the repression nor undo its effects, as might perhaps be expected from the fact that the previously unconscious idea has now become conscious. On the contrary, all that we shall achieve at first will be a fresh rejection of the repressed idea. But now the patient has in actual fact the same idea in two forms in different places in his mental apparatus: first, he has the conscious memory of the auditory trace of the idea, conveyed in what we told him; and secondly, he also has—as we know for certain—the unconscious memory of his experience as it was in its earlier form. Actually there is no lifting of the repression until the conscious idea, after the resistances have been overcome, has entered into connection with the unconscious memory-trace. It is only through the making conscious of the latter itself that success is achieved. On superficial consideration this would seem to show that conscious and unconscious ideas are distinct registrations, topographically separated, of the same content. But a moment's reflection shows that the identity of the information given to the patient with his repressed memory is only apparent. To have heard something and to have experienced something are in their psychological nature two quite different things, even though the content of both is the same" (175–76).

40 Kimberlyn Leary, "Racial Insult and Repair," *Psychoanalytic Dialogues* 17, no. 4 (2007): 545.

41 Cheng, "Passing," 556; emphasis in original.

42 Craps, *Postcolonial Witnessing*, 6.

43 On the topic of "chosen traumas," see Vamik D. Volkan, "Transgenerational Transmissions and 'Chosen Trauma': An Element of Large-Group Identity," opening address of the XIII International Congress, International Association of Group Psychotherapy, August 1998, accessed December 10, 2015, http:// www.vamikvolkan.com/Transgenerational-Transmissions-and-Chosen -Traumas.php.

44 Michel Foucault, *The History of Sexuality*, vol. 1, *An Introduction* (New York: Vintage, 1978); and Gilles Deleuze and Félix Guattari, *Anti-Oedipus: Capitalism and Schizophrenia* (Minneapolis: University of Minnesota Press, 1983).

45 We thank Hirokazu Yoshikawa for this insight.

46 See Leary, "Race as an Adaptive Challenge," 282.

47 The "Black Lives Matter" (BLM) activist movement began in 2013 with the acquittal of George Zimmerman in the shooting death of an African American

teenager Trayvon Martin in Sanford, Florida. BLM became nationally recognized for its street demonstrations following the 2014 deaths of two African American males at the hands of police officers: Michael Brown in Ferguson, Missouri, and Eric Garner in Staten Island, New York. See Wikipedia, accessed December 10, 2015, https://en.wikipedia.org/wiki/Black_Lives_Matter.

48 See Williams, *Marxism and Literature.*

49 David L. Eng, *The Feeling of Kinship: Queer Liberalism and the Racialization of Intimacy* (Durham, NC: Duke University Press, 2010), 1.

50 D. W. Winnicott, *Playing and Reality* (New York: Brunner-Routledge, 1971), 64.

51 Long, "Transitioning Racialized Spaces," 49–70.

52 Christy Ling Hom, "The Academic, Psychological, and Behavioral Adjustment of Chinese Parachute Kids" (PhD thesis, University of Michigan: Thesis, 2002), 17.

53 Hom observes that "only 8% of 18-year-olds in Taiwan are enrolled in university, compared to 30% in Japan and 50% in the United States . . . . In Taiwan, less than half (44%) of those who graduate from high school ever go on to postsecondary schools, and a much smaller proportion are admitted to accredited universities and colleges. In Hong Kong, less than 10% of high school graduates are admitted to the few accredited universities, polytechnics, and colleges there. And in mainland China, only about 10 to 15% of high school graduates go onto college" ("Academic, Psychological, and Behavioral Adjustment," 37).

CHAPTER 1. RACIAL MELANCHOLIA

1 Danzy Senna, *Caucasia* (New York: Riverhead, 1998), 329. "Jesse" presents herself as Jewish (and thus not black), significantly complicating the racial complexities of whiteness in Senna's novel. Although "Jesse" is marked differently from the WASPs populating her New Hampshire environment, her part-Jewish background is mobilized so that she can pass and claim the privileges of whiteness. It is also used as an explanation for her darker skin tone and hair.

2 Senna, *Caucasia*, 329.

3 See, for instance, Desiree Baolian Qin, "Doing Well vs. Feeling Well: Understanding Family Dynamics and the Psychological Adjustment of Chinese Immigrant Adolescents," *Journal of Youth and Adolescence* 37 (2008): 22–35. See also Jennifer Lee and Min Zhou, *The Asian American Achievement Paradox* (New York: Russell Sage Foundation, 2015).

4 Melancholia as a theoretical concept in psychoanalysis and depression as a clinical diagnosis are not synonymous, although their sources and symptoms often overlap. The relationship between melancholia and processes of immigration, assimilation, and racialization is underdeveloped in both ethnic studies and psychoanalysis. We became interested in racial melancholia through our various case histories as well as through reading Asian American literature. We

suggest that those interested in this intersection read literature by authors such as Frank Chin, *The Chinaman Pacific and Frisco R. R. Co.* (Minneapolis, MN: Coffee House Press, 1988); Maxine Hong Kingston, *The Woman Warrior: Memoirs of a Girlhood among Ghosts* (1976; repr., New York: Vintage Books, 1989); Wendy Law-Yone, *The Coffin Tree* (1983; repr., Boston: Beacon Press, 1987); Fae Myenne Ng, *Bone* (New York: Hyperion 1993); and Chay Yew, *Porcelain* (New York: Grove Press, 1997).

5 See Raymond Williams, *Marxism and Literature* (New York: Oxford University Press, 1978), 128–34.

6 Sigmund Freud, "Mourning and Melancholia" (1917), in *The Standard Edition of the Complete Psychological Works of Sigmund Freud,* vol. 14, trans. and ed. James Strachey et al. (London: Hogarth, 1957), 243.

7 For a historical description of the emergence of white identity, see David R. Roediger, *The Wages of Whiteness: Race and the Making of the American Working Class* (New York: Verso, 1991); and Alexander Saxton, *The Rise and Fall of the White Republic: Class Politics and Mass Culture in Nineteenth-Century America* (New York: Verso, 1990).

8 See Neil Gotanda, "Citizenship Nullification: The Impossibility of Asian American Politics," in *Asian Americans and Politics: Perspectives, Experiences, Prospects,* ed. Gordon H. Chang (Stanford: Stanford University Press, 2002), 79–98.

9 Freud, "Mourning and Melancholia," 243.

10 Freud, "Mourning and Melancholia," 244.

11 Freud, "Mourning and Melancholia," 246.

12 Freud, "Mourning and Melancholia," 245; emphasis in original.

13 Here, Senna might be seen as reconfiguring a long history of "contamination" associated with race and racial purity—for instance, with the "one drop of blood" rule of blackness. There is also a long history of race and hygiene configuring immigrants as diseased and contaminated, as carriers of illness that infect the national body politic. Contamination is thus one theme for thinking about the intersections of African American and Asian American racialization processes.

14 Sigmund Freud, "Group Psychology and the Analysis of the Ego" (1921), in *The Standard Edition of the Complete Psychological Works of Sigmund Freud,* vol. 18, trans. and ed. James Strachey et al. (London: Hogarth, 1957), 75.

15 For a history of immigration exclusion and its legal categories and mechanisms, see Sucheng Chan, ed., *Entry Denied: Exclusion and the Chinese Community in America, 1882–1943* (Philadelphia, PA: Temple University Press, 1991); Bill Ong Hing, *Making and Remaking Asian American through Immigration Policy, 1850–1990* (Stanford, CA: Stanford University Press, 1993); Lisa Lowe, *Immigrant Acts: On Asian American Cultural Politics* (Durham, NC: Duke University Press, 1996); and Mae M. Ngai, *Impossible Subjects: Illegal Aliens*

and the Making of Modern America (Princeton, NJ: Princeton University Press, 2005).

16 Teemu Ruskola, *Legal Orientalism: China, the United States, and Modern Law* (Cambridge, MA: Harvard University Press, 2013), 141.

17 For an elaboration of "absent presence," see Anne Anlin Cheng, *The Melan-choly of Race: Psychoanalysis, Assimilation, and Hidden Grief* (New York: Ox-ford University Press, 2001); and Caroline Chung Simpson, *An Absent Presence: Japanese Americans in Postwar American Culture, 1945–1960* (Durham, NC: Duke University Press, 2001).

18 For a history of the model minority stereotype, see Bob H. Suzuki, "Educa-tion and the Socialization of Asian Americans: A Revisionist Analysis of the Model Minority Thesis," *Amerasia Journal* 4, no. 2 (1977): 23–51. For a critique of the model minority thesis in terms of Asian, white, and black relations, see Mari J. Matsuda, "We Will Not Be Used: Are Asian Americans the Racial Bour-geoisie?" in *Where Is Your Body? And Other Essays on Race, Gender, and the Law* (Boston: Beacon Press, 1996), 149–59; Vijay Prashad, *Karma of Brown Folk* (Minneapolis: University of Minnesota Press, 2000); and Ellen Wu, *The Color of Success: Asian Americans and the Origins of the Model Minority* (Princeton, NJ: Princeton University Press, 2014).

19 See W. E. B. Du Bois, *The Souls of Black Folk* (Chicago: A. C. McClurg, 1903), 1. Du Bois writes, "Between me and the other world there is ever an unasked question: unasked by some through feelings of delicacy; by others through the difficulty of rightly framing it. All, nevertheless, flutter round it. They ap-proach me in a half-hesitant sort of way, eye me curiously or compassionately, and then, instead of saying directly, How does it feel to be a problem? they say, I know an excellent colored man in my town; or, I fought at Mechanicsville; or, Do not these Southern outrages make your blood boil? At these I smile, or am interested, or reduce the boiling to a simmer, as the occasion may require. To the real question, How does it feel to be a problem? I answer seldom a word."

20 See Prashad, *Karma of Brown Folk*. Prashad writes, "Meanwhile, white America can take its seat, comfortable in its liberal principles, surrounded by state-selected Asians, certain that the culpability for black poverty and oppression must be laid at the door of black America. How does it feel to be a solution?" (6).

21 See Wu, *Color of Success*.

22 For an elaboration of the concepts of "heterogeneity, hybridity, and multiplic-ity," see Lowe, *Immigrant Acts*, 60–83.

23 Maxine Hong Kingston, *China Men* (1980; repr., New York: Vintage Books, 1989), 151.

24 Kingston, *China Men*, 145.

25 See Sigmund Freud, "Fetishism" (1927), in *The Standard Edition of the Com-plete Psychological Works of Sigmund Freud*, vol. 21, trans. and ed. James Strachey et al. (London: Hogarth, 1957), 152–57; and Sigmund Freud, "Splitting of the

Ego in the Process of Defence" (1938), in *The Standard Edition of the Complete Psychological Works of Sigmund Freud*, vol. 23, trans. and ed. James Strachey et al. (London: Hogarth, 1957), 275–78.

26 Stanley Sue and Derald W. Sue, "Chinese-American Personality and Mental Health," *Amerasia Journal* 1, no. 2 (1971): 42.

27 Toni Morrison, "Unspeakable Things Unspoken: The Afro-American Presence in American Literature," *Michigan Quarterly Review* 28, no. 1 (1989): 11.

28 Homi Bhabha, "Of Mimicry and Man: The Ambivalence of Colonial Discourse," *October* 28 (1984): 126, 130; emphasis in orginal.

29 Freud, "Mourning and Melancholia," 251.

30 Homi Bhabha (1983), "The Other Question: Stereotype, Discrimination, and the Discourse of Colonialism," in *The Location of Culture* (London: Routledge, 1994), 66.

31 We borrow this formulation from Desiree Baolian Qin. Although this pattern of "safe" professions continues today, data on second-generation Asian Americans also suggest patterns of resistance to these pressures—for instance, through careers in the arts. See Philip Kasnitz, John H. Mollenkopf, Mary C. Waters, and Jennifer Holdaway, *Inheriting the City: The Children of Immigrants Come of Age* (New York: Russell Sage Foundation, 2009).

32 See Antonio Viego, *Dead Subjects: Toward a Politics of Loss in Latino Studies* (Durham, NC: Duke University Press, 2007).

33 Sau-ling Cynthia Wong, *Reading Asian American Literature: From Necessity to Extravagance* (Princeton, NJ: Princeton University Press, 1993).

34 For an elaboration of this concept, see Wendy Brown, *States of Injury: Power and Freedom in Late Modernity* (Princeton, NJ: Princeton University Press, 1995). In particular, see chapter 3, "Wounded Attachments" (52–76).

35 See, for example, Julia Kristeva, *Desire in Language: A Semiotic Approach to Literature and Art* (New York: Columbia University Press, 1980).

36 The question of generational sacrifice is historically as well as ethnically specific. For example, during the exclusion era, many first-generation Asian immigrants barred from naturalization and citizenship exhibited a strong identification with their home country and considered themselves as "sojourners" in the United States. Consequently, it was the second generation during this historical period (especially those born on US soil) who exhibited the stronger characteristics of a lost generation—for instance, the second-generation Nisei interned during World War II.

After the reformation of the Immigration and Nationality Act in 1965, Asian immigrants were legally guaranteed—and in much larger numbers—access to the space of the nation-state as citizens. The narrative of sacrifice thus attaches itself more strongly to these first-generation immigrants whose hope for assimilation and integration into the national fabric is more manifest through the legal promise of citizenship and inclusion.

37 Rea Tajiri, dir. *History and Memory* (New York: Women Make Movies, 1991).

This reading of Tajiri's film comes from David L. Eng, *The Feeling of Kinship: Queer Liberalism and the Racialization of Intimacy* (Durham, NC: Duke University Press, 2010), 166–70.

38 Sigmund Freud, "The Unconscious" (1915), in *The Standard Edition of the Complete Psychological Works of Sigmund Freud*, vol. 14, trans. and ed. James Strachey et al. (London: Hogarth, 1957), 194.

39 Freud, "Mourning and Melancholia," 245; emphasis in original.

40 Freud, "Mourning and Melancholia," 248.

41 Judith Butler, *The Psychic Life of Power: Theories in Subjection* (Stanford, CA: Stanford University Press, 1997), 182; emphasis in original.

42 It is important to consider how the model minority stereotype dovetails with a Confucian tradition of filial piety in East Asian societies. This tradition mandates a strict hierarchical relationship between individual family members, and between individual family units and the political representatives of the state.

43 Lowe, *Immigrant Acts*, 63; emphasis in original.

44 See Freud's essay "The Uncanny" (1919), in *The Standard Edition of the Complete Psychological Works of Sigmund Freud*, vol. 17, trans. and ed. James Strachey et al. (London: Hogarth Press, 1955), 217–48. For a discussion of the uncanny and nation building, see Wong, *Reading Asian American Literature*, especially chapter 2; and Priscilla Wald, *Constituting Americans: Cultural Anxiety and Narrative Form* (Durham, NC: Duke University Press, 1995), especially chapter 1. See Mari J. Matsuda, Charles R. Lawrence III, Richard Delgado, and Kimberle Williams Crenshaw, *Words That Wound: Critical Race Theory, Assaultive Speech, and the First Amendment* (Boulder, CO: Westview Press, 1993).

45 Monique Thuy-Dung Truong, "Kelly," *Amerasia Journal* 17, no. 2 (1991): 42.

46 See Louis Althusser, "Ideology and Ideological State Apparatuses (Notes towards an Investigation)," in *Lenin and Philosophy and Other Essays*, ed. B. Brewster (New York: Monthly Review Press, 1971), 127–86.

47 Lowe, *Immigrant Acts*, 55.

48 Lowe, *Immigrant Acts*, 56.

49 Melanie Klein, "Mourning and Its Relation to Manic-Depressive States," (1940) in *The Selected Melanie Klein*, ed. Juliet Mitchell (New York: Free Press, 1987), 165–66; Klein's emphasis.

50 Melanie Klein, "A Contribution to the Psychogenesis of Manic-Depressive States" (1955), in *The Selected Melanie Klein*, ed. Juliet Mitchell (New York: The Free Press, 1987), 119.

51 Klein, "Psychogenesis of Manic-Depressive States," 121; Klein's emphasis.

52 Klein, "Psychogenesis of Manic-Depressive States," 125; Klein's emphasis.

53 Klein, "Psychogenesis of Manic-Depressive States," 123.

54 Klein, "Psychogenesis of Manic-Depressive States," 124.

55 José Esteban Muñoz, *Disidentifications: Queers of Color and the Performance of Politics* (Minneapolis: University of Minnesota Press, 1999), 74.

56 Klein, "Mourning and Manic-Depressive States," 164.

57 Hannah Arendt, "Was bleibt? Es bleibt die Muttersprache," a talk with Günter Gaus, initially aired on German television in 1964. The discussion was published in Munich in Günter Gaus, *ZurPerson,* and in French translation as "Qu'est-ce qui reste?: Reste la langue maternelle" in *La tradition cachée: Le Juif comme paria,* trans. Sylvie Courtine-Denamy (Paris: Christian Bourgois, 1987), cited in Jacques Derrida, *Monolingualism of the Other; or, The Prosthesis of Origin,* trans. Patrick Mensah (Stanford, CA: Stanford University Press, 1998), 84–90n2. We would like to acknowledge Patricia Gherovici for this insight.

58 On psychic resilience and race, see Beverly Greene, "African American Lesbians and Bisexual Women in Feminist-Psychodynamic Psychotherapies: Surviving and Thriving between a Rock and a Hard Place," in *Psychotherapy with African-American Women: Innovations in Psychodynamic Perspectives and Practices,* ed. Leslie C. Jackson and Beverly Greene (New York: Guilford Press, 2000), 82–125.

59 Freud, "Mourning and Melancholia," 249.

60 The phrase "His Majesty the Ego" comes from Sigmund Freud, "Creative Writers and Day-Dreaming" (1908), in *The Standard Edition of the Complete Psychological Works of Sigmund Freud,* vol. 9, trans. and ed. James Strachey et al. (London: Hogarth, 1957), 150.

61 See Jacques Lacan, *The Seminar of Jacques Lacan, Book II: The Ego in Freud's Theory and in the Technique of Psychoanalysis, 1954–1955* (New York: Norton, 1991).

62 Freud, "Mourning and Melancholia," 250.

63 See William Ronald Dodds Fairbairn, *An Object-Relations Theory of the Personality* (New York: Basic Books, 1954); Christopher Bollas, *The Shadow of the Object: Psychoanalysis of the Unthought* (New York: Columbia University Press, 1987); and Jessica Benjamin, *The Shadow of the Other: Intersubjectivity and Gender in Psychoanalysis* (New York: Routledge, 1998).

64 Freud, "Mourning and Melancholia," 248.

65 Freud, "Mourning and Melancholia," 257.

66 We draw this idea from Kathleen Pogue White, "Surviving Hating and Being Hated: Some Personal Thoughts about Racism from a Psychoanalytic Perspective," *Contemporary Psychoanalysis* 38, no. 3 (2002): 401–22.

67 Freud, "Mourning and Melancholia," 246.

68 Sigmund Freud, "On Narcissism: An Introduction" (1914), in *The Standard Edition of the Complete Psychological Works of Sigmund Freud,* vol. 14, trans. and ed. James Strachey et al. (London: Hogarth, 1957), 85.

69 Muñoz, *Disidentifications,* 73.

70 Butler, *Psychic Life of Power,* 185.

71 Douglas Crimp, "Mourning and Militancy," *October* 51 (1989): 18; emphasis in original.

1 These observations are borrowed from David L. Eng, *The Feeling of Kinship: Queer Liberalism and the Racialization of Intimacy* (Durham, NC: Duke University Press, 2010), 1–2.

2 See David L. Eng and Shinhee Han, "Desegregating Love: Transnational Adoption, Racial Reparation, and Racial Transitional Objects," *Studies in Gender and Sexuality: Psychoanalysis, Cultural Studies, Treatment, Research* 7, no. 2 (2006): 141–72.

3 On the concept of the "good-enough" mother, see D. W. Winnicott, "Ego Distortion in Terms of True and False Self" (1960), in *The Maturational Process and the Facilitating Environment: Studies in the Theory of Emotional Development* (New York: International Universities Press, 1965), 145–50.

4 Arguments from this section are derived from David L. Eng, "Transnational Adoption and Queer Diasporas," *Social Text 76* 21, no. 3 (fall 2003): 1–37.

5 Sigmund Freud, "Mourning and Melancholia" (1917), in *The Standard Edition of the Complete Psychological Works of Sigmund Freud*, vol. 14, trans. and ed. James Strachey et al. (London: Hogarth Press, 1957), 245.

6 See Kimberlyn Leary, "Racial Enactments in Dynamic Treatment," *Psychoanalytic Dialogues* 10, no. 4 (2000): 648.

7 This description of primary processes of splitting and idealization in Klein is drawn from David L. Eng, "Colonial Object Relations," *Social Text 126* 34, no. 1 (2016): 7.

8 Melanie Klein, "The Psycho-analytic Play Technique: Its History and Its Significance (1955), in *The Selected Melanie Klein*, ed. Juliet Mitchell (New York: Free Press, 1987), 48.

9 To return to a passage from Klein raised earlier in our analysis of Nelson: "In some patients who had turned away from their mother in dislike or hate, or used other mechanisms to get away from her, I have found that there existed in their minds nevertheless a beautiful picture of the mother, but one which was felt to be a *picture* of her only, not her real self. The real object was felt to be unattractive—really an injured, incurable and therefore dreaded person. The beautiful picture had been dissociated from the real object but had never been given up, and played a great part in the specific ways of their sublimations." Melanie Klein, "A Contribution to the Psychogenesis of Manic-Depressive States" (1935), in *The Selected Melanie Klein*, ed. Juliet Mitchell (New York: Free Press, 1987), 125; emphasis in original.

10 Kathleen Pogue White, "Surviving Hating and Being Hated: Some Personal Thoughts about Racism from a Psychoanalytic Perspective," *Contemporary Psychoanalysis* 38, no. 3 (2002): 403.

11 Peter Buckley, introduction to *Essential Papers on Object Relations*, ed. Peter Buckley (New York: New York University Press, 1986), xvii.

12 Freud, "Mourning and Melancholia," 251.

13   Klein, "Psychogenesis of Manic-Depressive States," 124.

14   Melanie Klein, "A Study of Envy and Gratitude" (1956), in *The Selected Melanie Klein*, ed. Juliet Mitchell (New York: Free Press, 1987), 217.

15   Klein, "Study of Envy and Gratitude," 217.

16   Klein, "Psychogenesis of Manic-Depressive States," 123.

17   Freud, "Mourning and Melancholia," 250.

18   Klein, "Psychogenesis of Manic-Depressive States," 131.

19   Klein, "Mourning and Its Relation to Manic-Depressive States" (1940), in *The Selected Melanie Klein*, ed. Juliet Mitchell (New York: Free Press, 1987), 173.

20   Klein, "Mourning and Its Relation to Manic-Depressive States," 173.

21   Donald Woods Winnicott, "Transitional Objects and Transitional Phenomena" (1951), in *Playing and Reality* (New York: Routledge, 1989), 3.

22   Winnicott, "Transitional Objects and Transitional Phenomena," 14–15.

23   Winnicott, "Transitional Objects and Transitional Phenomena," 10.

24   Winnicott, "Transitional Objects and Transitional Phenomena," 6.

25   Carol Long, "Transitioning Racialized Spaces," *Psychoanalysis, Culture, and Society* 16, no. 1 (2011): 50.

26   Leary, "Racial Enactments," 649.

27   Leary, "Racial Enactments," 649.

28   See Kimberlyn Leary, "Race, Self-Disclosure, and 'Forbidden Talk': Race and Ethnicity in Contemporary Clinical Practice," *Psychoanalytic Quarterly* 66 (1997): 163–89.

29   Long, "Transitioning Racialized Spaces," 67.

30   See Jessica Benjamin, "Beyond Doer and Done To: An Intersubjective View of Thirdness," *Psychoanalytic Quarterly* 73 (2004): 11.

31   Adam Phillips, *Winnicott* (Cambridge, MA: Harvard University Press, 1988), 114.

32   Long, "Transitioning Racialized Spaces," 51.

33   Long, "Transitioning Racialized Spaces," 67.

34   Winnicott, "Transitional Objects and Transitional Phenomena," 5.

35   Winnicott, "Transitional Objects and Transitional Phenomena," 13.

36   Donald Woods Winnicott, "Playing: A Theoretical Statement" (1968), in *Playing and Reality* (New York: Routledge, 1989), 38; emphasis in original removed.

37   Michelle E. Friedman, "When the Analyst Becomes Pregnant—Twice," *Psychoanalytic Inquiry* 13, no. 2 (1993): 226–39.

38   We borrow this formulation from Kaja Silverman, "Primal Siblings: George Baker in Conversation with Kaja Silverman," *Art Forum* (February 2010): 176–83.

39   Donald Woods Winnicott, "The Use of an Object and Relating through Identifications" (1969), in *Playing and Reality* (New York: Routledge, 1989), 87.

40   Winnicott, "Use of an Object," 89.

41   The notion of "positions" and the concept of "transitions" that we encounter in object relations—in contrast to Freudian theories of stages that are accom-

plished, lived through, and overcome—force our attention to the everyday mechanisms of psychic coping that patients repeatedly employ to negotiate the social realities and psychic pain of immigration, assimilation, and racialization. Like melancholia, positions and transitions do not have a temporal end. They are not stages to be mastered but are mechanisms fundamentally pertaining to psychic negotiation, adjustment, and coping.

42 Klein, "Study of Envy and Gratitude," 217.

43 Klein, "Study of Envy and Gratitude," 212.

44 Klein, "Study of Envy and Gratitude," 213.

45 We are indebted to Robert Diaz for raising this concept of envy and racial spoilage with us.

CHAPTER 3. RACIAL DISSOCIATION

1 This argument is borrowed from David L. Eng, *The Feeling of Kinship: Queer Liberalism and the Racialization of Intimacy* (Durham, NC: Duke University Press, 2010), ix-x.

2 The Immigration and Nationality Act of 1965 (Hart-Celler) abolished the earlier immigration quota system based on national origins, replacing it with a new system based on preferences. It favored the reunification of immigrant families and those with skilled, technical expertise. The act dramatically shifted patterns of immigration to the United States, spurring a "brain drain" of settlers from Asia, an area largely barred from immigration since the late nineteenth century. The act brought in large numbers of immigrants from both Asia and Latin America, resulting in the "browning" of the United States. See Sucheng Chan, *Asian Americans: An Interpretive History* (Boston: Twayne Publishing, 1991); and Mae Ngai, *Impossible Subjects: Illegal Aliens and the Making of Modern America* (Princeton, NJ: Princeton University Press, 2005).

3 David L. Eng and Shinhee Han, "Psychic Nowhere: Parachute Children, False Self, and the Politics of Attachment," paper delivered at the American Psychological Association Annual Meeting, Division 39, plenary session "Racism and Othering," Boston, MA), April 27, 2013.

4 The term "parachute children" (降落傘儿童)—and similar terms, such as "unaccompanied minors," "transnational students," and "early international students"—derives from two associated Cantonese neologisms: "astronaut families" (太空人) and "satellite people" (衛星人). Hong Kong journalists coined all three terms in the early 1990s to describe the contemporary dispersal of Chinese nuclear families across continents. "Astronaut families" describes the phenomenon of one spouse (usually the wife) who settles in a host country with the children, while the other spouse (usually the husband) continues working in Hong Kong, shuttling between both locations ("satellite people"). In Korea, "geese families" (기러기 가족) describes the phenomenon of mothers and children who settle in the West, with "goose dads" (기러기 아빠), "penguin

dads" (펭귄 아빠), or "eagle dads" (독수리 아빠) remaining in Korea. While goose dads fly in at set seasons (winter and summer breaks) to reunite with their families, penguin dads cannot afford family reunions, and eagle dads can afford to fly in anytime.

5 Boonsoon Byun, "South Korean High School Parachute Kids in Southern California: Academic, Psychological Adjustment and Identity Formation" (PhD diss., University of Southern California, Rossier School of Education, 2010), 2. Byun draws her statistics from figures provided by US Immigration and Customs Enforcement (US ICE). She writes, "Koreans holding active students visas comprised over 14.5 percent of the total student visa holders in the US. The number of students in grades 1–12 who sought educational visas increased from 7,944 in 2001 to 20,400 in 2005" ("South Korean High School Parachute Kids," 2).

6 Young-ee Cho, "The Diaspora of Korean Children: A Cross-Cultural Study of the Educational Crisis in Contemporary South Korea" (PhD diss., University of Montana, 2007), 7.

7 Byun, "South Korean High School Parachute Kids," 18. According to Huang et al., Asians now make up almost half of the streams of new settlers in the traditional migration receiving countries such as the United States, Canada, Australia, and New Zealand. See Shirlena Huang, Brenda S. A. Yeoh, and Theodora Lam, "Asian Transnational Families in Transition: The Liminality of Simultaneity," *International Migration* 46, no. 4 (2008): 3.

According to Hom, although "there are no official statistics on the number of parachute kids in the US, a 1990 study estimated that there were 30,000–40,000 Chinese children from Taiwan living in the United States without their parents." See Christy Ling Hom, "The Academic, Psychological, and Behavioral Adjustment of Chinese Parachute Kids" (PhD diss., University of Michigan, 2002), 6.

8 See also Cindy Chang and Howard Shyong, "Teens' Attack on Chinese Girl Draws Comparison to 'Lord of the Flies' from Judge," *Los Angeles Times*, July 2, 2015, http://www.latimes.com/local/california/la-me-chinese-bullying -20150702-story.html#page=1.

9 Byun, "South Korean High School Parachute Kids," 33.

10 See Brook Larmer, "The Parachute Generation," *New York Times Magazine*, February 5, 2017, https://www.nytimes.com/2017/02/02/magazine/the -parachute-generation.html.

11 Aihwa Ong, an early commentator on the phenomenon of parachute children, characterizes the networks and knowledge established by parachute children as an entrepreneurial strategy for expanding a family's field of economic operation, while acquiring "symbolic capital" in the West. See Aihwa Ong, *Flexible Citizenship: The Cultural Logics of Transnationality* (Durham, NC: Duke University Press, 1999).

12 Acceptance rates today at the most selective US universities hover between 5

and 10 percent, whereas at Peking University in China admissions are approximately .01 percent. See note 53 of the introduction in this book for statistics regarding the comparative university enrollments of Taiwan, Japan, Hong Kong, China, and the US.

13 In addition to Chang and Shyong, "Teens' Attack on Chinese Girl," see also Jiayang Fan, "The Golden Generation: Why China's Super-Rich Send Their Children Abroad," *New Yorker*, February 22, 2016, http://www.newyorker .com/magazine/2016/02/22/chinas-rich-kids-head-west.

14 Byun writes in the mode of model minority discourse, "Researchers and educators have likely paid scant attention to parachute kids because they do well academically and, therefore, do not draw attention to themselves" ("South Korean High School Parachute Kids," 50). Zhou observes that parachute children and immigrant children are "subject to similar demands and pressures imposed on them by their families, their American peers, and the host society." See Min Zhou, "'Parachute Kids' in Southern California: The Educational Experience of Chinese Children in Transnational Families," *Educational Policy* 12, no. 6 (November 1998): 682.

Newman and Newman write, "One might expect that being a parachute kid places a child at a very high risk. Parachute kids are separated from their parents at a relatively young age, without the social resources of family and community, in an ambiguous relationship with peers, and with intense pressures for academic success in a country where the language, values, and peer environment present significant challenges. Yet, the limited literature suggests that most parachute kids are successful in school, at least as successful as their peers who migrate to the US with their parents, and as well as American-born children of Asian descent. Overall, they do not have more emotional difficulties than their peers. Although they often do have conflicts around their relationship to family and their ethnic identification, parachute kids seem to manage these difficulties by demonstrating a high degree of flexibility and adaptive resilience"; Philip R. Newman and Barbara M. Newman, "Self-Socialization: A Case Study of a Parachute Child," *Adolescence* 44 (fall 2009): 535.

In contrast, Orellana et al. raise issues of unstable emotional and psychological adjustment. They write, "In making decisions about leaving kids, bringing them, or sending them back, adults are actively engaged in the process of 'developing' their children toward the goals and values they hold for them. Sometimes families may temporarily neglect the needs or presumed needs of their children (or, in the eyes of some observers, appear to be neglectful) in order to open up possibilities for their futures. Some transnational moves involve deliberate, long-term strategies; others represent forced choices based on limited options. Families who are pressed for household survival do not have the luxury to foreground a child's 'developmental needs.' Families that are divided across national borders, operating with minimal economic resources, do, however, make great sacrifices—including, perhaps, the loss of a certain quality in their own love for their children, and their children's love for them—in order to give their children opportunities, as parents told us, 'to come out ahead.'" Marjorie Faulstich Orellana, Barrie Thorne, Anna Chee, and Wan Shun Eva Lam, "Transnational Childhoods: The Participation of Children in Processes of Family Migration," *Social Problems* 48, no. 4 (November 2001): 587.

15 See Newman and Newman, "Self-Socialization," 523–37.

16 Hom, "Academic, Psychological, and Behavioral Adjustment," 17.

17 See W. E. B. Du Bois, *The Souls of Black Folk* (Chicago, IL: A. C. McClurg, 1903), 1. Du Bois writes, "Between me and the other world there is ever an unasked question: unasked by some through feelings of delicacy; by others through the difficulty of rightly framing it. All, nevertheless, flutter round it. They approach me in a half-hesitant sort of way, eye me curiously or compassionately, and then, instead of saying directly, How does it feel to be a problem? they say, I know an excellent colored man in my town; or, I fought at Mechanicsville; or, Do not these Southern outrages make your blood boil? At these I smile, or am interested, or reduce the boiling to a simmer, as the occasion may require. To the real question, How does it feel to be a problem? I answer seldom a word."

18 See Vijay Prashad, *Karma of Brown Folk* (Minneapolis: University of Minnesota Press, 2000), 6. Prashad writes, "Meanwhile white America can take its seat, comfortable in its liberal principles, surrounded by state-selected Asians, certain that the culpability for black poverty and oppression must be laid at the door of black America. How does it feel to be a solution?" See also Robert G. Lee, "The Cold War Origins of the Model Minority," in *Orientals: Asian Americans in Popular Culture* (Philadelphia, PA: Temple University Press, 1999), 145–79.

19 D. W. Winnicott, "Ego Distortion in Terms of True and False Self" (1960), in *The Maturational Process and the Facilitating Environment: Studies in the Theory of Emotional Development* (New York: International Universities Press, 1965). Winnicott observes, "The best example I can give is that of a middle-aged woman who had a very successful False Self but who had the feeling all her life that she had not started to exist, and that she had always been looking for a means of getting to her True Self" (142).

20 Winnicott, "Ego Distortion," 145.

21 Winnicott, "Ego Distortion," 146. See also D. W. Winnicott, "The Use of an Object and Relating through Identifications" (1969), in *Playing and Reality* (New York: Brunner-Routledge, 1989), 86–94.

22 Winnicott, "Ego Distortion," 146; emphasis in original.

23 Winnicott, "Ego Distortion," 147.

24 See Dorothy M. Jones, "Bulimia: A False Self Identity," *Clinical Social Work Journal* 13, no. 4 (winter 1985): 305–16.

25 Winnicott, "Ego Distortion," 151. In this context, Bromberg writes, "One exam-

ple of this is those individuals whose characteristically easy-going manner and reliability are so congenial to the analyst's feeling of well-being that the analyst doesn't notice his own complicity in failing to address a stalemate treatment"; Philip M. Bromberg, *Standing in the Spaces: Essays on Clinical Process, Trauma, and Dissociation* (New York: Psychology Press, 2001), 125.

26 Winnicott notes that one of the hardest personality types to work with in the space of the clinic is false self, as you are not treating the real patient but the false self who presents him or herself to the world. That is, in such circumstances, "the fact must be recognized that the analyst can only talk to the False Self of the patient about the patient's True Self" ("Ego Distortion," 151).

27 Bromberg, *Standing in the Spaces*, 7.

28 Bromberg, *Standing in the Spaces*, 186.

29 Bromberg, *Standing in the Spaces*, 273.

30 Bromberg, *Standing in the Spaces*, 274.

31 Bromberg, *Standing in the Spaces*, 186.

32 Bromberg, *Standing in the Spaces*, 182.

33 D. W. Winnicott, "Playing: A Theoretical Statement," in *Playing and Reality* (New York: Brunner-Routledge, 1989), 38.

34 Winnicott, "Ego Distortion," 143.

35 Winnicott, "Ego Distortion," 142.

36 Winnicott is careful to emphasize that the true self is not a hidden or essential identity masked behind gestures of compliance to the Other's demands. He writes, "There is but little point in formulating a True Self idea except for the purpose of trying to understand the False Self, because it does no more than collect together details of the experience of aliveness" ("Ego Distortion," 148).

37 Winnicott writes, "The world may observe academic success of a high degree, and may find it hard to believe in the very real distress of the individual concerned, who feels 'phoney' the more he or she is successful" ("Ego Distortion," 144).

38 Winnicott, "Ego Distortion," 144.

39 Winnicott, "Ego Distortion," 150.

40 See Antonio Viego, *Dead Subjects: Toward a Politics of Loss in Latino Studies* (Durham, NC: Duke University Press, 2007).

41 See Mimi Thi Nguyen, *The Gift of Freedom: War, Debt, and Other Refugee Passages* (Durham, NC: Duke University Press, 2012).

42 Winnicott, "Ego Distortion," 144.

43 Frantz Fanon, *Black Skin, White Mask*, trans. Charles Lam Markmann (1952; repr., New York: Grove, 1963), 110.

44 Michelle Stephens, "The Affective Difference: Reading Blackness through Psychoanalysis and Performance," lecture at University of Pennsylvania, Department of English Lecture Series, November 20, 2014.

45 See Roberto A. Gonzales, "Learning to Be Illegal: Undocumented Youth and

Shifting Legal Contexts in the Transition to Adulthood," *American Sociological Review* 76.4 (2011): 602–19.

46 Immigrant kids and parents often looked down on parachute children: "'Because we live without our parents' supervision, they think we are doing something bad. They do not want their children to play with us.' Daniel's position of feeling caught between two nations, educational systems, and ways of growing up, conveys one of the risks of transnational childhoods—feeling marginal in both places" (Orellana et al., "Transnational Childhoods," 583).

47 Seen as academic failures in Korea, they are scorned in their homeland. In the United States, they are often shunned by Asian American communities who see them as spoiled children of the rich, who are irresponsible and behave poorly without proper parental supervision. Many immigrant parents do not want their kids associating with parachute children, fearing such negative influences. Unlike most Asian immigrant children who experience high levels of parental involvement, parachute children experience comparatively little. Like many Asian immigrant children, they are generally ignored or scorned by dominant US society, as well.

48 Michelle Stephens, "The Affective Difference: Reading Blackness Through Psychoanalysis and Performance," lecture at University of Pennsylvania, Department of English Lecture Series, November 20, 2014.

49 Stephens, "Affective Difference."

50 John Bowlby, "The Making and Breaking of Affectional Bonds," *British Journal of Psychiatry* 130, no. 3 (1977): 201.

51 Winnicott, "Ego Distortion," 151.

52 Bowlby, "Making and Breaking of Affectional Bonds," 207–8.

53 Bromberg, *Standing in the Spaces*, 173.

54 Kathleen Pogue White, "Surviving Hating and Being Hated: Some Personal Thoughts about Racism from a Psychoanalytic Perspective," *Contemporary Psychoanalysis* 38 (2002): 406.

55 Bowlby, "Making and Breaking of Affectional Bonds," 203.

CHAPTER 4. (GAY) PANIC ATTACK

1 Suffice it to say, while many of our students and patients constitute the United States, and the West more generally, as a site of freedom, the meaning of living free and independently differs greatly according to each person. Some consider a dense network of family and kinship ties at home, as well as their implicit social obligations and implications, more easily managed from abroad. Others who come from religious backgrounds immigrate to avoid sexual stigma or arranged marriages. Others are sent away because parents are ashamed of their "sexual flamboyance." Yet, in other cases, the issue of sexual freedom is not connected at all to immigration or to the West. To the contrary, home is

constituted as a safe and nurturing sexual space, and migration is precisely the mechanism by which this safety is rendered precarious.

The politics of homosexuality and coming out as a story of civilization, progress, and development in the West is historically and theoretically complex. Recent publications in anthropology and cultural studies have done much to analyze the politics of sexual comparison. For instance, see Gayatri Gopinath, *Impossible Desires: Queer Diasporas and South Asian Public Cultures* (Durham, NC: Duke University Press, 2005); Petrus Liu, *Queer Marxism in Two Chinas* (Durham, NC: Duke University Press, 2015); Martin Manalansan, IV, *Global Divas: Filipino Gay Men in the Diaspora* (Durham, NC: Duke University Press, 2003); and Lisa Rofel, *Desiring China: Experiments in Neoliberalism, Sexuality, and Public Culture* (Durham, NC: Duke University Press, 2007).

2 See David L. Eng, *Racial Castration: Managing Masculinity in Asian America* (Durham, NC: Duke University Press, 2001); and Shinhee Han, "Gay identity disclosure to parents by Asian American gay men," PhD diss., New York University School of Social Work, 2001.

3 See David L. Eng, *The Feeling of Kinship: Queer Liberalism and the Racialization of Intimacy* (Durham, NC: Duke University Press, 2010). See also Lisa Duggan, *The Twilight of Equality? Neoliberalism, Cultural Politics, and the Attack on Democracy* (Boston: Beacon Books, 2003).

4 See Shinhee Han, "Gay identity disclosure to parents."

5 Ang Lee, dir. *The Wedding Banquet* (喜宴), Ang Lee Productions, 1993.

6 Such an outcome is not uncommon for gay men in general. See Ken Corbett, *Boyhoods: Rethinking Masculinities* (New Haven, CT: Yale University Press, 2009). Writing in the context of the feminine son, Corbett observes, "The creation of this transforming nexus is undertaken with both parents, but it may have a particular significance for mothers and their feminine sons. In direct contrast to Richard Green's suggestion that feminine boys do not need their mothers, it has been my overwhelming clinical experience that those boys who can, along with their mothers, create a holding environment fare much better as they move into the outside world" (*Boyhoods*, 114).

7 Eng had described this phenomenon as "racial castration." See Eng, *Racial Castration*.

8 Kimberlé Crenshaw, "Mapping the Margins: Intersectionality, Identity Politics, and Violence against Women of Color," *Stanford Law Review* 43 (1990–91): 1252.

9 Donald Woods Winnicott, "Ego Distortion in Terms of True and False Self" (1960), in *The Maturational Process and the Facilitating Environment: Studies in the Theory of Emotional Development* (New York: International Universities Press, 1965), 144.

10 Winnicott, "Ego Distortion," 148.

11 Melanie Abeygunawardana, "(Gay)(Asian)(Human)," response paper for David Eng's "Psychoanalysis and Critical Race Theory" graduate seminar, Depart-

ment of English, University of Pennsylvania, spring 2017; emphasis in original. We thank Abeygunawardana for allowing us to cite her unpublished work. We also thank the other students in the seminar for their thoughts, feedback, and insight on this case history.

12 Neil Gotanda, "A Critique of 'Our Constitution Is Color-Blind,'" *Stanford Law Review* 44, no. 1 (November 1991): 5.

13 See Rachel Moran, *Interracial Intimacy: The Regulation of Race and Romance* (Chicago, IL: University of Chicago Press, 2001).

14 Jay Caspian Kang, "What a Fraternity Hazing Death Revealed about the Painful Search for Asian-American Identity," *New York Times Magazine*, August 9, 2017.

15 Freud, "The Unconscious" (1915), in *The Standard Edition of the Complete Psychological Works of Sigmund Freud,* trans. and ed. James Strachey et al., vol. 14 (London: Hogarth, 1957), 175–76.

16 Jean Laplanche, *Essays on Otherness,* ed. John Fletcher (New York: Routledge, 1999), 120.

17 See Pamela Kyle Crossley, *A Translucent Mirror: History and Identity in Qing Imperial Ideology* (Berkeley: University of California Press, 2002); Frank Dikötter, *This Discourse of Race in Modern China* (Stanford: Stanford University Press, 1992); Mark C. Elliott, *The Manchu Way: The Eight Banners and Ethnic Identity in Late Imperial China* (Stanford: Stanford University Press, 2001); Dru C. Gladney, *Dislocating China: Muslims, Minorities, and Other Subaltern Subjects* (Chicago: University of Chicago, 2004); and Thomas S. Mullaney, *Coming to Terms with the Nation: Ethnic Classification in Modern China* (Berkeley: University of California Press, 2011).

18 Eve Kosofsky Sedgwick, *Between Men: English Literature and Male Homosocial Desire* (New York: Columbia University Press, 1985), 20.

19 Sigmund Freud, "Psycho-Analytic Notes on an Autobiographical Account of a Case of Paranoia" (1911), in *The Standard Edition of the Complete Psychological Works of Sigmund Freud,* trans. and ed. James Strachey et al., vol. 12 (London: Hogarth, 1957), 49.

20 Freud, "Psycho-Analytic Notes," 71; emphasis in orignal deleted.

21 We thank Michelle Stephens for this elegant formulation.

22 Angela Davis, "Interview with Lisa Lowe, Angela Davis: Reflections on Race, Class, and Gender in the USA," in *The Politics of Culture in the Shadow of Capital,* edited by Lisa Lowe and David Lloyd (Durham, NC: Duke University Press, 1997), 303-23. Davis writes, "A woman of color formation might decide to work around immigration issues. This political commitment is not based on the specific histories of racialized communities or its constituent members, but rather constructs an agenda agreed upon by all who are a part of it. In my opinion, the most exciting potential of women of color formations resides in the possibility of politicizing this identity—basing the identity on politics rather than the politics on identity" (318).

23 Freud, "Psycho-Analytic Notes," 71.

24 See Toni Morrison, *The Bluest Eye* (New York: Holt, Rinehart and Winston, 1970), 15–16.

25 The arguments in this section are borrowed from Eng, *Feeling of Kinship*, "Introduction," 1–22.

26 Cheryl I. Harris, "Whiteness as Property," *Harvard Law Review* 106, no. 8 (June 1993): 1714.

27 Jodi Melamed, "The Spirit of Neoliberalism: From Racial Liberalism to Neoliberal Multiculturalism," *Social Text* 24, no. 4 (2006): 3.

28 See Anne Anlin Cheng, "American Racial Grief, a Reprisal," *Huffington Post*, March 16, 2016, accessed June 3, 2016, http://www.huffingtonpost.com/anne-a -cheng/american-racial-grief-a-r_b_9467348.html.

29 Freud, "Unconscious," 190–91.

EPILOGUE

1 See Stefano Harney and Fred Moten, *The Undercommons: Fugitive Planning and Black Study* (New York: Autonomedia, 2013).

2 The origins of college counseling date back to the 1930s, with a focus on general guidance and career counseling. The clinic's historical transformation in the university over the decades to its current array of mental health services encompassing individual counseling, crisis management, psychopharmacological consultations, support groups, and campus outreach programs is notable.

3 A 2014 review of college counseling services' directors survey of 275 colleges and universities showed that 87 percent of the directors are white while, seven percent are African American, three percent Latino, and two percent Asian Americans. Moreover, the gender of the university clinic staff was seventy percent female over thirty percent male. The staff racial diversity category included over seventy percent white, ten percent African American, ten percent Latino, and less than five percent Asian American. Over ninety percent of the staff's sexual orientation reported as heterosexual. See Alison M. LaFollette, "The Evolution of University Counseling: From Educational Guidance to Multicultural Competence, Severe Mental Illnesses and Crisis Planning," *Graduate Journal of Counseling Psychology* 1.2 (Spring 2009): 113–20. See also www.collegecounseling.org.

4 Carol Long, "Transitioning Racialized Spaces." *Psychoanalysis, Culture and Society* 16, no. 1 (2011): 49–70.

5 Kimberlyn Leary, "Racial Enactments in Dynamic Treatment," *Psychoanalytic Dialogues* 10, no. 4 (2000): 641, 647.

6 Donald Woods Winnicott, *The Maturation Process and the Facilitating Environment* (New York: International Universities Press, 1965).

BIBLIOGRAPHY

Althusser, Louis. "Ideology and Ideological State Apparatuses (Notes towards an Investigation)." In *Lenin and Philosophy and Other Essays*, edited by B. Brewster, 127–86. New York: Monthly Review Press, 1971.

Altman, Neil. "Black and White Thinking: A Psychoanalyst Reconsiders Race." *Psychoanalytic Dialogues* 10 (2000): 589–605.

Baucom, Ian. *Specters of the Atlantic: Finance Capital, Slavery, and the Philosophy of History*. Durham, NC: Duke University Press, 2005.

Benjamin, Jessica. "Beyond Doer and Done To: An Intersubjective View of Thirdness." *Psychoanalytic Quarterly* 73 (2004): 5–46.

Benjamin, Jessica. *The Shadow of the Other: Intersubjectivity and Gender in Psychoanalysis*. New York: Routledge, 1998.

Bergner, Gwen. *Taboo Subjects: Race, Sex, and Psychoanalysis*. Minneapolis: University of Minnesota Press, 1997.

Bhabha, Homi K. "Of Mimicry and Man: The Ambivalence of Colonial Discourse." *October* 28 (spring 1984): 125–33.

Bhabha, Homi K. "The Other Question: Stereotype, Discrimination, and the Discourse of Colonialism." 1983. In *The Location of Culture*, 66–84. London: Routledge, 1994.

Blackstone, William. *Commentaries on the Laws of England, Book II: Of the Rights of Things*. Oxford: Oxford University Press, 2016.

Bollas, Christopher. *The Shadow of the Object: Psychoanalysis of the Unthought*. New York: Columbia University Press, 1987.

Bowlby, John. "The Making and Breaking of Affectional Bonds." *British Journal of Psychiatry* 130, no. 3 (1977): 201–10.

Bromberg, Philip M. *Standing in the Spaces: Essays on Clinical Process, Trauma, and Dissociation*, New York: Psychology Press, 2001.

Brown, Wendy. *States of Injury: Power and Freedom in Late Modernity*. Princeton, NJ: Princeton University Press, 1995.

Buckley, Peter. Introduction to *Essential Papers on Object Relations*, edited by Peter Buckley, xi–xxv. New York: New York University Press, 1986.

Bullard, Alice. "L'Oedipe Africain: A Retrospective." *Transcultural Psychiatry* 42, no. 2 (2005): 171–203.

Butler, Judith. *The Psychic Life of Power: Theories in Subjection.* Stanford, CA: Stanford University Press, 1997.

Byun, Boonsoon. "South Korean High School Parachute Kids in Southern California: Academic, Psychological Adjustment and Identity Formation." PhD diss., University of Southern California Rossier School of Education, 2010.

Chan, Sucheng. *Asian Americans: An Interpretive History.* Boston: Twayne Publishing, 1991.

Chan, Sucheng, ed. *Entry Denied: Exclusion and the Chinese Community in America, 1882–1943.* Philadelphia, PA: Temple University Press, 1991.

Chang, Cindy, and Howard Shyong. "Teens' Attack on Chinese Girl Draws Comparison to 'Lord of the Flies' from Judge." *Los Angeles Times,* July 2, 2015, http://www.latimes.com/local/california/la-me-chinese-bullying -20150702-story.html#page=1.

Cheng, Anne Anlin. "American Racial Grief, a Reprisal." *Huffington Post,* March 16, 2016. Accessed June 3, 2016. http://www.huffingtonpost.com/anne-a -cheng/american-racial-grief-a-r_b_9467348.html.

Cheng, Anne Anlin. *The Melancholy of Race: Psychoanalysis, Assimilation, and Hidden Grief.* New York: Oxford University Press, 2001.

Cheng, Anne Anlin. "Passing, Natural Selection, and Love's Failure: Ethics of Survival from Chang-rae Lee to Jacques Lacan." *American Literary History* 17, no. 3 (fall 2005): 553–74.

Chin, Frank. *The Chinaman Pacific and Frisco R. R. Co.* Minneapolis, MN: Coffee House Press, 1988.

Cho, Young-ee. "The Diaspora of Korean Children: A Cross-Cultural Study of the Educational Crisis in Contemporary South Korea." PhD diss., University of Montana, 2007.

Corbett, Ken. *Boyhoods: Rethinking Masculinities.* New Haven, CT: Yale University Press, 2009.

Craps, Stef. *Postcolonial Witnessing: Trauma Out of Bounds.* London: Palgrave Macmillan, 2013.

Crimp, Douglas. "Mourning and Militancy." *October* 51 (1989): 3–18.

Crossley, Pamela Kyle. *A Translucent Mirror: History and Identity in Qing Imperial Ideology* (Berkeley: University of California Press, 2002).

Dalal, Farhad. "Racism: Processes of Detachment, Dehumanization, and Hatred." *Psychoanalytic Quarterly* 75 (2006): 131–61.

Davis, Adrienne D. "The Private Law of Race and Sex: An Antebellum Perspective." *Stanford Law Review* 51 (1998–99): 221–88.

Deleuze, Gilles, and Félix Guattari. *Anti-Oedipus: Capitalism and Schizophrenia.* Minneapolis: University of Minnesota Press, 1983.

Dikötter, Frank. *This Discourse of Race in Modern China* (Stanford: Stanford University Press, 1992).

Du Bois, W. E. B. *The Souls of Black Folk.* Chicago, IL: A. C. McClurg, 1903.

Duggan, Lisa. *The Twilight of Equality? Neoliberalism, Cultural Politics, and the Attack on Democracy.* Boston: Beacon Books, 2003.

Elliott, Mark C. *The Manchu Way: The Eight Banners and Ethnic Identity in Late Imperial China* (Stanford: Stanford University Press, 2001).

Eng, David L. "Colonial Object Relations." *Social Text 126* 34, no. 1 (2016): 1–19.

Eng, David L. *The Feeling of Kinship: Queer Liberalism and the Racialization of Intimacy.* Durham, NC: Duke University Press, 2010.

Eng, David L. *Racial Castration: Managing Masculinity in Asian America.* Durham, NC: Duke University Press, 2001.

Eng, David L. "Transnational Adoption and Queer Diasporas." *Social Text 76* 21, no. 3 (fall 2003): 1–37.

Eng, David L., and Shinhee Han. "Desegregating Love: Transnational Adoption, Racial Reparation, and Racial Transitional Objects." *Studies in Gender and Sexuality: Psychoanalysis, Cultural Studies, Treatment, Research* 7, no. 2 (2006): 141–72.

Eng, David L., and Shinhee Han. "A Dialogue on Racial Melancholia." *Psychoanalytic Dialogues* 10, no. 4 (2000): 667–700.

Fairbairn, William Ronald Dodds. *An Object-Relations Theory of the Personality.* New York: Basic Books, 1954.

Fan, Jiayang. "The Golden Generation: Why China's Super-Rich Send Their Children Abroad." *New Yorker*, February 22, 2016. http://www.newyorker.com/magazine/2016/02/22/chinas-rich-kids-head-west.

Fanon, Frantz. *Black Skin, White Mask.* Translated by Charles Lam Markmann. 1952. Reprint, New York: Grove, 1963.

Forbes, Jack D. *Africans and Native Americans: The Language of Race and the Evolution of Red-Black Peoples.* Urbana: University of Illinois, 1993.

Foucault, Michel. *An Introduction.* Vol. 1 of *The History of Sexuality.* New York: Vintage, 1978.

Freud, Sigmund. "Creative Writers and Day-Dreaming." 1908. In *The Standard Edition of the Complete Psychological Works of Sigmund Freud*, translated and edited by James Strachey et al., 141–54. Vol. 9. London: Hogarth, 1957.

Freud, Sigmund. "Fetishism." 1927. In *The Standard Edition of the Complete Psychological Works of Sigmund Freud*, translated and edited by James Strachey et al., 152–57, Vol. 21. London: Hogarth, 1957.

Freud, Sigmund. "Group Psychology and the Analysis of the Ego." 1921. In *The Standard Edition of the Complete Psychological Works of Sigmund Freud*, translated and edited by James Strachey et al. 69–143. Vol. 18. London: Hogarth Press, 1955.

Freud, Sigmund. "Mourning and Melancholia." 1917. In *The Standard Edition of the Complete Psychological Works of Sigmund Freud*, translated and edited by James Strachey et al., 243–58. Vol. 14. London: Hogarth, 1957.

Freud, Sigmund. "On Narcissism." 1914. In *The Standard Edition of the Complete Psychological Works of Sigmund Freud,* translated and edited by James Strachey et al., 73–102. Vol. 14. London, Hogarth Press, 1957.

Freud, Sigmund. "Splitting of the Ego in the Process of Defence." 1938. In *The Standard Edition of the Complete Psychological Works of Sigmund Freud,* translated and edited by James Strachey et al., 275–78. Vol. 23. London: Hogarth Press, 1964.

Freud, Sigmund. "The Uncanny." 1919. In *The Standard Edition of the Complete Psychological Works of Sigmund Freud,* translated and edited by James Strachey et al., 217–48. Vol. 17. London: Hogarth Press, 1955.

Freud, Sigmund. "The Unconscious." 1915. In *The Standard Edition of the Complete Psychological Works of Sigmund Freud,* translated and edited by James Strachey et al., 159–215. Vol. 14. London: Hogarth, 1957.

Friedman, Michelle E. "When the Analyst Becomes Pregnant—Twice." *Psychoanalytic Inquiry* 13, no. 2 (1993): 226–39.

Fujitani, Takashi. *Race for Empire: Koreans as Japanese and Japanese as Americans during World War II.* Berkeley: University of California Press, 2013.

Gladney, Dru C. *Dislocating China: Muslims, Minorities, and Other Subaltern Subjects.* Chicago, IL: University of Chicago Press, 2004.

Gonzales, Roberto A. "Learning to Be Illegal: Undocumented Youth and Shifting Legal Contexts in the Transition to Adulthood." *American Sociological Review* 76, no. 4 (2011): 602–19.

Gopinath, Gayatri. *Impossible Desires: Queer Diasporas and South Asian Public Cultures.* Durham, NC: Duke University Press, 2005.

Gotanda, Neil. "A Critique of 'Our Constitution Is Color-Blind.'" *Stanford Law Review* 44, no. 1 (November 1991): 1–68.

Greene, Beverly. "African American Lesbians and Bisexual Women in Feminist-Psychodynamic Psychotherapies: Surviving and Thriving between a Rock and a Hard Place." In *Psychotherapy with African-American Women: Innovations in Psychodynamic Perspectives and Practices,* edited by Leslie C. Jackson and Beverly Greene, 82–125. New York: Guilford Press, 2000.

Grey, Thomas C. "The Disintegration of Property." *Nomos XII* (1980): 69–85.

Han, Shinhee. "Gay Identity Disclosure to Parents by Asian American Gay Men," PhD diss., New York University School of Social Work, 2001.

Harbison, John S. "Hohfeld and Herefords: The Concept of Property and the Law of the Range." *New Mexico Law Review* 22 (1992): 459–99.

Harney, Stefano, and Fred Moten. *The Undercommons: Fugitive Planning and Black Study.* New York: Autonomedia, 2013.

Harris, Cheryl I. "Whiteness as Property." *Harvard Law Review* 106, no. 8 (June 1993): 1709–91.

Hing, Bill Ong. *Making and Remaking Asian American through Immigration Policy, 1850–1990.* Stanford, CA: Stanford University Press, 1993.

Hohfeld, Wesley. "Faulty Analysis in Easement and License Cases." *Yale Law Journal* 27 (1917): 66–101.

Hohfeld, Wesley. "Fundamental Legal Conceptions as Applied in Judicial Reasoning." *Yale Law Journal* 26 (1917): 710–70.

Hohfeld, Wesley. "Some Fundamental Legal Conceptions as Applied in Judicial Reasoning." *Yale Law Journal* 23 (1913): 16–59.

Holmes, Dorothy E. "The Wrecking Effects of Race and Social Class on Self and Success." *Psychoanalytic Quarterly* 75 (2006): 215–35.

Hom, Christy Ling. "The Academic, Psychological, and Behavioral Adjustment of Chinese Parachute Kids." PhD diss., University of Michigan, 2002.

Huang, Shirlena, Brenda S. A. Yeoh, and Theodora Lam. "Asian Transnational Families in Transition: The Liminality of Simultaneity." *International Migration* 46, no. 4 (2008): 3.

Huntington, Samuel P. *The Clash of Civilizations and the Remaking of World Order.* New York: Simon and Schuster, 1996.

Jen, Gish. *Typical American.* Boston: Houghton Mifflin, 1991.

Jones, Dorothy M. "Bulimia: A False Self Identity." *Clinical Social Work Journal* 13, no. 4 (winter 1985): 305–16.

Kazanjian, David. "'When They Come Here They Feal So Free': Race and Early American Studies." *Early American Literature* 41, no. 2 (June 2006): 329–37.

Khanna, Ranjana. *Dark Continents: Psychoanalysis and Colonialism.* Durham, NC: Duke University Press, 2003.

Kingston, Maxine Hong. *China Men.* 1980. Reprint, New York: Vintage Books, 1989.

Kingston, Maxine Hong. *The Woman Warrior: Memoirs of a Girlhood among Ghosts.* 1976. Reprint, New York: Vintage Books, 1989.

Klein, Melanie. "A Contribution to the Psychogenesis of Manic-Depressive States." 1935. In *The Selected Melanie Klein,* edited by Juliet Mitchell, 116–45. New York: Free Press, 1987.

Klein, Melanie. "Mourning and Its Relation to Manic-Depressive States." 1940. In *The Selected Melanie Klein,* edited by Juliet Mitchell, 146–74. New York: Free Press, 1987.

Klein, Melanie. "The Psycho-analytic Play Technique: Its History and Its Significance." 1955. In *The Selected Melanie Klein,* edited by Juliet Mitchell, 35–54. New York: The Free Press, 1987.

Klein, Melanie. "A Study of Envy and Gratitude." 1956. In *The Selected Melanie Klein,* edited by Juliet Mitchell, 211–29. New York: Free Press, 1987.

Kristeva, Julia. *Desire in Language: A Semiotic Approach to Literature and Art.* New York: Columbia University Press, 1980.

Lacan, Jacques. *The Seminar of Jacques Lacan, Book II: The Ego in Freud's Theory and in the Technique of Psychoanalysis, 1954–1955.* New York: Norton, 1991.

LaFollette, Alison M. "The Evolution of University Counseling: From Educational Guidance to Multicultural Competence, Severe Mental Illnesses and Crisis Planning." *Graduate Journal of Counseling Psychology* 1, no. 2 (spring 2009): 113–20.

Lane, Christopher J., ed. *The Psychoanalysis of Race*. New York: Columbia University Press, 1998.

Laplanche, Jean. *Essays on Otherness*. Edited by John Fletcher. New York: Routledge, 1999.

Law-Yone, Wendy. *The Coffin Tree*. 1983. Reprint, Boston: Beacon Press, 1987.

Layton, Lynne. "Racial Identities, Racial Enactments, and Normative Unconscious Processes." *Psychoanalytic Quarterly* 75 (2006): 237–69.

Leary, Kimberlyn. "Race as an Adaptive Challenge: Working with Diversity in the Clinical Consulting Room." *Psychoanalytic Psychology* 29, no. 3 (2012): 279–91.

Leary, Kimberlyn. "Race, Self-Disclosure, and 'Forbidden Talk': Race and Ethnicity in Contemporary Clinical Practice." *Psychoanalytic Quarterly* 66 (1997): 163–89.

Leary, Kimberlyn. "Racial Enactments in Dynamic Treatment." *Psychoanalytic Dialogues* 10, no. 4 (2000): 639–53.

Leary, Kimberlyn. "Racial Insult and Repair." *Psychoanalytic Dialogues* 17, no. 4 (2007): 539–49.

Lee, Ang, dir. *The Wedding Banquet* (喜宴). Ang Lee Productions, 1993.

Lee, Robert G. "The Cold War Origins of the Model Minority." In *Orientals: Asian Americans in Popular Culture*, 145–79. Philadelphia, PA: Temple University Press, 1999.

Liu, Petrus. *Queer Marxism in Two Chinas*. Durham, NC: Duke University Press, 2015.

Long, Carol. "Transitioning Racialized Spaces." *Psychoanalysis, Culture and Society* 16, no. 1 (2011): 49–70.

Loomba, Ania. "Race and the Possibilities of Comparative Critique." *New Literary History* 40 (2009): 501–22.

Lowe, Lisa. *Immigrant Acts: On Asian American Cultural Politics*. Durham, NC: Duke University Press, 1996.

Lowe, Lisa. "The Intimacies of Four Continents." In *Haunted by Empire: Geographies of Intimacy in North American History*, edited by Ann Laura Stoler, 191–212. Durham, NC: Duke University Press, 2006.

Manalansan, Martin, IV. *Global Divas: Filipino Gay Men in the Diaspora*. Durham, NC: Duke University Press, 2003.

Martínez, María Elena. "The Language, Genealogy, and Classification of 'Race' in Colonial Mexico." In *Race and Classification: The Case of Mexican America*, edited by Ilona Katzew and Susan Deans-Smith, 25–42. Stanford, CA: Stanford University Press, 2009.

Marx, Karl. *A Critique of Political Economy: Part 2*. Vol. 1 of *Capital*. New York: Penguin, 1992.

Matsuda, Mari J. "We Will Not Be Used: Are Asian Americans the Racial Bour-geoisie?" In *Where Is Your Body? And Other Essays on Race, Gender, and the Law*, 149–59. Boston: Beacon Press, 1996.

Melamed, Jodi. "The Spirit of Neoliberalism: From Racial Liberalism to Neo-liberal Multiculturalism." *Social Text* 24, no. 4 (2006): 1–24.

Memmi, Albert. *The Colonizer and the Colonized*. 1957. Reprint, New York: Orion Press, 1965.

Memmi, Albert. *Dependence: A Sketch for a Portrait of the Dependent*, translated by Philip A. Facey. 1979. Reprint Boston: Beacon Press, 1984.

Moran, Rachel. *Interracial Intimacy: The Regulation of Race and Romance*. Chi-cago, IL: University of Chicago Press, 2001.

Morrison, Toni. *The Bluest Eye*. New York: Holt, Rinehart and Winston, 1970.

Morrison, Toni. "Unspeakable Things Unspoken: The Afro-American Presence in American Literature." *Michigan Quarterly Review* 28, no. 1 (1989): 11.

Moynihan, Daniel Patrick. *The Negro Family: The Case for National Action*. Washington, DC: Office of Policy Planning and Research, United States Department of Labor, 1965.

Mullaney, Thomas S. *Coming to Terms with the Nation: Ethnic Classification in Modern China* (Berkeley: University of California Press, 2011).

Muñoz, José Esteban. *Disidentifications: Queers of Color and the Performance of Politics*. Minneapolis: University of Minnesota Press, 1999.

Musser, Amber Jamilla. *Sensational Flesh: Race, Power, and Masochism*. New York: New York University Press, 2014.

Myrdal, Gunnar. Assisted by Richard Sterner and Arnold Rose. *An American Dilemma: The Negro Problem and Modern Democracy*. New York: Harper and Brothers, 1944.

Newman, Philip R., and Barbara M. Newman. "Self-Socialization: A Case Study of a Parachute Child." *Adolescence* 44 (fall 2009): 523–37.

Ng, Fae Myenne. *Bone*. New York: Hyperion 1993.

Ngai, Mae. *Impossible Subjects: Illegal Aliens and the Making of Modern America*. Princeton, NJ: Princeton University Press, 2004.

Ong, Aihwa. *Flexible Citizenship: The Cultural Logics of Transnationality*. Dur-ham, NC: Duke University Press, 1999.

Orellana, Marjorie Faulstich, Barrie Thorne, Anna Chee, and Wan Shun Eva Lam. "Transnational Childhoods: The Participation of Children in Pro-cesses of Family Migration." *Social Problems* 48, no. 4 (November 2001): 587.

Phillips, Adam. *Winnicott*. Cambridge, MA: Harvard University Press, 1988.

Prashad, Vijay. *Karma of Brown Folk*. Minneapolis: University of Minnesota Press, 2000.

Robinson, Cedric J. *Black Marxism: The Making of the Black Radical Tradition*. Chapel Hill: University of North Carolina Press, 2000.

Roediger, David R. *The Wages of Whiteness: Race and the Making of the American Working Class*. New York: Verso, 1991.

Rofel, Lisa. *Desiring China: Experiments in Neoliberalism, Sexuality, and Public Culture*. Durham, NC: Duke University Press, 2007.

Rothberg, Michael. *Multidirectional Memory: Remembering the Holocaust in the Age of Decolonization*. Stanford, CA: Stanford University Press, 2009.

Ruskola, Teemu. *Legal Orientalism: China, the United States, and Modern Law*. Cambridge, MA: Harvard University Press, 2013.

Saxton, Alexander. "Introduction: Historical Explanations of Racial Inequality." In *The Rise and Fall of the White Republic: Class Politics and Mass Culture in Nineteenth-Century America*, 1–20. New York: Verso, 1990.

Senna, Danzy. *Caucasia*. New York: Riverhead, 1998.

Seshadri-Crooks, Kalpana. *Desiring Whiteness: A Lacanian Analysis of Race*. New York: Routledge, 2000.

Simpson, Caroline Chung. *An Absent Presence: Japanese Americans in Postwar American Culture, 1945–1960*. Durham, NC: Duke University Press, 2001.

Stephens, Michelle Anne. "The Affective Difference: Reading Blackness through Psychoanalysis and Performance." Lecture at University of Pennsylvania, Department of English Lecture Series, November 20, 2014.

Stephens, Michelle Anne. *Skin Acts: Race, Psychoanalysis, and the Black Male Performer*. Durham, NC: Duke University Press, 2014.

Suchet, Melanie. "A Relational Encounter with Race." *Psychoanalytic Dialogues* 14 (2004): 423–38.

Sue, Stanley, and Derald W. Sue. "Chinese-American Personality and Mental Health." *Amerasia Journal* 1, no. 2 (1971): 36–49.

Suzuki, Bob H. "Education and the Socialization of Asian Americans: A Revisionist Analysis of the Model Minority Thesis." *Amerasia Journal* 4, no. 2 (1977): 23–51.

Tajiri, Rea, dir. *History and Memory*. New York: Women Make Movies, 1991.

Trenka, Jane Jeong. *The Language of Blood*. Minneapolis: Graywolf Press, 2005.

Truong, Monique Thuy-Dung. "Kelly." *Amerasia Journal* 17, no. 2 (1991): 41–48.

Tummala-Narra, Pratyusha. "Skin Color and the Therapeutic Relationship." *Psychoanalytic Psychology* 24 (2007): 255–70.

Vaughan, Alden T. "The Origins Debate: Slavery and Racism in Seventeenth-Century Virginia." In *The Roots of American Racism: Essays on the Colonial Experience*, 136–74. New York: Oxford University Press, 1989.

Viego, Antonio. *Dead Subjects: Toward a Politics of Loss in Latino Studies*. Durham, NC: Duke University Press, 2007.

Volkan, Vamik D. "Transgenerational Transmissions and 'Chosen Trauma': An Element of Large-Group Identity." Opening address of the XIII International Congress, International Association of Group Psychotherapy, London, August 1998. Accessed December 10, 2015. http://www.vamikvolkan.com/Transgenerational-Transmissions-and-Chosen-Traumas.php.

Wald, Priscilla. *Constituting Americans: Cultural Anxiety and Narrative Form*. Durham, NC: Duke University Press, 1995.

Walton, Jean. *Fair Sex, Savage Dreams: Race, Psychoanalysis, Sexual Difference*. Durham, NC: Duke University Press, 2001.

White, Kate, ed. *Unmasking Race, Culture, and Attachment in the Psychoanalytic Space*. London: Karnac Books, 2006.

White, Kathleen Pogue. "Surviving Hating and Being Hated: Some Personal Thoughts about Racism from a Psychoanalytic Perspective." *Contemporary Psychoanalysis* 38 (2002): 401–22.

Williams, Raymond. *Marxism and Literature*. New York: Oxford University Press, 1977.

Winnicott, Donald Woods. "Ego Distortion in Terms of True and False Self." 1960. In *The Maturational Process and the Facilitating Environment: Studies in the Theory of Emotional Development*, 140–52. New York: International Universities Press, 1965.

Winnicott, Donald Woods. *The Maturation Process and the Facilitating Environment*. New York: International Universities Press, 1965.

Winnicott, Donald Woods. *Playing and Reality*. New York: Brunner-Routledge, 1971.

Winnicott, Donald Woods. "Playing: A Theoretical Statement" (1968). In *Playing and Reality*, 38–52. New York: Brunner-Routledge, 1989.

Winnicott, Donald Woods. "Transitional Objects and Transitional Phenomena." 1951. In *Playing and Reality*, 1–25. New York: Routledge, 1989.

Winnicott, Donald Woods. "The Use of an Object and Relating through Identifications." 1969. In *Playing and Reality*, 86–94. New York: Brunner-Routledge, 1989.

Wong, Sau-ling Cynthia. *Reading Asian American Literature: From Necessity to Extravagance*. Princeton, NJ: Princeton University Press, 1993.

Wu, Ellen. *The Color of Success: Asian Americans and the Origins of the Model Minority*. Princeton, NJ: Princeton University Press, 2014.

Yew, Chay. *Porcelain*. New York: Grove Press, 1997.

Zhou, Min. "'Parachute Kids' in Southern California: The Educational Experience of Chinese Children in Transnational Families." *Educational Policy* 12, no. 6 (November 1998): 682–704.

INDEX

Dalal, Farhad, 5, 181n5
Davis, Angela, 170, 201n22
death drive, 46, 64, 86–87, 96–97, 120
Deleuze, Gilles, 21
depression. *See* mental health issues
depth psychology, 135
"A Dialogue on Racial Melancholia" (Eng and Han), 3, 34–35
diaspora, 5, 8–12, 23, 104, 109, 116–17, 129, 135–40, 168. *See also* Asian Americans; immigration
Diaz, Robert, 194n45
discrimination: accents and, 54–55, 62, 110, 133, 150; antidiscrimination protections and, 145–47; against Asian Americans, 2–7, 35–41, 55, 102, 115, 148, 159, 167. *See also* homosexuality; race and racialization
Disidentification: Queers of Color and the Performance of Politics (Muñoz), 61
dispersion, 1, 91, 143, 170–71
displacement, 4–5, 10, 59, 78, 109, 116–23, 130, 138, 162–63
dissociation. *See* Bromberg, Philip M.; racial dissociation; Winnicott, D.W.
double consciousness, 18–19, 125. *See also* Du Bois, W.E.B.
double inscription, 19, 161–62. *See also* Freud, Sigmund
Du Bois, W. E. B., 18, 41, 114–15, 117, 125–26, 197n17. *See also* double consciousness

early study abroad programs (ESA), 106, 111–12
"Ego Distortion in Terms of True and False Self" (Winnicott), 101, 118, 197n19, 198n26
Eng, David L., 192n1, 192n4, 192n7, 194n1
English (language), 54–55, 59, 70, 105–16, 127, 132–33, 138, 150
ethnic studies, 6, 177–78, 186n4

Fairbairn, W. R. D., 17, 63
False Self, 23, 27, 108, 117, 119–31, 135,

139, 155, 198n26. *See also* racial dissociation
Fanon, Frantz, 18, 125–26
Feeling of Kinship, The (Eng), 192n1, 194n1
feminism, 14, 50, 56–59, 144, 146
fetishism, 23, 42–43
filial piety, 190n42
Foucault, Michel, 21
Freud, Sigmund: consciousness and, 160–62; double inscription and, 161–63; the ego and, 62–63; hysteria and, 23, 160, 180; melancholia and, 3, 25, 35–38, 51, 61, 63, 92, 94; mourning and, 37–38, 48, 57, 67; paranoia and, 169–70; the unconscious and, 28, 160–62, 172–73, 185n39. *See also* double inscription; *specific works*

"gay is the new black," 103, 163
Generation X: civil rights movement and, 102–4; coming out and, 143–50; homosexuality and, 142, 149, 156, 162, 164; racial melancholia and, 22–24, 35, 156, 168–69; second-generation dynamics and, 77, 128. *See also* parachute children; racial dissociation; racial melancholia
Generation Y: homosexuality and, 143–50, 156; parachute children and, 22, 24; race and racialization, 102, 156; racial dissociation and, 4, 169, 172. *See also* millennials
globalization. *See* neoliberalism
Gonzales, Roberto, 127
good enough. *See* Winnicott, D.W.
good mother, 58. *See also* Klein, Melanie; mothers
Gotanda, Neil, 37, 159, 162
Green, Richard, 200n6
Greene, Beverly, 62
Grey, Thomas C., 14
"Group Psychology and the Analysis of the Ego" (Freud), 38
Guattari, Félix, 21
guilt, 26, 49, 57–61, 68, 81–82

Japanese internment, 39, 50–53
Jen, Gish, 46–47
Jews, 73, 186n1
Jim Crow regime, 14–15
Judeo-Christian traditions, 35

Kang, Jay Caspian, 160
Karma of Brown Folk (Prashad), 197n18
Kazanjian, David, 12
"Kelly" (Truong), 55–56
Kingston, Maxine Hong, 42–44
Klein, Melanie: beautiful picture and,
    58–59, 62, 83–84, 192n9; envy and, 96–97;
    infant development and, 67, 81–82, 86;
    mother-child relationships and, 59,
    80–82, 84; mourning and, 58, 62, 192n9;
    object relations and, 23, 26, 57, 60, 68,
    80, 86; racialized objects and, 80–82, 94.
    See also bad mother; good mother
Korea/n, 26–27, 49–50, 67–87, 90, 92–97,
    106–19, 127–29, 136–37, 151
"Koreanness," 78, 85

Lacan, Jacques, 17, 19, 46, 62, 125, 135,
    184n34
language: belonging and, 54–57, 74,
    106–7, 134–38, 178; of the closet, 67;
    feelings and, 153–57; mourning and,
    64, 128, 138, 153; of neoliberalism, 159,
    163, 174, 178
Language of Blood, The (Trenka), 65
Laplanche, Jean, 161
Latino/as, 16, 34, 40, 46, 73, 149, 176,
    194n2, 202n3
law: antidiscrimination protections and,
    145–47; Constitutional, 6, 28, 130;
    critical race theory and, 4–8, 24, 29;
    exclusionary immigration acts and,
    39, 42, 48, 102; hate crimes and, 166,
    174; national belonging and, 39, 42,
    48, 102; property law and, 8–15; queer
    liberalism and, 28–29, 143–48, 156–58,
    162–63, 171. *See also* neoliberalism;
    queer liberalism; race and racializa-
    tion; whiteness

Lawrence v. Texas, 102, 146–47
Layton, Lynne, 181n5
Leary, Kimberlyn, 5, 19, 88
Lee, Ang, 144, 200n5
LGBTQ rights, 103
Long, Carol, 26, 88–89, 176, 179
loss. *See* mourning; racial melancholia
Loving v. Virginia, 102
Lowe, Lisa, 13, 41, 53, 57

Martin, Trayvon, 185n47
Marx, Karl, 11–12
Matsuda, Mari, 55
Melamed, Jodi, 172
melancholia: Freud and, 3, 25, 35–38, 51,
    61, 63, 92, 94; mourning and, 47–57, 61.
    See also mourning; racial melancholia
Memmi, Albert, 18
mental health issues: alcohol abuse,
    113–14; anxiety, 28, 58–59, 81, 85–87,
    136, 148–55, 161–65, 171; depression
    and, 24–26, 34–38, 46–59, 108–10,
    166–69, 186n4; eating disorders (bu-
    limia), 112–14, 120; panic attacks and,
    132–33, 148–54, 158–64, 171; parachute
    children and, 108, 111–19, 129; purging
    and, 111–12; suicide and, 38, 111, 121,
    126, 129
millennials: homophobia and, 157–60;
    homosexuality and, 24, 143, 148–49,
    157–60, 163; immigration and, 102–5;
    parachute children and, 27–28; racial
    dissociation and, 1, 130, 136; racial
    melancholia and, 1, 102. *See also* Gen-
    eration Y
Milne, A. A., 150
mimicry, 44–47, 61
model minority status, 2, 16, 40–42,
    114–16, 124–25, 138, 155, 190n42.
    See also Asian Americans; race and
    racialization
Moran, Rachel, 159
Morrison, Toni, 44, 171, 175
mothers: adoptive mothers and, 26,
    68, 74–77, 80, 82, 84, 93–94, 97;

racial melancholia (*continued*)
    intergenerational trauma and, 48–49,
    52; intersubjectivity and, 23, 51, 61,
    67; loss and, 36–37, 59, 62, 78, 86, 90;
    mimicry and, 44–47, 54–55; mourn-
    ing and, 1, 47–50, 60–61, 180; paranoia
    and, 169–70; psychic pressures and, 22,
    84–85, 115; suicide and, 125; transna-
    tional adoption and, 78–79, 94. *See also*
    mourning; transnational adoption
racial reparation, 4, 23–25, 59, 68, 81–87,
    94–97, 175
racial transitional objects, 87–94
refugees, 55–56, 115, 124
reparation: psychological dynamic of,
    generally, 4, 23–26, 57, 59, 61, 67; racial,
    4, 23–25, 59, 68, 81–87, 94–97, 175. *See
    also* guilt; Klein, Melanie
repression, 10, 21, 23, 41, 43, 50, 53, 68, 84,
    86, 122, 135, 143, 155, 160–71, 185n39
Robinson, Cedric, 12
Ruskola, Teemu, 39

schools: boarding, 106, 109, 111–12, 132,
    150–51, 165, 138n; public, 132; segrega-
    tion and, 15, 18, 102
Schreber, Daniel Paul, 169–70
Scott, Ridley, 157
Sedgwick, Eve Kosofsky, 169
segregation: assimilation and, 9; emo-
    tional, 26, 79–87, 95–96, 163; mental
    health issues and, 53; racial difference
    and, 10, 14–15, 18, 60, 97, 102, 175; sexual
    difference and, 60
Senna, Danzy, 33–34, 186n1, 187n13
sexuality: bodies and, 28, 36; HIV and
    AIDS, 38, 73, 102, 145, 154–56; Oedipus
    complex and, 10, 18, 184n35; race and
    racialization, 19, 50, 142–43, 145–46,
    158; relationships and, 69, 71–72,
    119–20. *See also* homosexuality; queer
    liberalism
shaming, 25, 54–59, 62, 67, 144, 159, 177.
    See also Asian Americans; immigration
Silverman, Kaja, 193n38

Singapore, 27, 105, 107, 150–51, 167–68
slavery, 10–13, 15–16, 21, 168
Souls of Black Folk, The (Du Bois), 41, 114,
    188n19, 197n17
"South Korean High School Parachute
    Kids in Southern California" (Byun),
    195n5, 195n7
spaces: classroom and, 55–56; clinical
    and, 10, 21, 53, 94, 121–22, 175, 177,
    202n2; for creativity and play, 64,
    131–35; family and, 55, 78–79; homo-
    sexuality and, 148, 199n1; infant
    development and, 86, 118; Internet
    as, 148–51; public, 176, 178; race and
    racialization and, 14, 89, 102, 175, 179;
    racial dissociation and, 136–37; repres-
    sion and, 169–71; standing in, 109,
    125–28, 155–58; transitional, 25–27,
    67–68, 87–91, 95, 118, 140, 168–70. *See
    also* Bromberg, Philip M.; segregation;
    Winnicott, D.W.
spontaneity, 89, 118–26, 152, 155, 158, 175
sports, 132–35, 152, 157
Standing in the Spaces (Bromberg), 109,
    122, 125, 148, 197n25
Stephens, Michelle, 125–26, 135, 158,
    201n21
*Studies in Gender and Sexuality: Psycho-
    analysis, Cultural Studies, Treatment,
    Research* (journal), 67
subjects: history and, 16–22, 35, 116,
    138–40, 174; homosexuality and,
    143–46, 158–60; immigration and,
    78–80; intersubjectivity and, 23, 37,
    48–51, 55, 60–61, 67, 78–79, 82, 91, 126,
    129, 136–37; intrasubjectivity and, 23,
    25, 36–37, 44, 48, 51, 55, 60–61, 67–68,
    79, 129–30; race and racialization,
    1–22, 40, 42–46, 60–62, 102, 128, 156,
    171, 175–77. *See also* infant develop-
    ment; law; neoliberalism; property
Sue, Derald, 43
Sue, Stanley, 43
suicide. *See* mental health issues; racial
    dissociation; racial melancholia

"Surviving Hating and Being Hated" (White), 191

Taiwan, 27, 105, 107, 144, 186n53, 195n12
Tajiri, Rea, 50–51, 53
therapy, 21, 28, 52–53, 113, 122, 129, 142, 148, 153–54. *See also* psychotherapy
transference, 49, 68, 87, 92
transition (in object relations), 25–27, 67–68, 87–95, 118, 140, 168–70. *See also* objects and objectification
transitional objects. *See* objects and objectification; transition (in object relations)
transitional space. *See* spaces
transnational adoption: adoptive mothers and, 26, 68, 74–77, 80, 82, 84, 93–94, 97; birth mothers and, 26, 67–87, 90, 92–97; "coming out" and, 25–26, 67; family dynamic and, 69, 79–80; idealization and, 92–93; intersubjective struggles and, 67, 78–79; mothering and, 4, 25–26, 67, 71, 74–76, 80–81, 83; passing and, 3, 14, 19, 34, 38, 79, 125, 148, 157, 179, 184n34, 186n1; pregnancy and, 26, 68–73, 93, 112, 120; psychic development and, 68, 79–81; racial melancholia and, 77–81, 84; whiteness and, 26, 68, 74–77, 80, 82, 84, 93–94, 97, 115
"Transnational Childhoods" (Orellana, Thorne, Chee, and Lam), 196n14
trauma, 19–20, 23, 48–60, 122, 128–30, 138, 156
Trenka, Jane Jeong, 66
True Self, 26–27, 89, 114, 118–19, 121–25, 128, 136–38, 155, 197n19, 198n26, 198n36. *See also* racial dissociation
Trump, Donald, 166, 174–75
Truong, Monique T.D., 55–56
Tydings-McDuffie Act, 39

"The Unconscious" (Freud), 51–52, 141, 160–61, 184n39
unconscious racism, 6, 19, 22–25, 28, 56, 143, 155–63, 172–74

United Kingdom, 106, 165
United States: American exceptionalism and, 40, 110, 117; racial melancholia of, 38–44
US Supreme Court, 102–3

Viego, Antonio, 46, 124
Vietnam/ese, 56, 151

Wall Street, 157
The Wedding Banquet (Lee), 144
White, Kathleen Pogue, 83, 140, 191n66
whiteness: adoptive mothers and, 26, 68, 74–77, 80, 82, 84, 93–94, 97; passing and, 3, 14, 19, 34, 38, 79, 125, 148, 157, 179, 184n34, 186n1; as property, 15–21, 29, 39, 53–54, 63, 115, 143, 159, 163, 171–79; race as relation and, 9, 13, 16, 18–19, 23, 29, 40, 61, 64, 157, 171–79. *See also* Asian Americans; colorblindness; homosexuality; law; race and racialization
Williams, Raymond, 7, 25, 35, 61
Winnicott, D.W.: dissociation and, 122–23; False Self and, 23, 27, 108–9, 117, 119–31, 135, 139, 148, 155, 198n26; good-enough and, 22, 71; holding environment and, 144, 178–79, 200n6; infant development and, 23, 26; model minorities and, 124; playing and, 21, 89; spaces and, 68, 178; spontaneity and, 89, 118–26, 152, 155, 158, 175; transitional objects and spaces, 67, 87–88, 90, 94; True Self and, 89, 109, 118–19, 121, 123, 137, 155, 198n36. *See also* spaces
Winnie the Pooh (Milne), 150
Woman Warrior: Memoirs of a Girlhood among Ghosts, The (Kingston), 44
Wong, Sau-ling, 46
World War II, 39, 50
Wu, Ellen, 41

Yoon, Shirley, 3

Zimmerman, George, 185n47